Starting Out Right: Your Child's First Seven Years

Doris E. Durrell, Ph.D.

Copyright © 1989 by Doris E. Durrell

New Harbinger Publications
5674 Shattuck Ave.
Oakland, CA 94609
All Rights Reserved
Printed in the United States of America

To my daughter Sherri, my son Ian,
and my dear Mom and Dad.

ACKNOWLEDGMENTS

I would like to thank my friends Pat Wright, Kay Adler, and Janet Patterson for their help. Thank you Evan, Dylan, Kristen, and all Ian's friends for all the insights you gave me.

Contents

I
Basic Childrearing Facts

1

The First Three Years

Your child's first three years are critical. The investment of time and attention that you make to help your child become a happy, healthy, whole person will never again be so profitable. Your dedication to understanding your child and to teaching language, intellectual, and social skills in the first three years will have lasting effects.

Throughout my years of experience in raising children and treating children in a clinical setting, I have been continually impressed with the degree to which personality has been formed by the time a child is three years old. By this time, certain positive behaviors will have been established which will continue to bring your child positive responses, and negative behaviors may have been established which will cause your child problems with peers and adults.

By age three, many children have developed aggressive or assaultive behaviors which result in years of problems and struggles, some of which even require treatment by a psychologist. Such behavior problems can occur in fundamentally normal children whose parents have simply been unsophisticated in teaching social skills. Similarly, I have seen children whose language development has been slow and whose social skills with peers and with adults have been limited as a result.

On the other hand, when you know how to draw out your child's language capacity and how to teach social skills, the results can be remarkable. Two year olds can converse as freely as the average four year old. Your baby can ask you nicely for food or toys instead of screaming for them. Your child will be welcome and

popular in playgroups because you have taught sharing and cooperation from the start. You can bring out your child's maximum potential for creativity, scholastic achievement, and responsible decision
making.

What Makes a Dedicated Parent?

The nature of parenthood has changed for many of today's parents.
They are not having children simply because it is the natural order
of things. They have waited for the right time and circumstances
and really want to have a child. People are more likely than ever
to complete their educational and career goals and to travel and
broaden themselves in other ways before having children.

The birth of a truly wanted child to mature and settled parents
is frequently the most significant and meaningful experience of their
entire lives. They attend childbirth preparation classes together.
Fathers coach during the pregnancy and the birth. During childbirth
the mother is awake and aware. The birth is a peak experience in
their lives. Many women are so euphoric after the experience that
they are unable to sleep for days, and fathers leave the birth room
skipping and twirling around in the streets. The enthusiasm and
joy associated with the birth of the baby is carried over in some
degree to the raising of that child for the rest of his or her life.

These intelligent and informed parents are eager to do the absolute best for their babies. They find the information in most
childcare books insufficient. They want a book like this one, which
begins where other books end. They want to know what methods
are recommended by research in psychology. Even though the ideal
methods are not always possible to follow, they are goals toward
which dedicated parents wish to strive. They have the time, circumstances, and dedication which will permit them to attend to
the finer points of childrearing.

If you are a dedicated parent, you want to know what psychology can offer in the way of advice in your efforts to develop a well-
rounded child. You are interested not only in your son learning to
talk, but in his talking early, clearly, and with a wide vocabulary.
You want your child to be not only intelligent but also creative and
motivated to do well in school.

If you're dedicated, you're not content to let your daughter "fight
it out" but rather wish to teach her the social skills of shar-

ing, cooperative play, and empathy. You probably feel uncomfortable with using physical punishment as a means to control your child's behavior and would rather use other effective means of control.

To be a dedicated parent, you must realize that your child is an individual, with a unique personality and temperament. You need to always take into consideration such things as what your son thinks is a joke, what makes him angry, and what he finds difficult to do. His particular nature and style of reacting in any given situation must always be considered when setting your behavioral requirements. These individual personality characteristics may frequently determine where, when, with whom, and how you will spend your time. His personality may determine whether or not you take a walk, go for a drive, or extend a visit.

To people who have never had to deal with another little life, it may appear that you are being controlled by your child unnecessarily. The fact is that your child's individual personality and reaction tendencies must be considered in every decision which affects both you and your child. It is best to add up all the factors before deciding whether or not a certain behavioral requirement of your child is worth the stress that it will cause for both of you. When the figures don't add up, it is senseless to make the demands.

What Makes This Book Unique

Through the years of my university teaching career, many parents have asked me to recommend a book that would help them to understand the research findings in child psychology and their application to childrearing. When I would give them a copy of my favorite child psychology text, they were seldom impressed with the book, and usually did not read more than a chapter or two. The information I wanted to give them was in the textbooks, but hidden in obscure terminology and tedious explanations of research procedures. I found it necessary to translate the research findings into practical terms with examples of specific childrearing techniques or behaviors. A book whose purpose is to present research findings is far too abstract and academic for the needs of most parents. In this book I translate the research findings into terms understandable to most parents.

Other times, friends would come to me in my other role as a clinical psychologist to ask for help with problems which were not yet troublesome enough for them to seek psychological counseling in an office setting. The problems often were not only easily treated, but also ones that might have been prevented altogether with the application of a few simple psychological principles. These principles, used regularly by child psychologists in child therapy and treatment, are explained thoroughly in this book and may be easily grasped and successfully used by most parents.

The parent who will appreciate this book will be exceptional. Not exceptional in terms of education, but exceptional in terms of interest. The reader of this book will probably already have read other childcare books written for the average reader, but will have found them insufficient. My readers will already know that children need love and warmth, will have strong reservations about the use of physical punishment, and will be spending quality time with their children. This book begins where the others end.

This is an advanced childcare book with specific information, suggestions, and examples pertaining to issues such as promoting early language development, stimulating your child intellectually, encouraging creativity, fostering self-esteem, dealing with aggressive behavior, and encouraging sharing and generosity.

Here I am presenting what appear to me to be ideal methods. Few parents will be in a position to adhere to all my advice at all times. Sometimes the exigencies of life will make following these techniques very difficult. The needs of spouses, other children, and your own personal needs will make perfect adherence impossible.

Many children do manage to grow up well in far less than perfect circumstances. However, the extent to which you can maximize the application of the research and clinical information presented here will be the extent to which you will maximize the likelihood that your children will achieve their intellectual, social, and creative potential.

Although the approach of this book is very strongly influenced by my training in the area of behavior modification, it is an exceptionally sensitive and positive approach. I encourage parents to respond sensitively to the *individual* child and to positively reinforce desirable behavior rather than to punish or criticize. Parents who are not familiar with behavior modification will inevitably find themselves needing to respond with more coercive, restrictive, and punishing techniques than parents who familiarize themselves with the behavior modification techniques as described in this book.

Some parents initially reject the idea of using behavior modification with their children because they detect among behavior modifiers a tendency to be very insensitive to the individuality of the child. Typically people trained in behavior modification focus on behavior and disregard the individual motivational state of the baby. They tend to ignore internal conditions such as fatigue or hunger as causes of unacceptable behavior and often fail to consider individual personality factors. In treating abnormal or disturbed child behavior, a hard, tough approach is sometimes necessary to be able to eliminate some very undesirable behaviors. But, when you are using behavior modification to promote the growth and development of a normal, average baby, there must be a great deal more sensitivity to individual differences.

My Own Background

Since I received my Ph.D. in 1971, I have been employed, all but one year, as a full-time professor of psychology teaching child psychology classes. As I present the experimental data and research in the area of child psychology, my students always want to know what this means for parenting. Therefore, I have been thinking through the practical applications of the research for over ten years.

Another part of my work includes a small private practice in clinical psychology, treating children and adults with emotional problems. My clinical experience in treating children with behavior problems has given me insight into the way loving parents with typically "normal" children can run into difficult problems because of mismanagement. Here I have been able to see how the lives of so many parents and children are unhappy because parents are missing just a few pieces of information that would help them to handle their child's behavior.

As part of my training, I did a one year post-doctoral internship in behavior modification at the Center for Behavior Therapy in Beverly Hills, California. This training in a clinical setting made me aware of the value of applying the same methods with normal children to prevent problems before they begin.

All of this information would not have been enough for me to write this book. I also obtained necessary practical experience by raising my own two children, Sherri and Ian. I began to be aware of the importance my education had in my raising of my daughter in 1967, and at that time I decided that one day I would write a book for parents. With the birth of my second child in 1979, I began to take notes and write daily as I creatively applied my knowledge to my childrearing with Ian. I could not have written this book without being in the process of raising a child. Teaching him language, social skills, and how to use a potty were all essential to the step-by-step descriptions of the applications of the research to such important matters. My interactions with the parents of children his age and with their children in playgroups gave me wonderful examples of how to apply my academic information and clinical experience to the everyday problems of raising a normal child.

In this book I have something important to say. It has been a very rewarding experience for me to share my ideas on childrearing.

How To Use This Book

This book is organized around techniques, developmental stages, and the principles of learning. It is meant to be read carefully and in sequence. After that, if you wish to review everything pertaining to a specific problem, such as toilet training, you may consult the index at the back of the book.

Part One—Basic Childrearing Facts

This first section has three chapters: this introductory chapter, a discussion of Easy, Slow to Warm Up, and Difficult Babies, and a chapter on Attachment, Substitute Care, and Sleep Behavior.

Chapter Two explores the inborn differences among babies. Babies differ from birth in their eating and sleeping patterns, their reactions to new persons or objects, their adaptability, their intensity of response, and their general mood. Your child's inborn temperament will greatly determine your application of all the techniques taught in the rest of the book.

Chapter Three explains how and when attachments are formed, and the implications for working mothers and for choosing substitute caregivers. This chapter also answers basic questions about sleep patterns and what to do about night waking.

Part Two — Advanced Childrearing Techniques

Chapter Four, Promoting Language Development, goes into great detail to show you how to stimulate your child for early language acquisition. It discusses the many advantages to you and your child of early talking, and presents research that indicates that early language development is the best strategy for promoting high intelligence.

Can any child be a genius? Chapter Five gives techniques for fostering the early and complete flowering of intelligence. An analysis of Glenn Doman's controversial "Better Baby" course probes its strengths and weaknesses and shows how you can adapt some of his techniques for your own use.

Intelligence is not the same thing as creativity. Chapter Six explains the difference between convergent and divergent thinking. It describes games you can play with your child to spark creative thought and offers advice on encouraging and coping with your child's often quirky sense of humor.

Chapter Seven shows you how you can prepare your child to do well in school by starting at age one to encourage independent decision making and self-control. As your child grows older, you can use puzzles, toys, games, and books to effectively prepare your child for reading.

Part Three — Socialization

Children begin learning very early about what society expects of them. This can be a reasonable or a very stormy process, depending on your child's temperament and on the way you handle disobedience, tantrums, and aggressive behavior.

Chapter Eight shows how to prevent or minimize tantrums in young children. For older children it advises the use of reasoning in setting and enforcing rules, as opposed to the authoritarian style in which rules and punishments are arbitrary. Methods for promoting cooperation and family participation are also discussed.

Chapter Nine teaches the best methods for curbing aggressive behavior and developing alternative behaviors of empathy, sharing, and cooperation. Although children usually do not develop a true sense of empathy until about age seven, the foundation for this important development is laid starting at age one.

Part Four—Behavior Modification

Your child's behavior is constantly being modified by your actions and reactions. It doesn't matter whether you're conscious of what's going on or not. The modification of behavior goes on regardless. Your choice is not between using or not using behavior modification on your child. Rather, your choice is between using it consciously by plan or unconsciously by accident.

This last section of the book takes you step-by-step through the principles and techniques of behavior modification, so that you can have a conscious, informed plan for how you want to affect your child. Chapter Ten, Increasing Desirable Behavior, uses toilet training as an example of how you teach a very desirable behavior to your child.

Chapter Eleven is about Modeling, or teaching by example. It explains about how to talk and act to teach your child complex notions about violence, sex roles, assertiveness, and getting along in peer groups.

Chapter Twelve is on Decreasing Undesirable Behavior and focuses on the use of "time out," a nonviolent, nonjudgmental, and effective punishment procedure that has dozens of practical, everyday applications. For young children, the extinction of behaviors like tantrums at bedtime is fully explained.

Chapter Thirteen, Choosing Behavioral Goals for Older Children, focuses on the kinds of behaviors that will help your child be successful and happy in school and with peers.

Chapter Fourteen discusses techniques for changing the behavior of older children and helping them achieve the goals you've set.

Chapter Fifteen shows how children learn fears and how you can prevent or eliminate fear of the dark, fear of animals, fear of separation, fear of water, and so on. Sections on helping children change their negative thinking and on eliminating school phobias are also included.

2

Easy, Slow to Warm Up, and Difficult Babies

Babies are not all the same. It is neither desirable nor possible to expect the same sleeping and eating habits, degree of obedience, cheerfulness, cooperation, or other behaviors from all children. Inborn differences in babies require different methods of handling.

When my first child, Sherri, was a baby I visited a friend who also had a baby of three months. She was overjoyed with her baby and asked me, "Isn't motherhood wonderful?" For her, it was. Her daughter, Kimberly, slept four to six hours at a time, drank an eight-ounce bottle of milk and went back to sleep for another four to six hours. She almost never cried, but rather was happy, smiling, and pleasant most of the time. She loved other people and was very friendly.

From the beginning, my baby cried most of her waking hours. Her wake and sleep cycle was reversed and she was up most of the night. She appeared to be under a lot of stress. She drank two ounces of milk every two hours, never any more. Every night I walked the floor with her, patting her on the back and singing to her, trying to comfort her until one, two, or three o'clock in the morning.

Motherhood was not a "wonderful experience" for me. I wondered about myself. Why was I not enjoying this experience? What kind of mother and woman was I that I was not as happy and overjoyed as my friend?

Other friends advised me not to reinforce the crying. "Just let her cry, and only pick her up when she isn't crying," they said. I knew that this was not right. If I waited for her to stop crying, I might never pick her up. I carried her for the first four to five months of her life, trying to comfort her distress. Naturally, I was very anxious.

My friends in graduate school told me I was probably making her upset *because* I was anxious. I think the reverse was true. I think I was made anxious by my stressed and crying baby. I knew Sherri came into the world with a certain personality and temperamental characteristics to which I was responding. No amount of advice from the strict behavior modifiers or the helpful mothers could convince me that I was reinforcing crying behavior and creating the personality or temperament of my child.

Twelve years later when I had my second child, Ian, I received the same kind of "helpful advice" regarding his sleep behavior. He woke four to six times each night for the first two and a half years of his life. Experienced mothers and fathers advised, "He's just spoiled and in control of you. Let him cry it out. Any baby will wake up all night if you go to him and reinforce him."

Unfortunately for Ian, my husband and I succumbed to the pressure. When Ian was fourteen months old, I let him cry. For three nights he cried nearly the whole night with no sign of decreasing frequency. His waking was obviously not controlled by positive reinforcement, but by some inner biological rhythm.

Never forget that people are biological organisms subject to inborn biological determinants of behavior as well as environmental influences. To be most effective as a parent, you must tailor your expectations of children according to their individual personalities. *Babies are not all the same.*

Individual Differences in Babies

Psychologists have finally realized what parents have known all along: *babies are really different from the moment of birth.* From the late 1940s to the late 1960s, psychologists talked about parenting as if the infant were completely passive and had no influence on the parent. Parenting was a one-way street. Recently psychology has come to emphasize the two-way interaction between parents and child. Research has confirmed that a child has a very powerful influence on the parents' behavior.

Certain temperamental characteristics seem to be inborn and not a result of any specific childcare practices of the parents. Based on these characteristics, Thomas, Chess, and Birch found that babies can be classified as *Easy, Moderate,* or *Difficult.* The characteristics which differentiate babies are:

1. Rhythm — How regular and predictable are the child's patterns of hunger, excretion, and periods of sleep and wakefulness?
2. Approach / Withdrawal — How does the baby respond to new persons or objects?
3. Adaptability — How easily does the baby adapt to changes in the environment?
4. Intensity of Reaction — How intense are the baby's reactions? How much energy goes into such responses as laughing or crying?
5. Quality of Mood — How much of the time would the baby's behavior be described as friendly, pleasant, or joyful, as contrasted with behavior such as crying, whining, or fussing?

According to the way babies rate in these characteristics they may be classified as "easy," "slow to warm up," or "difficult." Some children will be categorized as clearly easy or clearly difficult; however, some will be easy in some ways and difficult in others. Of the 141 subjects in the original study of Thomas, Chess, and Birch, 65% of them were clearly categorized.

The Easy Baby

Suppose, for example, that you have a son who is a classic "easy" baby. His temperament has these characteristics:

Rhythmicity: The easy baby is very regular in his eating habits, periods of sleep and wakefulness, and time of excretion.

Approach/Withdrawal: His response to new persons and objects can be expected to be positive. He generally approaches new people or objects. He seems to enjoy people, to smile easily, and to exhibit little or no stranger anxiety. If stranger anxiety does occur, it is usually short-lived, and his reaction to strangers will not be very intense even at its strongest.

Adaptability: Your easy baby is very adaptable. He can easily adjust to changes in the environment. A change in babysitters will not be difficult for him to handle. He will relate to the new caregiver quickly. If he cannot take a nap on schedule, he can sleep earlier or later with little distress. If he cannot sleep in his own room or bed he will be able to fall asleep somewhere else relatively easily. He is likely to fall asleep almost anywhere, when he is tired, especially if you give him his bottle or nurse him. If he doesn't get his usual nap, he may have red eyes and yawn frequently, but there will be very little in the way of fussy behavior. He will tend to be his usual good-natured self, just a little more tired.

Intensity of Reactions: The intensity of his reactions is low or mild. If he falls, he cries only when really hurt. He will cry when he feels pain, but soon learns to say "ouch" and often may not even cry at all. At the age when most babies object to a diaper being changed, he is easy to distract and pacify during the process. He may protest, but not violently. When he is hungry he may signal his hunger by crying or whining, but this is mild and he is easy to distract while his lunch or dinner is being prepared.

Mood: Most of the time he is in a good mood. He smiles easily and is easy to pacify. Even when he is tired or hungry he can be pacified. Rarely is his behavior described as "fussy" or "whiny," and he is a joy to you.

Parenting the Easy Baby

A parent of this easy boy will be particularly likely to enjoy the experience of parenting. Your child quickly develops his own schedule, is generally glad to meet new people, and is basically a happy baby with very little in the way of unhappy or "fussy" periods. Friends and relatives will usually give you credit for being such a "good parent" when they see the smiles of your baby. Many people will assume that your infant's good nature reflects that you are doing a good job. They will believe that your nurturance and attentiveness is what makes your son happy.

It is very rewarding to care for an infant like this, since it is easy to make him happy. Very little in the way of attention and care will get warm sounds and happy smiles. Even when you mistakenly stick a pin in him, his reaction is mild and there is only a modicum of screaming. For a first-time parent this is a particularly wonderful experience. Contrast this with raising a slow to warm up or difficult baby.

The Slow To Warm Up Baby

If, for instance, you have a daughter who is slow to warm up, you learn to expect these inborn characteristics:

Rhythm: She is somewhat more variable with regards to her schedule of feeding, excreting, and sleep and wakefulness.

Approach/Withdrawal: She tends to initially withdraw from new persons or objects, but then gradually approaches them. This baby needs some time to look over a new situation, new babysitters, or preschool from a distance. Gradually, as she feels more comfortable, she will begin to approach. She is not generally as friendly and outgoing as the easy baby, but is more reserved in her initial reactions to new people and places.

Adaptability: It takes this baby longer to adjust to new situations such as changes in babysitters, or entering preschool. With care and encouragement, she will gradually adapt.

Intensity of Reaction: Her reactions are usually mild to most situations.

Mood: She is slightly negative in mood. Although she is usually fairly happy, she has more fussy times and days than the easy baby.

Parenting the Slow to Warm Up Baby

Because your slow to warm up daughter is likely to withdraw from or reject new experiences, you must present any new situation with frequency so that she may warm up to the event. If you have discerned that this is her temperament, you know that she will first withdraw from new situations and then *slowly* adapt. It is a mistake, however, to assume that her initial withdrawal means that she will not enjoy that experience in the future. For example, when this type of child is presented with a new food, she is very likely to spit it out and reject it. It would be a mistake for you not to present this food again, assuming that your baby does not like it. When you offer the new food over a period of time, with patience rather than with pressure or insistence, eventually she may accept the new food, and it may even become a favorite. Similarly, when the slow to warm up baby is bathed for the first time, and every time for a month after, she may scream and cry and appear to be very upset. Eventually she may come to thoroughly enjoy her bath. Because of the necessity of bathing, the initial withdrawal and gradual adjustment pattern may first become apparent in this situation.

The temperamental patterns of initial withdrawal and nonparticipation in new experiences can be distressing and upsetting if you do not understand your daughter's needs. When you first expose her to the company of peers and later to nursery school, her withdrawal and slow adaptation may set her apart from the other children. You may feel that her behavior reflects upon your childrearing or that she is insecure. Try to view her as an individual, be patient, and remind yourself of her tendency to be slow to warm to new situations.

When you first invite another child to your home, your daughter will not be happy and joyful about the visitor, and she will probably withdraw. This simply means that you must continue to introduce the playmate, be patient, and allow your little one to hang on your leg or bury her face in your skirt while the visitor is present for the first several times. It is a mistake to insist that she play while the visitor is present, or to coax or criticize her. If you continue to bring in the new playmate, eventually your baby will relax, play, and enjoy the company.

Similarly, when your slow to warm up daughter begins nursery school for the first time, she probably will be more upset than many of the other children. She may cry longer and louder than others, stand on the sidelines, and not participate for some time. Relax and remind yourself of her pattern and *keep taking her to school.* If possible, attend nursery school with her for the first week or so. Stay for part of each morning, gradually leaving earlier and earlier. Be sure your child's nursery school will cooperate with this approach.

Badgering, pressuring, or criticizing will not help. Allow your daughter to observe the situation on the fringe of the activity. As she feels more comfortable she will gradually warm up and begin to participate. If you try to change her way of coping with newness by pressuring her, she may become negative about the situation. Because the slow to warm up child will generally be mild in her responses, her initial negative reaction to a new situation will be relatively quiet and not intense. Unnecessary pressure, cajoling, begging, or ordering will probably turn a quiet withdrawal into active resistance.

The key to successfully coping with a slow to warm up child is patience. If you can frequently remind yourself that your daughter will gradually enjoy new situations as she begins to feel comfortable, you may be able to avoid rushing the process. Continue to re-expose your child to a new experience in a non-stressful way. With repeated exposure, you'll soon see her positive interest in the experience appear. If she is not re-exposed to the situation from which she initially withdraws, her experiences will be very limited.

Once the slow to warm up child makes an adjustment to a new situation such as a preschool or a new babysitter, missing school or not having a babysitter for even a week may require the whole adaptation process again. Because an extended absence requires a difficult readjustment period it is probably wise to place your child in a smaller school where the likelihood of colds or other illnesses requiring time at home would be diminished. Scheduling your vacations to coincide with school vacations will cut down the number of difficult adjustment periods.

Parenting a child who is slow to warm up is not as much fun as parenting a child who is easy. When you take her to the carnival or circus for the first time, expecting her to be thoroughly exhilarated and to participate in the games and activities, it is disappointing to find her arms securely fastened to your leg or her face buried in your skirt. At birthday parties you may feel embarrassed by your child's nonparticipation in the games or activities and when other parents ask if she's shy you may feel anxious or even angry. Always remind yourself that your most important concern is the long-term adjustment of your child, and not what someone else thinks of her behavior at a party.

A worry frequently expressed by parents of slow to warm up children is that their behavior looks terribly insecure. You may worry that you're making mistakes in your childrearing techniques. However, if you are sensitive to your child's needs, loving and attentive, and she is still slow to warm up, then she is simply this way by nature. Show patience and accept her as she is. By the time she is three years old there will be fewer new situations and, hopefully, fewer stressful times.

The Difficult Baby

If you have a difficult son, he has these characteristics:

Rhythm: He is irregular in terms of schedule. It is difficult to predict the time he will eat, excrete, or sleep.

Approach/Withdrawal: The typical reaction of a difficult baby is to withdraw from new people or situations and to take considerably longer to adjust to changes than either the easy or slow to warm up baby. New experiences such as separation from primary attachment figures, being left with a babysitter for the first time, changing babysitters, or entering preschool, are exceptionally upsetting.

He'll probably form a strong specific attachment to one parent. He will then protest very loudly and intensely when being left with the other parent. One boy cried from ten to thirty minutes every time his father, to whom he was specifically attached, left for work. An easier baby may protest for two or three seconds and then be fine.

Stranger anxiety usually emerges with great intensity in the difficult child. Whenever a stranger comes near him, he screams and cries, even when in your arms. If it is necessary to change babysitters, your son will be very disturbed by the change and will cry longer, louder, and a greater number of times than an easy child.

Adaptability: When your son is taken to a preschool for the first time, his difficulty in adapting is clearly seen. He will be likely to stand by the door and cry bitterly for a longer period of time than most children. When he finally becomes less tearful upon being left at the preschool, he will stand on the sidelines and observe for a long time. When he finally makes friends, he may become very strongly attached to one or two children and play and participate only when these two children are present. If his two regular playmates are absent on the same day, this is enough to disrupt his participation. He may once again withdraw, stand on the sidelines sucking his thumb, and appear depressed.

Intensity of Reaction: The energy behind a difficult child's responses is usually intense. If he hurts himself or falls, he screams as though severely injured, regardless of the degree of damage to his body. This intense reaction includes a long period of crying after each fall. Your child is not easily comforted.

If your son misses a nap, you are in for a very unpleasant afternoon. When your difficult son is off schedule and tired, he whines, cries, and fusses. He may be fussy for the next three days. He responds similarly to hunger, becoming easily upset, frustrated, and fussy when he is hungry.

When he gets close to the age of two and a half, when most babies become domineering, insist upon sameness, and have tantrums over things not going exactly the way they want them, your difficult baby is DIFFICULT. He will insist that *only* the specific attachment figure serve him breakfast, butter his toast, pour his milk, tie his shoe. If his French toast, after being cut, does not remain in a perfect square, he will cry and refuse to eat it. These incidents occur with most two-and-a-half-year-old children, but in the difficult child they produce intense tears and screaming when things don't go precisely his way.

Mood: Most difficult babies come into the world screaming and continue that way for quite some time. As a tiny infant your son is rarely content and often fusses and cries. As he gets older he is still frequently negative in mood, often whiny or unhappy. Regardless of where your son is for the first three years, there will be more unhappy sounds coming from him than from other children. Many times the difficult child is impossible to please. He cries for you to pick him up and then wants to get down. No matter what you do, no matter how you hold him, cuddle him, play with him, smile at him, he remains fretful.

Parenting the Difficult Baby

Avoid Difficult or Upsetting Situations. It is much easier to adjust your demands for mature behavior to the particular disposition of your baby than to try to make him like your other children or your friends' children. Your difficult son needs far more patience and careful handling. Whenever possible, you should avoid difficult situations rather than try to insist that he learn to cope with them. For example, if you know your son becomes whiny and fussy in the car on a long ride, it is foolish to make him accompany you for an unnecessary ride with your friends. His whining and crying will not extinguish within that half-hour ride and no one will enjoy it.

Adhere to a Routine. The difficult child needs a routine. He needs his nap when he needs it, and if he doesn't get it, he is miserable, fussy, and very hard to handle. If he stays up too late on one evening it may take him two or three days to get back on schedule, and for that next two or three days he can be expected to whine, fuss, and be very unhappy. Because life is so unpleasant for both you and your baby when his routine is disrupted, try to keep to a schedule as much as possible. When other children seem to adapt easily to changing bedtimes or varied nap times, take solace in the knowledge that this flexibility is a result of inborn temperamental factors and not a result of the parents having "trained" the child to be flexible.

Adapt to His Needs. Recognize the individuality of your child and adapt to his needs. For example, if your child does not handle hunger well, you may have to insist that you stop to eat when someone else wants to wait. Don't worry that you will be spoiling the baby, that he will always want to have his own way. These kinds of special considerations really need to be made only in the first two and a half to three years. By the time he is three years old, he will be far more easy to handle, and many of these temperamental characteristics will be less pronounced.

Give Him All the Attention You Can. Your difficult boy needs an incredible amount of attention. Other parents or childcare books may suggest ignoring the child's demands for attention, claiming that the demands will soon extinguish. Unfortunately, the extinction procedure just does not seem to be effective for difficult children. Because their need for attention is so intense, and their persistence in whining or crying for that attention is so great, it is nearly impossible to withhold your attention. The crying or whining will often persist until the child is so hungry that you really need to feed him or is so wet or soiled that you really must change him. In the process of taking care of these needs, you also reinforce whining. Because his needs for attention are so intense, it is usually far simpler to give him whatever attention you possibly can *immediately* when he asks for it. Sometimes a little attention will do the trick, and you can divert him into playing with something else.

Difficult children are simply not independent, and usually do not get involved in playing by themselves. You need to lead your child to an activity and help him become engaged in the activity. Then he will be likely to play by himself for a little while. When he tires of that activity, however, he is likely to need your attention again to redirect him towards some other activity. He seems to need this attention even if it is only to show him something else he can be doing.

Help Him to Adjust. All along the way, your child's difficulties in adapting to strange situations present problems that require patience and understanding. Because your child finds it difficult to adapt to new situations such as a new babysitter or preschool, it is best if you can stay with him for a couple of hours each day for a week or two to help him get used to that situation. Take extra care to make the new situation as pleasant as possible, and plan to remain there for longer than the parent of an easier child might. Help him feel comfortable and part of the group. Try to promote a friendship between your child and another child by pushing them on swings, talking to both. Knowing another child tends to make your child's adjustment to the new place a little easier. However, you should expect that even with carefully planned, gradual introduction to a new situation, your child will probably have a hard time. If he has to miss school for even a week, he'll have to make a readjustment all over again.

Your difficult baby's intense attachment to you and his withdrawal from new people make many situations very traumatic for both him and you. He simply does not warm up easily to others, and his crying and whining makes him particularly unattractive to other adults who have to handle him. It is no wonder you are anxious about leaving him with a babysitter or preschool. It is wise for you to take a great deal of care in helping your child adjust to a new situation so that some of his more positive behavior can be displayed for the other adults who will be caring for him in your absence.

Accept the Fact that Your Baby Is Difficult. It is very disheartening when you try your best to comfort a baby and are unsuccessful. It is especially depressing if you believe you should have control over this kind of behavior. Unless you recognize that there are simply some children who are temperamentally difficult, you can feel a great deal of guilt in raising such a child.

Parents of a difficult child typically go through a great number of feelings. You can expect to be frustrated and exhausted most of the time. You will feel responsible for your child's comfort and constantly be searching for something else to make him happier. You may wonder if you did something wrong during pregnancy, or blame his problems on difficulties in labor. You may worry that your own stresses or anxieties have caused the problem.

Research has turned up no reliable causes of the "difficult" temperament. Difficult babies are born to carefree women and women under stress, in both complicated and uncomplicated deliveries. Difficult children are firstborns, secondborns, and so on. They are both boys and girls. Statistics indicate that one child in ten is "difficult."

Recognize His Individuality. Do not compare your child to anyone else's and don't expect him to behave the same way other people's children behave in any given circumstance. Be prepared for advice from well-meaning friends and relatives regarding your childrearing. People will probably tell you that you must be reinforcing his crying, that you should probably just ignore the whining, that your child is spoiled and has to learn that he can't always get what he wants, and that he is being reinforced for being too demanding. Be assured that there are just some children who are demanding, who whine more than others, who need more attention, and who are very difficult to please. These factors are a result of inborn temperamental differences and are not related to your childrearing methods.

Consistency Is Essential. Consistency is important for most children, but it is *absolutely essential* for the difficult child. If you are consistent you will find your child as happy, socialized, and well behaved as any other child once this particularly rough period from birth to three years is passed.

Tailor your expectations of your difficult son's behavior according to what he can do without being miserable all day, and according to your own needs for establishing some behavioral requirements and control. Because your baby is unhappy so much of the time, and finds so many situations hard to adjust to, you will be more consistent if you decide in *advance* which behaviors are worth making an issue of and which are not.

Determine a certain number of behavioral requirements: things your child must *never* do, things he must *always* do. These behaviors should be required and treated the same way all the time. If you change your behavioral expectations on a day-to-day basis, because he wears you down or because you decide you are demanding too much, he will become more and more difficult to handle.

You can indulge those behaviors you have decided are not a big issue, such as demands for attention or for his television show or his milk in only *one* cup poured by mommy. Give in *immediately* to demands you decide to indulge.

If certain of his demands will not be met, then do not respond to them, *ever*. For example, if he wants you to sit beside him to watch a certain program on television and you do not want to watch it, then don't. Don't watch it today, tomorrow, or ever. When he has a tantrum to try to get you to watch it, put him in "time out" (see the chapter on Eliminating Undesirable Behavior for an explanation of time out).

Sometimes you hear so much crying and whining and fussing in a day that you'd do anything to prevent another episode. But if you give in to demands on one day that you will not want to satisfy on subsequent days, you will guarantee later tantrums. Because the difficult child is so demanding and persistent, you cannot afford to deviate from your rules. A rigid adherence to the principles of behavior modification is necessary.

Sometimes inconsistent parents of difficult children get so frustrated and angry that they resort to physical punishment. Experts in the area of child abuse believe many abused children are temperamentally difficult. Their whining and crying provoke the parents' rage.

Inconsistency is very damaging to children in the long run. In the study by Thomas, Birch, and Chess, 141 difficult children were followed through up to their elementary-school days. By the time they were school age, 70 percent of them had developed behavior problems. The authors found that the parents of the problem children had been very inconsistent, trying a variety of approaches to deal with their behaviors. They went from indulging to screaming to spanking. This inconsistency produced behavior disorders serious enough for the parents to seek treatment for the children.

When difficult children are handled consistently, lovingly, and with patience and understanding, they become quite normal. With age, they learn to adapt more and more easily to new situations. However, certain personality traits carry on to adulthood. Difficult children tend to become emotionally intense adults. They are intensely happy, angry, scared, or sad.

There is a bright side to raising a difficult baby. With loving care and consistency, the difficult baby develops a close bond to his parents and is *very expressive* of his love and attachment. When he feels love for you, it will be intense and you will hear about it! When his intensity becomes channelled into productive activity, he can accomplish great things. Both as a child and an adult, he may be an exciting, vibrant, and enthusiastic person. As an adult, his intensity may make him a leader in whatever he attempts.

Mixed Types

At least half the readers of this book will have babies who are easy in some ways, slow to warm up in others, and difficult in still others. The most important task for you as a parent is to always consider the individual reaction tendencies of *your* baby in each situation. Set your standards of behavior according to your child's personality. Make an issue of only those behaviors which are important to you, and be certain that you have some wonderful, happy, tension-free time to enjoy your baby. If this means that your baby's table manners will still be uncivilized at age three, so be it.

Temperament in Older Children

Although the more intense aspects of your difficult baby's temperament will even out after age three, temperamental differences in children do not disappear. Your easy, slow to warm up, and difficult babies will become easy, slow to warm up, and difficult children. What does change is the degree to which a child's behavior is controlled by temperament. Temperament should not be viewed as something immutable, unchangeable, and leading to a certain course of development. Both normal development and behavior disorders are a result of a complicated interaction between the characteristics or temperament of the child and the system of rewards and punishments that parents provide. See Chapter 13 for a further discussion of the temperaments of children aged four to seven.

3

Attachment, Substitute Care, and Sleep Behavior

Attachment

At two weeks of age most babies begin gazing more at their mothers' faces than at strangers' faces. At about three months old they begin to smile more for mother than for an unfamiliar female. They also respond more to mother's voice than to a strange one and "talk back" in coos and gurgles more to her voice. Before six months of age, babies clearly recognize and prefer their mothers, but they do not usually make a great effort to be with her and will not protest when she leaves.

Most babies show signs of specific attachment at around six months of age. When with someone else, they reach out to their mothers (or in some cases to their fathers). They actively look for their mothers and protest when she leaves their sight.

About a month after babies develop specific attachment they may begin to demonstrate *stranger anxiety*. Even babies who have previously been friendly to everyone will suddenly begin to cry when a stranger approaches. Not all babies develop stranger anxiety, and those who do usually get over it in a month and are once more friendly to strangers.

Once children have formed a specific attachment, usually to the mother, they need her to remain available to them until they are two and a half to three years told. Until then, separation will be difficult and must be handled carefully.

Fathers and Babies: A Relationship Worth Promoting

One of the biggest problems with dads getting involved with their babies seems to be their overwhelming sense of inadequacy in dealing with the young infant. Men seem to think that women automatically have experience and knowledge, that they know what to do with an infant from the beginning. Perhaps you feel inadequate, as do many dads, and worry that you won't handle the baby properly or that the mother can do it better. We all know that just about every little girl was given a doll to carry around from the time she was able to walk. She'd had years of coaching from her mother to "love the baby, rock the baby, take the baby for a walk in the stroller." Unfortunately, all this doll play doesn't seem to help women at all in knowing how to handle a real baby; that's why they call *their* mothers.

New mothers are just as frightened as new fathers are with their babies. They only face the fear and do it because all that doll play has taught them that they must.

Psychologists know quite a bit about the process of bonding and attachment between parent and baby, and this information may help you develop a more rewarding relationship with your baby in the first year.

Promoting Attachment

The research on infant attachment shows that babies become attached to people 1) Who respond immediately to their cries for food, diaper change, or consoling attention, and 2) Who spontaneously seek social interaction with them. This means that if you want your baby to become attached to you, then try to be the one to pick him up often. When he cries, you be the one who consoles him. You must also play with him and stimulate him when he is in the right mood.

Father Feeding the Baby: A Time to Bond.

With all the emphasis on women breast-feeding the baby, many people seem to have forotten about developing fathers' relationships to their babies via feeding. One of the earliest purposive behaviors that a baby under six months of age can do is to eat. Additionally, in the early months about the only time she wakes up is when she's hungry. So if the mother is the only one who ever gets to feed the baby, then she is the only one who will be forming a relationship. Around six weeks of age most babies make eye contact; they begin to focus on the eyes of the person who feeds them. Even mothers who have not been particularly bonded to their babies up to this time seem to fall in love with their babies once they make eye contact. As the mother holds her infant in her arms in the nursing position, the baby stares into her mother's eyes, and the mother feels her love grow.

Knowing how important eye contact is in meaningful relationships, dad should do some of the feeding so that he can also enjoy this eye contact and fall in love with the baby. A nursing mother will have to express some milk so that the father can give a bottle each day. The Leche League may not approve of bottles, but the benefits of that father's bonding to the baby are so important that you may want to introduce the bottle right from the beginning. It is important that you give the baby one bottle a day from the third or fourth week, or she very quickly will learn to want only the breast and to refuse the bottle. Every now and then you may go a couple of days without giving the baby a bottle, but in most cases if you go as long as a week without giving a bottle, the baby will no longer accept it and will only nurse from the breast. If dad has to be gone for a week, make sure that mom gives her that bottle each day until he gets back so the baby doesn't forget.

Notice that it's the parents becoming bonded to the baby in the early months. The baby really doesn't attach to the parent for several more months.

Consoling the Baby

Your baby will become attached to you if you are the one to console him when he is stressed. When a baby cries, he may want his diaper changed, a bottle or breast, or he may simply want to be held and cuddled. He can't ask you to give him a hug or hold him; the only way he can communicate is to cry. So when you hear your newborn cry, pick him up. Don't worry about whether or not you will be adequate for the job. You will learn how to console him just as his mother does. She learns to do what makes him stop crying: it could be rubbing his back, patting his head—you won't know until you experiment. You can always check his diaper or try a bottle but sometimes just holding him is enough. Even if your baby doesn't stop crying immediately, the fact that you are there is important to your baby. Because your baby doesn't stop crying doesn't mean you've failed or are somehow less skilled than his mother. Often a baby cries because he's stressed either physically or emotionally. He might be experiencing some pain or he may be tense from the activity of the day. In either case your holding him, rocking him, and consoling him will let him know that you care about his stress even if you can't make it go away.

The Importance of Play

As you talk to and play with your baby you learn what makes her smile or get excited. You become aware of what she likes and doesn't like so that a special little interaction develops over time. Your baby rewards you when she likes what you do. When you make certain noises or faces for her or tickle her in certain ways and get good smiles, you know that she likes these things and you'll keep doing them. When you make another face or sound, and she frowns or doesn't smile, you gradually stop doing it. This is why by the time a baby is four or five months old the baby seems to respond differently to her mother than she does to other people. By this time she has had hours and hours of interaction with her mother, during which she's let mom know time and again which kind of tickles, noises, sounds, and faces she likes and which she doesn't. Remember, a mother has *no particular training* for this special baby.

Both parents need to learn the likes and dislikes of their baby. The baby dolls, doll carriages, and pretend bottles do nothing to teach the mother the things that she will have to know about her own particular baby, so both of you are starting from square one on day one.

When to Play: The Quiet Alert State

Research has determned that there are five different infant states. Three of these you already know and can recognize immediately: sleeping, crying, and drowsiness, when baby's eyes are at half-mast with a dull and glazed look to them. The other two states are of particular interest to us in this discussion. The more important of these states is that of *quiet alertness*. During this state the baby lies quietly awake, is fully alert; his eyes are wide open and he seems to be paying attention to the sounds and sights around him. A baby in this state shows responsiveness to your talking, and to the faces and noises you make for him. A baby only spends about 10 percent of his time in this quiet alert state in the first month after birth. If you'd like to have your baby and his dad form a relationship, try to engineer it so dad gets to spend time with the baby when he's in the quiet alert state. When the baby is in that state and interested in interacting he should be rushed to his dad.

The *active awake state* is not a particularly important one for interacting with the baby. In this state she's usually wiggling her arms and legs, and although she is awake, her eyes are unfocused and she doesn't seem interested in the sights and sounds around her. Your faces and cooing and voice will probably not attract her interest very much when she is like this.

Research has shown that the best way to produce the state of quiet alertness is to pick up your baby when he's crying and put him to your shoulder. When a crying baby is held so that he can look over the mother's or father's shoulder, he is generally comforted and changes to a state of quiet alertness. This position is better for producing the state of quiet alertness than any other positions studied. Other positions studied in this research were 1) Holding the baby in the nursing position, 2) Pushing the baby horizontally, as in a stroller, 3) Moving the baby to a sitting position, 4) Leaning over the baby and embracing him without picking him up, and 5) simply verbal interaction, that is talking to the baby without picking him up. None of these other methods of consoling were as effective in producing the state of quiet alertness as was putting the baby to the shoulder. In fact in the research, 76.7 percent of the babies went into a state of quiet alertness from a state of crying when they were picked up and put to the shoulder. So to promote the relationship between the baby and his dad, dad should learn to console the baby using this position. Mothers can also get the baby in this position then hand him over to his dad for playful interaction.

If you want to have your baby to have a strong attachment to you, all you have to do is respond to her when she cries and initiate social play with her when she is in the quiet alert state. Your baby will spend increasing time in this state as she gets older. If you make faces for her, talk to her, and show her things in her environment when she is in the quiet alert state, you will become an important person for her and build the foundation for attachment.

In the beginning all you have to do is talk to her in a high-pitched voice and move your face around in front of hers, and she will respond to you. Somewhere between five and seven weeks of age she will smile for you. So nod yes and shake your head no and talk baby talk to her in a high-pitched voice. Don't worry about sounding unmasculine; go to a quiet corner where no one can hear you if you're embarrassed (Your baby will love it. This will be part of the foundation for that attachment that you want.) As she gets to three or four months, other sights and sounds will also amuse her and she will appreciate your efforts to stimulate her. As you carry her around and show her leaves blowing in the wind or the venetian blinds clacking in the breeze or the kitty meowing, you are providing stimulation. Remember everything is new for your baby and things that seem ordinary and routine to you are all fresh and exciting for this little person.

Separation

The way a baby reacts to separation depends first of all on the baby's temperament. If, for example, you have a daughter who is a difficult child, and you are the primary attachment figure, you're in for a trying time. Your daughter will form a strong attachment as you spend hours trying to comfort and sooth her. When you leave the room she'll respond with her usual vigor, screaming and refusing all attempts to quiet her until you return. Even when she's two years old she will fuss if you're away for more than a couple of hours.

If your daughter is less difficult, you may find that you can be gone for four or five hours before she misses you. If you're lucky enough to have an easy daughter who is friendly and outgoing, you may find that you can leave her for a whole day or even overnight without causing distress. The only danger with such an easy child is that you may overextend the limits of her ability to tolerate separation. Even though she may appear to be happy and untroubled during her stay away from you for a weekend, anything more than a weekend is likely to result in a detached and aloof reaction when you return, followed by a period of excessive clinginess and dependent behavior. This kind of reaction to separation indicates that there has been trauma as a result of the separation. For this reason, unless babies have developed strong multiple attachments, it is best not to leave them for even a weekend until they reach two and a half years.

The other factor that determines your baby's reaction to separation is the availability of other attachment figures. If your son is attached to his older sister, grandmother, or friend living with the family, he may be relatively unaffected if you and your spouse are gone for a weekend.

If you do not have a relative to whom you can promote another attachment, promote an attachment to a friend with a child the same age. You and your friend can make excursions with both children on a regular basis to a park, zoo, lake, or beach where the child will have a lot of fun. Visit at one another's homes with the children. Deliberately take care of one another's child so that each child becomes accustomed to having his needs met by the other's mother. Over time, your boy will develop an attachment to the second mother and it will be easy to leave him with her. Begin with a brief period of separation and gradually extend the length of time. The goal is simply to teach your son that he can count on someone other than you to take care of his needs. Even a difficult baby may be encouraged to form an attachment to an agemate and his mother so that by two and a half years old he may happily remain for a weekend at his friend's home.

To encourage an attachment to a babysitter, have her share some of your son's favorite activities. Let the babysitter help him fingerpaint, make play dough, or do drawing. Try to arrange for the sitter to take the child someplace special. For a child under two years, a trip to a pet store, a nature walk, or visiting a neighbor's cat may be special. A trip to the zoo is perfect.

Many parents mistakenly assume that children feel more comfortable with a babysitter when they are in their own homes. Actually, children usually experience being in their own homes with a babysitter as a big minus in their lives. The most important element of home—Mommy or Daddy—is gone. It is far better to have your child experience the excitement and fun of an interesting place outside the home so that some of the enjoyment of being there gets associated with the babysitter.

Working Mothers and Attachment

How a child is affected by a mother's working depends on the amount and quality of time she has available for interacting with her child, the particular setting in which her child is spending time while she works, and the temperament of her child. Infants are capable of forming multiple attachments and their attachments are related more to the quality of the interaction than to the number of hours spent with them. Therefore, it is clear that a mother may work and still be a very strong attachment figure for her infant.

If you are a working mother and wish to be certain of attachment, then you must spend a couple of hours each day in communication and interaction with your baby. This requires planning. For example, you can arrange for your daughter to take a very long nap in the afternoon while you are at work so that she will be awake to play with you in the evening.

Although it is difficult when you are tired and stressed after work, you must allow time for close communication and interaction with your baby if she is to develop a strong attachment. Your daughter's early feelings of attachment to you form the foundation for her later identification with you and her modeling of your values, attitudes, and behavior. Your hours spent with her will be rewarded in later years.

Substitute Care

The most important consideration in choosing substitute care for your child is stability. Whoever takes care of your child should be there consistently. An ever-changing succession of caregivers creates a situation similar to that of institutionalized children. They never develop any depth of emotional involvement because they don't have the opportunity to form deep attachments to their caregivers.

The next most important consideration is how much individual adult attention your child will receive. From this point of view, the best caregiver would be a grandmother or other relative who could devote all of her attention to your child alone. Almost as good would be someone who is caring for only one other child. A daycare center with a very low child-to-adult ratio is better than one with fewer adults and more children.

Finally, select your substitute caregiver according to the quality of care she can provide: consider her experience, competence, general level of nurturance, and her willingness and ability to learn to do things the way you want them done.

An important thing to notice with a caregiver is the way she talks to your baby. If she talks a lot, but not at the baby's level of language need, then teach her how to talk to your child. Give examples of the kind of sentences you want her to use. Be sure to emphasize repetition. Get her to read the chapter in this book on language development. A great deal of individual attention is important for language development, particularly in the first eighteen months. Studies of the effects on children of group daycare settings find some negative effect on language development.

With a child over one year of age another important thing to work out is the way you want your caregiver to handle certain inappropriate behaviors. If the caregiver allows your child to hit her, to hit others, or to get things by throwing tantrums, these behaviors will persist later.

This is especially important if you must change caregivers, because most children go through a testing period with a new person. In order to find out what the rules will be and what kind of person this is, your child may hit, slap, throw things, have tantrums, and go through many behaviors you have prohibited. Once it is clear that the new caregiver will not accept such behaviors either—that the rules are the same—your child will return to normal behavior.

Group Daycare

The quality of daycare settings varies enormously. When evaluating the results of research on daycare centers, you must consider the *kind* of daycare center in the study. For example, an extensive study by Kagan, Kearsley, and Zelazo compared daycare children with children who stayed at home with their mothers. The children were from three and a half to five and a half months old and were involved in the experiment until they reached thirty months. This study found no difference in a variety of cognitive, language, and social measure between daycare children and home-raised children. The two groups of children responded similarly even on tests measuring attachment, indicating that the daycare experience did not weaken infants' attachment to their mothers. Furthermore, the infants did not develop attachment to their teachers in preference to their mothers. It should be noted, however, that the daycare center in this study was superior, with a low child/adult ratio, a well-trained staff, and a wonderful setting. The results of this study can be generalized only to equally superior circumstances and not to the average daycare setting.

Long-Term Effects

The issue of daycare and working mothers involves children's adjustment not only in the first three years, but also throughout middle childhood, adolescence, and young adulthood. Unfortunately, the studies of the children in daycare follow them only a short time and not into adolescence. I believe that the issue of attachment and daycare is more complicated than it seems at first, and needs more attention. It may be that working parents can raise happy, well-adjusted children with a minimum of time and involvement, especially with good, consistent daycare. However, do spend all the time you possibly can to encourage attachment, develop a strong bond in the early years, and maintain it later. Particularly with a child of difficult temperament, you will need the strongest bond you can get when your child reaches adolescence.

For example, in middle childhood and adolescence a girl who has formed a strong attachment to you is more likely to identify with you and take on your values, attitudes, and behaviors as her own. A strong bond and identification with you makes discipline during the adolescent years far easier. If you are working parents, try to devote the maximum time possible to joyful interaction with your baby. Take your baby with you whenever you can: to dinner, to visit friends, and on vacations. If you work all day during the week, you need this time with your baby to develop a close attachment.

This may mean not reading the paper, not talking to one another very much, and little quiet relaxing time alone. It will be worth giving up some personal pleasure in these early years if by doing so you can increase the likelihood that your child will get through adolescence without serious problems.

Sleep Behavior

Some children begin to sleep through the night even in their first week of life. Other infants wake up every hour or two for months and then every four hours for the next two years. By the time they are three years old they finally begin to sleep for the better part of the night. There is really nothing you can do about babies who are night-wakers. They are not waking up because of positive reinforcement for waking. They are waking up because of some internal biological rhythm. In these cases it is not wise to try letting them cry it out.

There is a difference between protest at *going down to sleep* for the evening and *night-waking*. It is usually a simple matter to extinguish tantrum behavior at bedtime (see the Behavior Modification Section). In a matter of a week, tantrums at bedtime usually drop out altogether, and if your son is tired when you put him down, he will go right to sleep.

However, if your son is a night-waker, his waking at two a.m. is no different for him than his waking at seven a.m. If you want him to go back to sleeep, then you must attend to him, let him know that you are there, and somehow reintroduce the context of sleep for him. This may require giving another bottle, nursing him again, or rocking him so that he will once again become sleepy. It is important to realize that his cries for attention and comfort in the middle of the night are not manipulative behavior. He is not aware of any day and night schedule or of your views of the appropriate or inappropriate timing of his waking, and he does not *voluntarily* awaken. His internal rhythm wakes him at that time and he can do nothing to change it.

Some sources suggest that infants may become trained to awaken at a given hour because of being fed at that hour. To determine whether being fed during the night actually reinforces waking, someone other than the nursing mother should go to the baby when he cries during the night. Let daddy comfort the child and lull him back to sleep by patting him on the back, singing to him, or rocking him. If, after ten consecutive days of not being fed when he awakens at night, your child is still a night-waker, then his waking is not being maintained by being fed. He will probably continue to awaken during the night for some unpredictable period of time.

What should you do for the night-waking? It may be more difficult for the father, grandmother, or sibling to rock, comfort, or hold the child until he falls asleep than it would be to give him a bottle or nurse him again. The easiest solution is often to nurse him back to sleep. Many parents keep the baby in their own bed or on a mattress on the floor of their room for the first two or three years.

Will He Ever Sleep through the Night?

Often night-wakers change sleep patterns by the time they are two and a half years old. By that age many light sleepers seem to sleep more deeply than before and are less easily awakened. Sometimes children who have been taking very brief naps begin to take naps of two to three hours in the afternoon. It may be worth waiting for the child to make some internal biological changes which will enable him to sleep longer through the night, rather than fight the situation.

If by age two and a half your child still awakens during the night, you can reason with him and he will be able to control his own behavior when he awakens. Tell him, "You can't wake me up in the night anymore. I'm very, very tired. If you wake up in the night you can come see that I'm here, but don't wake me. When you see I'm here, you put your head back down on the pillow and go to sleep. Don't bother me, because I want to sleep."

Your child can be reminded of this before bed and then if he calls to you during the night you may say, "Don't bother me. Put your head down and go to sleep." If he continues to bother you, then remind him, "If you bother me and talk to me during the night I'll have to put you in time out." The next time he calls to you or tries to awaken you, place him in time out to discourage this behavior just as you would for any other unwanted or inappropriate behavior (see the chapter on Decreasing Undesirable Behavior for an explanation of time out).

Light and Deep Sleepers

Some babies simply sleep more deeply than others. Babies who awaken easily in the early months tend to be light sleepers through to adulthood, while those who are deep sleepers tend to be deep sleepers through to adulthood. There may be some change in the depth of sleep as the baby gets older, however, with light sleepers sleeping a little bit more soundly as they approach three years of age.

Parents of deep sleepers often pride themselves on having trained their baby to sleep through a party or through being carried or moved about during sleep. Actually, depth of sleep is an inborn characteristic. There's no way to train light sleepers to sleep through noise or even a blanket being placed over them or a window being closed in their room. Additionally, there are individual differences in sleep length that are inborn and persistent. Babies who are long sleepers tend to remain long sleepers through adulthood and those who are short sleepers tend to be short sleepers as adults.

II
Advanced Childrearing Techniques

4

Promoting Language Development

Why Encourage Early Language Development?

Since most children acquire language by the age of three without any specific language training, it is reasonable to ask, "Why should I promote early language development?" There are a number of immediate advantages to a child's developing language skills early. For example, through language your daughter will be able to convey her needs or wants. Once she has acquired the appropriate words, she can let you know when she is hungry, thirsty, tired, or cold without merely hoping that you will guess her needs correctly. As her verbal abilities progress, she will be able to tell you where she would like to be, with whom she would like to play, and when she is ready to go home.

With language she can ask for help. She can, once she has the appropriate words, request that you open a box, close the door, or put on the record. In this way, she becomes able to experience her ability to determine the behavior of other people. When she can ask you for help in locating a missing part of a toy, she can avoid much frustration and unhappiness.

Or, if your son can say to a playmate, "Come on, let's climb a tree," or "Do you want to play ball?" or "Do you want to play with me?" then he can initiate social interaction. This kind of sharing with others is difficult, if not impossible, without words. Nonverbal attempts such as pulling or pushing a playmate in one direction or another are very easily misinterpreted.

With increasing language skills, your son will be able to express himself as a unique individual with feelings, attitudes, and ideas. In his earliest utterances, such as "No like it!" as you try to brush his hair, or "Go see Evan" or "Go to the beach again" or "Go to Sluggo's and have some french fries," he will express to others who he is as a person. People who interact with your child will be more likely to respond to him as an individual when he can communicate his preferences and feelings verbally. It is through this use of language that he establishes himself as an individual with his own identity. Rather than being just "the baby," he then has an image of himself and others have an image of him as a person who likes to play with Evan, enjoys the beach, has french fries as a favorite food, and really does not like to have his hair brushed.

The more he can say, the more he can explore his environment through asking questions. When he can ask, "Where'd the ladybug go?" or "Does the kitty want some salad?" or "Why that bird eat dirty bread?" or "Can you touch a spider?" he will be able to encourage you to teach him about his world.

Language allows your daughter to pretend to be a lion or to feed pretend soup to her dolls. It enables her to play and to initiate games with you and with her playmates. She can say, "I'm an ugly old troll" as you have said in your play, and encourage you to again "be" the ugly old troll and engage in a game of chase. Thus the function of imagination and the interpersonal function interact. Now a whole new world of play, fun, and humor is available to your child and all those who interact with her. This imaginative function of language is enjoyed through adulthood in the forms of reading and poetry.

Through language she can tell people something new, something she has learned, or something she has experienced. After a trip to the zoo with Daddy, she can tell Mommy what she saw that day, what Daddy bought her to eat, and what the seal did.

The earlier your child acquires the ability to use language, the less likely it is that problem behaviors will develop from frustrated attempts to communicate. Many children whose speech and language development is slow acquire habits such as whining, screaming, grabbing things from other children, and full-blown temper tantrums when their attempts at communication through nonverbal means are misunderstood. Early language development can prevent many undesirable behaviors which, once present, are often difficult to eliminate.

Additionally, there is data to suggest that intense early language stimulation may actually increase a child's intelligence. Some psychologists believe that future research may demonstrate that intensive language stimulation actually increases brain weight, size, and chemical constitution.

There are still other advantages to early language development. The use of language greatly facilitates the socialization of your child because reasoning becomes possible. Research consistently shows that reasoning as a means of discipline is associated with the highest degree of self-control in children. Explanation and reasoning can help your child inhibit antisocial behaviors such as hitting, grabbing children or toys, or tantrum behavior, and can promote social behaviors such as sharing and cooperative play. With extensive language stimulation even an eighteen-month-old child can understand and respond to such reasoning as, "Your friend needs some toys to play with or he will want to go home to play with his own toys," or "You have to share, if you want him to stay." When words such as "this is dangerous," "we have to share our friends," or "we need shoes on because the ground is hot" come to exercise control over your child's behavior, the need for physical restraint or punishment is greatly reduced and the likelihood of crying and other tantrum behavior is minimized.

Another advantage of early language development is that language helps your child deal more effectively with waiting and other experiences of discomfort. For instance, once your son can understand and communicate, then when he is tired or angry about having a diaper changed or having to sit in a carseat, he can be helped to endure the discomfort through conversation. You can engage him in talking about something enjoyable he has just done: "What did you feed the horse? What else did he eat?" Or you can talk about something he is about to do: "Who do you want to see at the zoo? Who should we visit?" When your child becomes interested in your question and has to think to form the answer, this behavior is incompatible with tantrum behavior. Similarly, you may help him wait for food by asking him, "What would you like to eat? Would you like some cheese or some ham?" He may find it easier to wait to go outside if you engage him in conversation with questions like "Shall we bring our buckets and shovels outside? What else do we want to take? What do you want to bring outside? You get the toys while I fix our bag." Your child's response about his choice of toys and gathering the toys helps him to wait.

From your perspective, the earlier your child develops language and communication skills the more manageable, reasonable, interesting, and fun to be with you'll find him. Just help him learn the words and he will listen to reason, tell you jokes, make you laugh, and tell you, "I love you." Every bit of effort you put into his language stimulation will be returned to you in joy.

When Do Children Begin to Talk?

Children usually speak their first words somewhere between the ages of twelve and thirteen months. The next advance in language development usually occurs some three months after the single word phase, between the ages of fifteen and twenty months, when the child puts two words together. At eighteen months most children know ten words. Studies of the expected number of words for an average child of twenty-four months vary from fifty words (Lenneberg) to three hundred words (Dale), with most studies ranging between two hundred to three hundred words. The two year old is also expected to use many two-word phrases. By the time the child is three years old, the youngster will have a thousand-word vocabulary which will be understood by people unfamiliar with the child.

These statistics are certainly not to be understood as limitations of children's language development. The developmental timetables for language acquisition found in most child psychology books are merely averages. In reality, there is a considerable range of language ability in children from age ten months on. Some babies can speak ten words at ten months, at eighteen months have a vocabulary of greater than one thousand words, are understandable to strangers, and can ask questions such as "Do you want to go to a restaurant and have some eggs?" and "What are those guys doing on the beach?" On the other hand, many children at age two may speak only three or four single words.

To what do we attribute such variation in the language facilities of children? The most common assumption made by doctors, preschool teachers, and parents is that this range of ability reflects individual differences of an inborn nature, some children being "born talkers," others more quiet. Even some textbooks on developmental psychology suggest that language facility is an inborn capacity rather than a reflection of training.

On the contrary, I have found that training *does* make a difference. In 1981 I studied parents and their children at a parent participation group. I determined that those children who demonstrated advanced verbal development had mothers or fathers who used some or all of the techniques to be described in this chapter. Children with limited language ability had parents who had *not* been using these techniques. The range in verbal ability of the children reflected the range in the parents' sophistication in the use of language-teaching techniques.

All parents in the group of slow to speak children were interested in their children, spent time with them, and tried to teach them to talk. The problem was that their methods were ineffective, not that the effort was absent. Some parents read books far too advanced for the babies and spoke to them in sentences far too complex. Some parents had taped written labels on nearly every object in the home (taping the word "chair" on a chair, and the word "mother" on the mother's picture, and so on). This procedure may help children sightread after they have learned to speak, but it will not teach language. All parents had read several popular baby books which gave general advice to "talk and read to the baby," but provided little in the way of specific teaching techniques.

Certainly there are factors other than teaching which will produce differences in children's rate of language acquisition, such as the intelligence level of the child, the presence of older siblings, and probably some individual personality and temperamental differences. But for any particular child, the rate of acquiring language and the complexity of language used will reflect the degree of stimulation and language training received from the parents or caregiver. If you're not satisfied to hear placating statements such as "He'll probably start talking in sentences when he's two," or "Einstein didn't talk until he was three," I'm writing this chapter for you.

I am convinced that *any* child who would otherwise have acquired language by age three can be helped to acquire language earlier, to have a wider vocabulary, and to use more complex language structure with the specific language training outlined here.

Getting Started

The newborn infant seems to be programmed to acquire language. We have data that indicates that infants are attending to speech sounds in their environments well before they can speak. One important study (Condon and Sander) demonstrated that newborn infants will synchronize their body movement to coordinate with the pattern of sound made by adult speech to such an extent that they appear to be dancing in rhythm to music. By the time infants are one month of age, they respond differently to the voice of their mothers than to the voice of an unfamiliar female (Horowitz). Another important study demonstrated that infants as young as one month of age can discriminate among speech sounds such as "pah" and "bah" as well as adults can (Eimas). In other studies of visual preferences, infants of one to two months begin to prefer representations of a human face to any other pattern or to any color, and by two to three months of age, they demonstrate very clear preferences and look significantly longer at the human face. What does all this mean in terms of your interaction with your newborn?

Talk to Your Newborn

In order to develop speech, the newborn must pay attention to your face, particularly your mouth, and imitate the speech sounds that you make. Your newborn daughter's responsiveness to the human face and receptiveness to speech sounds mean that at birth she is ready for language stimulation to begin. Even though she cannot understand you or respond verbally to your words, talking to her is very important as a priming experience for her later language acquisition.

Reward Cooing

A very important antecedent to early language development is the cooing that is heard from all babies at around the end of the second month and the beginning of the third month. This cooing generally occurs even in deaf babies and seems to be something that programs the baby for communication. If your infant son's earliest cooing sounds are attended to immediately and frequently, then you are teaching him something very important: that his vocalizations will *have an effect on his environment*. This experience of having an effect on the environment is one of the motivating forces for acquiring language.

To assure that your son has significant experiences in having his cooing rewarded and attended to, you should provide stimuli that will elicit more cooing. The best stimulus for promoting cooing seems to be the human face. So, as often as possible, present yourself face to face to him and respond to his cooing with more cooing or speech sounds. This is a time when baby talk is desirable. It is a fact that infants at this age respond more to high-pitched voices and silly sounds than they do to normal adult speech. So at this time make whatever silly noises, cooing sounds, or squeals that seem interesting to your baby. Your goal in the first two months is to reinforce cooing, not to model correct adult speech.

Certain toys will be likely to promote cooing. For example, I've found that a Pooh bear with a large black nose, clear black eyes, and black eyebrows on a bright yellow face is a stimulus that seems to draw out cooing in most infants. When you hold this bear up before your baby's face and he begins to coo, you can respond with simple speech sounds or coos. Studies indicate that when infants' cooing is reinforced by attention, these babies coo more frequently than those whose cooing is not reinforced.

Teach Imitation

When the baby is three and a half to four months old, imitation training may begin. At this time, many babies will begin to make spitting sounds and enjoy the feeling and sound of their own motor behavior and noise. It is at this time you may begin the process which leads to imitation. This is a circular process. First your child will make a certain sound which, *face to face,* you will imitate. There will be a chain: Your child makes a noise, you imitate the noise, your child again makes the noise, you imitate the noise. After many of these chains, the sequence may change: Now you make the noise, your child makes the noise. When your noise precedes your child's noise in time, then you have imitation. On later occasions when you make the same noise, and this noise prompts your child to immediately make this noise, you have succeeded in teaching an imitative behavior. This is a very important prerequisite for the development of speech.

Babbling

When babies reach six months, another very important development occurs. They start babbling. At this time babies will make all the speech sounds which are used in all languages. Even deaf babies will babble, although not for long, since they can't hear any response. Babbling includes both vowels and consonants which eventually approximate words in various languages. For example, "da, ma, na." After a period of time, this babbling seems to focus on sounds that are interesting to the infant. Between six and ten months, the infant will begin to repeat a single syllable with slight alterations each time. For example, "ma" and "me" and all the sounds in between "ma" and "me." This emergence of babbling provides a wonderful opportunity to promote the imitations so important in the development of speech. With the same circular process as was described with cooing, you can imitate, *face to face,* your child's "ma, ma, ma." Your child will later imitate your "ma, ma, ma." Once your child imitates the syllables you present, these syllables may be attached to significant items in the environment.

Capturing the First Word

For example, when your child says, "ma, ma" you can run to the child and say, "Did you call Momma, Momma, Momma?" and begin to pair your child's saying, "ma ma" with Momma immediately appearing. By nine months of age many infants are capable of imitating simple sounds of adults and by ten months of age many infants are capable of communicative speech. Some advanced babies can be expected to say words such as "Momma" and "Dadda" in their eighth month and by ten months to have a vocabulary of ten words (with varying degrees of clarity) such as "kitty," "dadda," "momma," "dog," "hi," "bye-bye," "bottle," or "baby."

How do you decide which words to teach first? With or without specific language training, first words usually are social words such as *hi* and *bye-bye.* This shows the importance of interaction in a child's language development, the social function. The next words usually involve events or objects in the environment that are *important* to your youngster and involve *activity* in the life of your child rather than some stationary object. For example, frequent first words are "shoes," "dog," "ball," or "momma." Children are very unlikely to have as first words things such as "stove," "floor," or "house." Between the sixth and ninth month, you should select three or four items or people that command the attention of your infant. Usually this will be the parents, sibling, and perhaps a family pet or ball. Then each time your child's attention is clearly focused on that person or animal or object, you should repeat the name. For example, you could take your child for a daily stroll and bring the dog on a leash. Each time your child looks in the direction of the dog, you can say, "dog—dog—see the dog."

Capture a Sound

Another trick to pulling out the language capacity of your infant is to capture a sound which is very frequently made by your baby and make it a communicative sound. For example, some babies will make a growling sound on their own, with no prompting, in their play. It is a simple matter to take a book with a large picture of a lion, show your daughter the picture of the lion when she is making that growling sound, and say to her, "What does a lion say?" When she growls say, "Yes, that's right, that's what the lion says. What does a lion say?" You should then growl to prompt her. When she growls imitatively, reinforce it by saying, "Yes, that's right, that's what the lion says, the lion says *grrrrrr*."

Often children will grunt or make some other sound which can be attached to another animal such as a pig, or an approximation to a "whoof-whoof" can be attached to the dog. The process is the same. When the youngster makes a sound similar to "whoof," then you repeat, "whoof-whoof, that's what the doggy says, whoof-whoof. What does the doggy say? Whoof-whoof," and prompt the child to say "whoof-whoof."

The emphasis on animal sounds in the beginning is important not because these sounds are so practical in life, but because they are fun for the babies and they are very easy to extract from a child by capturing sounds already made. A very important reason to encourage these sounds is that they teach babies something about their voices: that they can communicate, that sounds have meaning, and that people will respond to the sounds that they can make. This is extremely important as an early language experience.

Echo the Child's Words

In the beginning, your daughter's attempt to repeat a word may consist of only the initial letter and a syllable. For example, "dog" may be heard as "do" or "da" or some other. You should echo her words but with the correct enunciation. When she says, "da" you should say, "that's right, *dog*," emphasizing the beginning and ending letters. This procedure, called echoing, is something that you will continue for a long time. Whenever your child says something, before you respond to it, it is a good idea to repeat what she has just said. In the beginning you will merely repeat the word, modeling the correct enunciation. When you echo a child's more complex language expressions, you will echo the intended meaning, correcting enunciation and use of English with your echo. For example, when your child asks "what he has?" You echo, "What does he have?" Then answer, "He has a cookie."

Repeat

Hundreds of times in the course of a month you will repeat "dog." After many repetitions, you may begin to ask, "Where is the dog?" when the dog is very near and in the periphery of your daughter's vision. When she focuses directly on the dog, reward that by saying, "Yes, that's right, that's the dog." Similarly, when playing with the ball you can bounce the ball and as she watches it, you repeat over and over again, "Ball, ball, see the ball—ball." And then ask her to orient to the ball by asking, "Where is the ball?" When she focuses on the ball say, "Yes, that's right, that's the ball." When she can crawl, ask her to "Get the ball." Teaching these first words utilizes the same principles used throughout this book: Start simply with small pieces of behavior, and be certain that the response is within the capability of the baby. Begin with only three or four words. Once these speech sounds are clearly understood and your baby is making some attempt to repeat them, then you may expand to other items.

Encourage Repetition of Words

One good way to incorporate new vocabulary words into your speaking vocabulary has been recommended by English teachers for years: repeat the word you want to learn ten times and the word will be yours. You can encourage your son to repeat words over and over again by continuing to echo his word beyond the first occurrence. For example, in the beginning when he says, "dog" you respond, "That's right, that's a dog, dog." If he doesn't repeat, you say, "What is that? It's a dog" and then try to encourage him to say, "dog" again. If he won't repeat it, ask him to orient toward it by saying, "Where is the dog?" and when he looks at it, you say, "That's right, that's the dog."

Gradually your son will begin to repeat words more and more. As his vocabulary increases you can have conversations which involve the use of the particular words at least ten times. When you take a first train ride, you say to your child, "This is a passenger train." He says "passenger train," you repeat, "That's right, this is a passenger train," and then when he repeats "passenger train" you say, "Yes, and you are a passenger, and I am a passenger, and Daddy is a passenger." Encourage him to repeat "Daddy is a passenger," using the word "passenger" over and over again.

Children who repeat a newly acquired vocabulary word over and over again have an enormously large speaking vocabulary. Those children who at eighteen months know a thousand words are the ones who repeat these words to themselves and in conversations with their mothers or fathers or caregivers.

Use Gestures and Action

Whenever possible, use some gestures or action to call attention to the word you are intending to teach. For example, to teach the word "water," run the water, splash it, put your son in it, pour it on his tummy, all the time saying, "water." To teach the word "run," take him in your arms and run with him, or, if he can walk, take him by the hand and say, "Let's run, run, run, run, run" as you run. As his speech develops say, "We are running." To teach the word "throw," take a ball and play with your dog. Put the ball in the baby's hand, hold his hand and the ball, and when you throw say, "Throw the ball, throw it, throw the ball to the dog."

Model Correct Enunciation

Some children can learn to pronounce a word without even looking closely at your mouth. For other children, articulation comes slowly but can be facilitated by encouraging the child to pay close attention to your mouth movements. Sometimes it is necessary to say, "Look at me," take your daughter's chin in your hand and direct her face toward your mouth. Then pronounce the word carefully. For example, the *l* sound in "blue" may be difficult for your child. She may be saying "bwue." It is frequently helpful to break the word into pieces to help the child make the individual sounds before putting them together. For example, you might help her to make an *l* sound by putting your tongue between your teeth and saying "la, la, la," several times, encouraging her to imitate your *l* sound with exaggerated tongue between teeth. Then put the *b* with it and say, "bla, bla, bla," after she correctly imitates the first sound. Then put it all together and help her to exaggerate it by saying "belue."

If your daughter's speech is at least somewhat understandable to the primary caregiver, then this effort should only be continued if it is well received by the child. Some children enjoy breaking words into parts and imitating your sound. Other children will resist having their face directed toward your face and will balk at this breaking down of words. It is a mistake to persist in this unless your child seems to enjoy it. Most children will improve in their articulation with time and errors such as substituting a *w* sound for *l* as in "blue" or *w* for *r* as in saying "wabbit" for "rabbit" are very common in children under three. Certainly, if your child's articulation can be improved without her resisting it, then there are advantages to doing so. Once the child's articulation improves, her speech will be understandable to strangers and many more interactions will be possible.

Excite Your Child

Another important aspect in teaching language involves providing exciting experiences, because children will be much more likely to learn to label those things which excite and interest them most. Therefore, if possible, frequent trips to the nearest zoo are highly recommended. For a baby nine to eighteen months old, a once-a-week trip to the zoo is highly desirable. In the beginning you should take your child to perhaps five or six significant animals and label those clearly and distinctly. For example, you might visit the elephants, lions, giraffes, zebras, and bears.

In any single trip to the zoo, it is unlikely that your baby will acquire the appropriate labels. So take along a camera and take a picture of each of these five animals, or if there are postcards available that give a good view of these animals, you can simply purchase them. At home, show the baby the pictures with the appropriate label. In this way, books and pictures take on greater significance for your baby and the use of books and pictures will become extremely important in your child's language development. With regular trips to the zoo and repeated presentation of these pictures or postcards, your baby will be able to name these animals.

If it is not possible to make a weekly excursion to a zoo, then think about the available resources in your area. Often there will be some very exciting experiences for babies right around the corner. For example, visit a kennel that takes in dogs to board. Seeing all the different types of dogs and hearing the label "dog" applied to all the varied-looking animals is a very important learning experience to a one-year-old child. Perhaps the animal shelter is not too far away. Perhaps there are ducks or chickens in the area that your child can feed or watch you feed. If there is a park nearby, feeding pigeons some wild birdseed is a very exciting experience to an infant. There may be a rabbit in the neighborhood to whom you can bring a carrot or some lettuce, or perhaps there is a stable which you can visit and show your child the horses. Not too far away there may be cows. In cold weather try a visit to a pet store or a friend's house to see a cat, a dog, or a bird.

The most important point here is that to really pull out the capabilities of a child, the necessary ingredient is excitement and interest. You must always be searching out experiences that will be exciting for your child.

Repeat the Experience

Repetition is important. It is not enough to expose your child to the stable with horses on only one occasion. Until your child has acquired the label "horse," learned to neigh like a horse, and is able to recognize the horse in a book, it is important to continue to make that excursion as often as possible, even every day. In fact, having a habit of taking a stroll to the stables to see the horses, a walk to the park to feed the pigeons, or a walk to the animal shelter to see the dogs, is very important in the development of anticipation and thinking about the future.

Speaking To Your Child

There are certain characteristics of adult speech to children that facilitate language development. They are simple:

1. Slow down your speech.
2. Articulate your words very clearly, emphasizing beginning and ending sounds.
3. Speak in simple, well-formed sentences.
4. Coordinate your statements with what you are doing, or with what captures the interest of the child at the moment.
5. Repeat your sentences three to four times.

A very effective device in teaching language is the repetition of very simple, well-formed sentences coordinated with activity. For example, in giving a fifteen month old boy his juice, you can say, "Would you like some juice?" or "Do you want some juice?" three or four times, repeating the same question while offering him juice. The effect of repetition is to intensify the child's focus of attention and to increase the probability that he will understand the message (Benedict). Additionally, you are modeling the use of question formation and the use of verbs which he will later imitate.

Whenever possible you should describe ongoing activity. For example, let your son watch as you make breakfast. As you crack the eggs, say, "See, Mommy's breaking the eggs" several times. Then as you scramble them, say, "See the eggs? The eggs are cooking, the eggs are cooking." When putting on his shoes, say, "Let's put on your shoes, put on your shoes."

Once your son has begun to acquire some words and to label the animals and the experiences that have been exciting to him, then on your way to visit the animal you should begin to talk about what you will be doing: "Let's go see the birds, let's go feed the birds" or "Let's go see the bears" or "Let's go see the lion." Keep this up all the way to the animal. After the excursion, you can talk about what you have seen: "Did you see the birds? Did you feed the birds? Did you see the horse? The horse said neigh."

In the one-word stage, it is important to realize that a single word may be used by your child in a variety of ways. Sometimes your daughter will identify a horse saying, "horse" emphatically. What she wants at this time is merely confirmation from you: "Yes, that is a horse." At other times, she may call a four-legged animal of some other species, such as a deer, a "horse." This time she probably knows that this is not a horse, but is asking you for some help in identifying what it really is. Merely to answer with, "No, that is not a horse" or worse yet to agree with her that it is, in fact, a horse, are both undesirable responses at this time. Tell her, "No, that's a deer, deer. See, it has horns. It's a deer." As soon as possible, provide her with a picture of a horse and a picture of a deer. Point to each animal and label each one repeatedly. Children at this time are hypothesis-testing, and look to you to correct them. The problem here is that you can vastly underestimate the understanding and language potential of your baby. Children really want to learn and to communicate and the more information you give them, *at their pace and level of understanding,* the more information they want. If their curiosity is discouraged, their motivation will not endure. At other times, your daughter will use a single word such as "horse" with an inflection or questioning tone in her voice. What she wants to hear in this case may be a description of what the horse is doing. Perhaps the horse is eating hay, jumping over rails, or carrying a rider who is someone your daughter knows. She is eager to learn and wants to be able to describe his experience and to hear you say, "Yes, the horse is eating hay, see the hay" or "Suzy is riding the horse. See Suzy ride the horse? Suzy is riding the horse" or "The horse is jumping, he's jumping." Note that the description of the behavior of the animal should be simple and descriptive and repeated several times.

Sing Songs and Chant

You may have begun singing to your newborn son to lull him to sleep but, once he begins to develop speech, songs may take on added significance. By singing songs which use words and describe experiences he can relate to, you can increase the phrases and words available to him in his own speech. After you sing to him many times, "I'm a little white duck swimming in the water" followed by "I'm a green frog," he may creatively begin to sing things like "I'm a black duck," "I'm a white frog," "I'm a brown dog," and to correctly use "I'm a . . . " as a phrase in a number of circumstances. You need not be limited by established songs, but you may create your own songs related to activities such as dressing the child or picking up toys. You may sing your own tune or make up your own verse to a nursery rhyme tune. After singing over and over again, "This is the way we comb our hair, comb our hair, comb our hair" or "This is the way we brush our teeth so early in the morning," many children will begin to appropriately use the pronouns "we" and "our" and other phrases used in the song.

Expansion

Some three months after your daughter has acquired a repertoire of single words, she will begin to put two words together. She will begin to say such things as, "see bird" or "more juice" or "get down." At this time it's a good idea to increase your description of events to include adjectives or adverbs. For example, if she says, "pet kitty,"

then you should respond, "Pet the *nice* kitty, pet the *nice* kitty *softly.*"
Or if your child responds, "more juice," then you should respond
with, "You want some more *apple* juice?" This technique is called
expansion in child psychology textbooks. It means that you increase
the complexity of a statement you make to your daughter to slightly
ahead of what she is capable of saying herself. When you speak
at a level of complexity slightly ahead of your child's it seems to
provide a maximum learning opportunity.

Elaboration

A related procedure is called elaboration. When your child says,
"There's tractor," you respond with "That's a yellow tractor, it's
cleaning the beach," and give a little more information. Again, your
statement should be repeated three or four times. If your child says,
"There's a fish," you respond with, "That's a little fish swimming
in the water," and repeat it three or four times. Be sure that you
elaborate according to the attention of your child. If your child is
looking at a large lizard in the zoo and the predominant activity
is that lizard's tongue darting in and out, then say, "See the lizard.
See him stick out his tongue. Look at his tongue. See the lizard's
tongue. He's sticking out his tongue." It's not helpful to point out
the dry terrain in which the lizard lives or the tracks the lizard has
made with his tail. Your child is focusing on the lizard's tongue,
so that's what you should describe in your elaboration.

No Baby Talk Now

Following the two-word stage, your child will continue to speak
in a manner which has been called "telegraphic speech." This refers
to the finding that children will omit prepositions such as "of," "by,"
"on," "through," articles such as "a," or "an," and word endings,
and will almost always simplify the verb to the present tense. Their
utterances do contain the most meaningful words in the sentence,
referred to by psychologists as "content words" (Slobin). Even when
your son is attempting to imitate you, his version will take the form
of telegraphic speech. For example, when you say, "Do you want
to throw the ball to the dog?" your son will imitate "throw ball
dog." When you say, "Let's get some water toys and play with some
water," he may respond with "play toys water." This telegraphic
speech seems to be something which all children do in whatever
happens to be their native language.

An important thing to remember is that you should *use the correct and completely full sentence.* Unfortunately, it is at this time that many parents begin to imitate their children's speech and to omit the plurals the children have omitted, to use the present tense at all times, and to omit articles such as "an" and "the." For example, the parents will offer the toddler an apple, saying "Suzy want apple?" or, "Baby want up?" instead of, "Suzy, do you want an apple? Do you want to get up? Does the baby want to get up?" Telegraphic communication by the parent will hinder the child's language development, whereas the full sentences will promote language development. It is this kind of communication which psychologists and writers on language development refer to when they suggest that you should not talk baby talk to children.

Ask Questions

Another helpful technique is to ask questions of your child even though you cannot expect an answer. For example ask your son, "Do you like the raisin toast? Is it good?" As he is riding his rocking horse ask him, "Are you riding a horse, John?" When he is swimming ask him "Are you swimming in the water? Are you a fish?" This helps him to learn important sentence structure.

Correct through Modeling

A uniform error in the language development of children is in the formation of negative sentences. Initially children say "no" before the sentence to make it a negative, resulting in "no like it," "no go outside," "no want juice." When you practice the important repetition of your child's utterances in this case, be certain to correct them grammatically, not by reprimanding or pointing out the error to the child, but by modeling the correct way of making that negative statement. For example, instead of responding to the child, "you no like it," or "you no want outside," or "you no want juice," you should respond, "You *don't* like it," "you *don't* want to go outside," "you *don't* want any juice."

Another error which seems to be universal in children is to over-regularize the rules of language. For example, a child who has previously learned the words "foot" and "feet" will, after having learned to add an "s" to make plurals, begin to say "feets." Similarly, a child who had previously correctly used the word "went" as in "he went outside," will, after having acquired the rules of adding "ed" to form the past tense, begin to say, "he go-ed outside." These cases of overregularization are cute, and you may be reluctant to provide the correct models, but this will handicap your child's verbal development.

Modeling the Use of Pronouns

One aspect of language acquisition which is very difficult for children is the correct use of pronouns. Many children confuse "you" and "me," "she" and "her," "I" and "you," "I" and "me," and "he" and "him" for a long time. The whole process of learning pronouns may be facilitated through the use of modeling. For example, when you ask your child questions or make statements, use your child's name and your name and then repeat the question or the statement using the pronoun. For example, "Does Jane want some juice?" Then ask "Do you want some juice?" Second example: "Does Jane want to give Mommy a bite? Do you want to give me a bite?" Or, "Mommy will get it for Jane. Mommy will get it for you. I will get it for you, Jane." When she asks about the cat, "Does Tuffy want some salad?" You would answer, "No, Tuffy doesn't want some salad, he doesn't like salad. Do you want to give it to him and see? Do you want to give it to Tuffy and see?"

Expanding Vocabulary Development

Once your daughter is communicating her needs and wants and appears to have conquered the basic structure of language, you can still work to advance her communication skills by helping her learn new words. You can do so by using new words and then giving their meanings while conversing with her. For example, playing with her by "tasting" her legs to see which one is better and saying, "I can't *decide*" [new word] which leg is better. Does this one taste better or does this one taste better? I can't make up my mind. I can't *decide*." Then "taste" each leg. As you offer her a choice of clothing you can say to her, "You can *choose* [new word] the shirt you want. Which one do you want? Would you like the red one or the blue one? You *choose,* you pick the one you want." When you cannot give her a pen to play with, you can tell her, "This ink pen is *permanent* [new word], it won't wash off—it stays there for good, it's *permanent*. If you get it on your clothes, it will be there, and stay there, and won't come off anymore—it's *permanent*." When you take her by a trailer where a construction crew is living for a time, you may tell her, "The workers are living in that trailer while they are building that house. It's their *temporary* house. They are only living there for a little while and then they'll move. It's their *temporary* house—it's only for a while."

Whenever you are unsure of whether or not your child can understand a particular word, use that word and give the definition simply as a matter of course. Use the more advanced word such as "decide" or "choose," then in the same discussion give a definition or a synonym just as part of your conversation. This is more effective than giving a definition in a more usual sense (for example, "You choose—that means you decide or you pick it out.") Once you hear your child using the word correctly alone, you no longer have to include the definition each time you use the word.

To increase and expand your child's understanding and use of words, continue to introduce new words daily, always speaking at a level slightly beyond your child's current level of language use.

A Sample Sequence For Teaching Language

The sequence will be used (1) to teach individual words, (2) To connect them to verbs using action to teach the verb, and finally, (3) To combine nouns and verbs already known with objects and prepositional phrases.

I. Teaching Individual Words

    A. Begin with three words: *dog, cat, ball.*

        1. Repeat word with appropriate accompanying action. Strive for ten repetitions each time a word is presented. Present each word a hundred times before using the word in a sentence.

            a. Examples of presentation:

                i. Take dog for a walk with baby in the stroller. Repeat "dog" each time the baby looks at the dog.

                ii. Dog barks and baby orients toward the dog, repeat the word *dog.*

                iii. As baby looks through the window at dog, repeat "dog."

            b. Repeat "cat" as cat walks by and baby's attention is focused on cat. Pick up cat and bring it to baby, repeating "cat" as the child focuses on it. As cat meows for food and child orients to it, repeat "cat."

            c. Bounce or roll ball while saying "ball."

2. Teach questions: "Where is the dog," "Where is the cat," "Where is the ball." As child orients correctly to the dog [cat or ball], you say, "Yes, there is the dog [cat or ball]."

3. Continue using first three words with requests: "Get the dog," "Get the ball," "Get the cat." Use appropriate gestures pointing to the cat or dog or rolling the ball near the baby as you give your request. When baby reaches for the dog [ball or cat] say "Yes, you got the dog [ball or cat]."

4. Each day repeat each word, *dog, cat, ball,* at least ten times in these simple sentences. Emphasize the word *dog.*

See the dog.
Where is the dog?
Yes! There is the dog.
Get the dog.
You like the dog.
That is a dog, dog.

Do the same for cat and ball.

5. Model and reward imitation of the word.

a. Get baby's attention to focus on your mouth, repeat "dog, dog, dog." Look into baby's eyes and say "Ian, say dog, dog, dog." Model the word *dog* and request him to say the word as described above ten times per day.

b. When baby repeats "duh" or "da" or any *d* sound, reinforce the approximation, saying "That's right! Dog!"

c. Continue to model and request imitation of the word *dog.* Once baby more closely imitates the word, only reinforce the *closer imitation* from that point on. Gradually reward as close to perfect imitation as baby can make, but do not require perfect imitation.

d. Ask the question "What is that?" Then answer it yourself. "That is a dog. Dog." Encourage imitation: "Say dog."

   e. When baby responds correctly to the question "What is that?" (referring to dog) and says "Duh" or some approximation to dog, or spontaneously says "Duh" when she sees the dog five times, she knows the word.

   f. When baby knows three words—*dog, cat,* and *ball*—introduce three new words or sounds.

B. Teach three animal sounds.

   1. Begin with sounds of cat, dog, and cow. Buy small plastic models of these animals.

      a. Show baby the plastic cat and say, "See the cat. The cat says meow, meow, meow. The cat says meow, meow. Meow meow cat." Then place the cat among the dog and cow. Ask baby to "Get the cat." When baby gets the cat say, "That's right, that's the cat. The cat says meow, meow. The cat says meow." Then ask and answer the question "What does the cat say?" The cat says meow."

      b. Show the baby the plastic dog and repeat the above procedure with "woof, woof" for the dog.

      c. Teach the word *cow* with the actual animal if possible. Be there at feeding time so the cow will moo. Bring along a tape recorder so you can tape the sound of the cow mooing. When the cow moos for you and your child, you say, "The cow says moo, the cow says moo. Listen, the cow says moo" and record your mooing as well. Then show baby the plastic cow and repeat above procedure. Play the tape for the baby while you show her the plastic animal.

   2. Model animal and reward imitation of the animal sounds. Ask "What does the cat say?" Then help baby focus on your face and model "meow." Tell him to "Say meow." Reward any *m* sound or attempt at *m* sound at first. Later, reward imitations that are closer to "meow." Continue to ask the question and request imitation of your meow ten times daily until learned. Baby knows the animal sound when he answers the question, "What does the cat say?" without your modeling "meow" or when he picks up the plastic cat or looks at the cat and says "meow" spontaneously. Strive for ten repetitions each time a word is presented.

C. Following the same structure, add three more words: *baby, shoes, airplane.*

1. Present new words by using them often. Be playful and have fun as you repeat the word at least ten times in each training session. For example, give the baby her shoe to hold while you say "shoe, shoe" repeatedly. When an airplane flies overhead, point to it and repeat "airplane, airplane, airplane."

2. Ask questions: "Where is the baby?" "Where is the shoe?" "Where is the airplane?" When baby correctly orients or points to baby, shoe, or airplane, say "That's right, that is the baby [shoe or airplane]."

3. Request the baby to "Get the shoe." "Get the baby." Review previous words: "Get the ball." "Get the dog." "Where is the dog?" Reinforce correct responses: "Yes, that is the dog!" "You got the shoe!"

4. Repeat the new words in simple sentences at least ten times a day. For example: "See the airplane!" "Bye-bye airplane." "Where is the airplane?"

5. Model words and reward imitation of words. Get the baby's attention to focus on your mouth and repeat the new words. Look into the baby's eyes and repeat the new words. Model each word and request baby to imitate ten times per day. When the baby gives any approximation of the word, such as "pane" or "apane" for "airplane," reinforce the approximation, saying "That's right! Airplane!" Continue to model and request imitation of the new words, reinforcing closer approximations each time. Prompt the answer to "What's that?" Ask your baby "What's that?" Answer yourself "Airplane." Tell your child to say "airplane."

6. When baby responds correctly to the questions, "What is that?" or spontaneously says the word when she sees the object, she knows the word.

7. Continue using words which have been learned previously, repeating them and asking questions about them daily. Encourage your baby to use the words learned.

D. Add three more words: *cup, telephone, hat.*

E. Add three more words: *bus, bird, water.*

F. Add three more words: *truck, bunny, fish.*

G. Add three more words: *car, duck, boat.*

H. Add three more animals: *elephant, lion,* and *seal.*
1. Take a trip to the zoo and observe three new animals. Observe the elephants, lions, and seals on one day and then show the child the cow and the ducks he already knows on the same day. As your child is focusing on the elephant, repeat "elephant" at least thirty times. As your child focuses on the lion, again repeat "lion" at least thirty times. Try to tape-record the lion roaring, the elephant trumpeting, and the seal barking.
2. With lifelike plastic animals, practice the child's retrieving the animal by name by asking "Where is the elephant?" Lead his hand to the elephant and say "That's right. That is the elephant." When the child can correctly reach for all three animals, then teach the animal sounds. Do not add any new animals until the child can correctly reach for and name each of the six already presented (dog, cat, cow, elephant, lion, seal) from a group of five animals. As many trips to the zoo as possible and as many play sessions as possible with plastic animals or pictures of animals are recommended. Try for at least one fifteen-minute session per day.
3. Teach baby to make *sounds* of elephant, lion, and seal. Show baby the plastic lion and say, "See the lion. The lion says grrr, grrr, grrr. The lion says grrr, grrr. Grrr, grrr lion." Then place the lion among the dog and cow. Ask baby to "Get the lion." When baby gets the lion, say "That's right, that's the lion. The lion says grrr, grrr. The lion says grrr." Then ask and answer the question "What does the lion say? The lion says grrr." Repeat the sequence with the plastic elephant and seal.

I. Following the same structure add three new animals: *giraffe, bear, hippo.*
J. Add three new animals: *chick, goat, zebra.*
K. Add three new animals: *horse, rooster, tiger.*

L. When your baby can say fifty words (including animal sounds), introduce sentences by attaching verbs to nouns that your baby already knows. Although you will use articles such as *the,* your baby will probably use two-word sentences only. For example, when you will say "get the ball," your baby will repeat "get ball." Continue to use the article *the.*"

II. Attaching Verbs to Nouns Baby Knows.

    A. Theme 1: playing ball.

        1. Throw the ball. As you throw the ball, take the baby's hand and help him throw the ball and say "Throw the ball." Repeat the throw and say "Throw the ball" at least ten times.

        2. Running. Take the child's hand and run with him, saying "run, run, run."

        3. As you reach for the ball with the baby, repeat "Get the ball." Continue this sequence, repeating each phrase: "Throw the ball," "Run, run, run," "Get the ball," each time. You can repeat each segment two or three times each time you do it, "Throw the ball, throw the ball, throw the ball." "Run, run, run. Run, run, run. Run, run, run."

    B. Teach the present tense and the present participle with each verb presented.

        1. Teaching the verb *drink*. As the dog is drinking his water, repeat "See the dog drinking. He is drinking. See the dog drink." When your baby drinks his juice, say "You want to drink?" "[Child's name] is drinking." "See the baby drink." "The baby is drinking." As the cat drinks, say "See the cat drink. The cat is drinking. See the cat drink." Any of the animals that you have already presented may be now used in sentences with the word *drink*. The sentences, "See the _____ drink. The _____ is drinking." Be certain to use words that the child already knows with the words *drink* and *drinking*.

        2. Teaching the verb *run*. "See the dog run. The dog is running. See the boy run. The boy is running." Again, use all the animals that the child already knows when the opportunity arises.

        3. Use the same structure with the new verb *swim*.

        4. Use the same structure with the new verb *jump*. At this point, you might have a boy or girl in the neighborhood jump over small hurdles for the child to watch as you repeat the words, "The boy is jumping" and "The girl is jumping." Boy and girl are new vocabulary words which could be introduced at this time.

        5. Use the same structure with the new verb *eat*. Introduce new vocabulary words that go with the verb *eat*. Ex-

amples might be "The seal eats fish." "The baby eats cookies."

6. Use the same structure with the new verb *play*.
7. Use the same structure with the new verb *dance*. Again, you could have a neighborhood boy or girl dance for you while you play music for the child.
8. Use the same structure with the new verb *sit down*.
9. Use the same structure with the new verb *walk*.
10. Use the same structure with the new verb *stand up*. Most zoos will have a bear that stands up or you might be able to get your dog to stand up on its hind legs for a cookie.
11. Use the same structure with the new verb *fly*. Introduce the word *kite* here as new vocabulary: "See the kite fly, the kite is flying."
12. Use the same structure with the new verb *feed*.

III. **Combining a Noun and a Verb with a Prepositional Phrase or Object.**

A. Join one known noun and one known verb to make a longer sentence. As you say, "Throw the ball to the dog," help the baby to throw the ball to the dog. As you say "Throw the shoe to the dog," help the baby to throw the shoe. You may have a ball and a shoe at the same time and alternate asking the baby to throw the ball and then the shoe to the dog. Sometime have another boy and a dog together and ask you baby to throw the ball to the boy instead of the dog.

B. Combining known words in new phrases. The *known noun + known verb + known object*

Examples: The boy throws the ball.
The boy is throwing the ball.
The baby throws the cup.
The baby throws the ball
The seal eats the fish.
The seal is eating fish.
The bear eats the fish.
The bear is eating fish.
The dog eats the shoe.
No, no, dog. Don't eat the shoe.
The elephant eats the hay.
The elephant is eating hay.
No, no baby, don't eat the hay.

C. Combine known words with new object. The *known animal* is *new verb[ing] new object*
   Examples: The dog is drinking water.
             The baby is drinking water.
             The lion is drinking water.
             The elephant is drinking water.
             All the zoo animals are drinking water.

D. Combine known nouns, verbs, and prepositional phrases. The *known noun + known verb + prepositional phrase with known object* (prepositional phrase = in the water)
   Examples: The baby is swimming in the water.
             The fish are swimming in the water.
             The dog is swimming in the water.
             The green frog is swimming in the water.
             The seal is swimming in the water.
   (New prepositional phrase = with the ball)
             The kitten plays with the ball.
             The puppy plays with the ball.
             The baby plays with the ball.
             The elephant plays with the ball.

E. Combine known noun, new verb, and prepositional phrase (prepositional phrase = with the dog).
   Examples: The boy dances with the dog.
             The girl is dancing with the dog.
             The boy is dancing with the girl.

Introduce new verb *ride* and *rides* with known words.
   Examples: See the girl ride the horse.
             The girl rides the horse.
             The girl is riding the horse.
             See the boy ride the car.
             The boy is riding the car.
             See the boy ride the horse.
             See the boy ride the elephant.
             The boy rides the elephant.
             The boy is riding the elephant.

Introduce new verb *fly* and new prepositional phrase *in the sky*
   Examples: See the bird fly in the sky.
             The bird flies in the sky.
             The bird is flying in the sky.
             See the airplane fly in the sky.
             The airplane flies in the sky.

F. Presentation of pronouns *him, her, them*. Add new words to known words and phrases when actions make meaning clear. For example, while feeding animals say:

> Feed the horse some bread.
> Feed him some bread.
> Feed the birds some bread.
> Feed them some bread.
> Feed the birds some cookies.
> Feed them some cookies.
> Feed the bunny some carrots.
> Feed her some carrots.

G. Reviewing verbs and pronouns to teach feelings. *Pronouns + known verbs + new words of feelings or states of being*

1. Drinking: "See the dog drink. The dog is drinking water. The dog is thirsty. He is thirsty."
2. Eating: "See the man eating watermelon. See the baby eating watermelon. The baby likes watermelon. The man is hungry. The baby is hungry. They are all hungry."

IV. **Introduce Questions and Answers.**

> Is the seal eating watermelon?
> No, the seal is not eating watermelon.
> The seal is eating fish.
> Is the baby eating hay?
> No, the baby is not eating hay.
> The baby is eating watermelon.
> Is the dog eating a bone?
> No, the dog is not eating a bone.
> The dog is eating a shoe.
> No, no, dog, don't eat the shoe.

V. **Teaching words of emotion.**

A. Teach the verbs *waiting, wanting,* and *liking*.

Examples: The dog gets the ball.
> See the baby throw the ball to the dog.
> The dog is waiting. The dog is waiting.
> He wants that ball. He wants that ball.

And as the dog runs:
> You see, he likes that ball, the dog likes the ball.
> The baby's waiting for his juice.
> The baby wants his juice.
> He is thirsty.
> The baby wants his juice.

Show a picture of a boy waiting to ride the pony. Say "He wants to ride the pony. See. He is happy. He likes to ride the pony. He likes to ride the pony." When your child or another child is sleepy and wants to go to sleep, say "He is tired. He wants to sleep. Night-night baby. He wants to sleep. He is tired."

B. Teach the verbs *love* and *loving*.

    Examples: When the baby puts his head on the dog. You say, "The baby loves the dog. Nice dog. When you are holding the baby, say, "See the mommy loving the baby. The mommy hugs the baby."

C. Teach the verb *crying*.

D. Teach the adjective *angry*.

VI. **Introduce Classification of Known Items.**

A. While shopping introduce the class of fruit. "Let's get some fruit. Do you want some oranges? Or do you want some bananas? Or do you want some peaches? What kind of fruit do you want? Do you want oranges, or bananas, or peaches?" The same can be done in a toy store. "See all the toys. There are balls, trucks, riding toys. What would you like? What toys would you like?"

Using Books To Teach Language

Why should you promote an interest in books? There are a number of reasons:

1. Early interest in books and pictures is extremely valuable in promoting language development.
2. Children who have been frequently read to as toddlers are themselves good readers in school.
3. Reading increases your child's general information and knowledge.
4. A love for books in childhood provides a wonderful means of entertainment which can last a lifetime.

Start using books to teach language when your child is around six to eight months old. In the beginning, select books which have only one realistic picture of a single item per page. Try to find for example, an ABC book which has for the letter *A*, a large red apple, for *B*, a large bird, for *C*, the face of a clown, for *D*, a dog, and so on. Look for a book which contains items which are realistic, interesting, and exciting to your baby. You will not be mentioning the letters at this early stage but will be focusing on the large, colorful, realistic pictures found in such books.

When you "read" the book to your baby, you must *use single words*. Whenever possible, integrate real-life experience with the pictures. For example, if on the page for *W* there is a watermelon, then get some watermelon and say, "Watermelon, see the watermelon? This is a watermelon, Do you want some watermelon?" Point to the picture while your child is eating the watermelon. Similarly, when you arrive at the *X* for xylophone, dig your child's xylophone out of the toy box and show the xylophone in the picture while you play a few notes. When you arrive at the clown, bring out your child's toy clown and set it down beside the picture.

In your early use of books, the procedure should be the same as in teaching language at any other time. You really want to be teaching only one thing at a time. Therefore, until your child learns to correctly identify "clown" do not introduce a more complicated study of the clown. Later on, you may begin to label the clown's nose or eyes. A common mistake of parents trying to teach language to their children and introducing books to their children is to bombard them with far more than they can assimilate at one time. Rather than facilitating language acquisition, this only confuses your child. Richard Scarry's *Best First Book Ever* is not a good first book by these criteria. If you use books appropriately from the time your child is eight months of age, the Scarry book is good at about eighteen months.

Select Books According to Your Child's Experiences

Another criterion in selecting books for your child is to be guided by what your child knows. If you have been taking your daughter to a nearby duck pond, then find a book with pictures of ducks. She will attend more to a book with something *meaningful* in each picture. If a page shows ducks swimming in a pond similar to one she has seen,then she will be interested in other things on the page which she may not have seen, like a frog sitting on a lily pad. If you have taken a trip to the zoo, then to sit down with a book about zoo animals is very meaningful and relevant.

When you are attempting to introduce something new by way of a book, be sure to introduce the new word along with some familiar words and experiences. For example, if your daughter knows the word "horse" but does not know the word "barn," show her the picture of the horse with the barn and tell her that the horse lives in the barn. Then, as soon as possible, relate a new experience to the picture she has seen. Try to take her to a stable where the horses live in the barn.

The relationship between books and experiences, particularly for a child of eight to eighteen months, should be very interactive. When your daughter has a new experience, you should try to find a related picture in a book. If something in a book is new to her, attempt to provide the related experience. With this approach, you can create a genuine love for books. When the picture of the horse helps her to remember seeing a horse and creates in her some fraction of the excitement she felt when she saw a real, live horse, then her excitement and interest in books increases.

Describe Action in the Picture

Let's say your son has a substantial picture vocabulary (that is, when you ask him "What is this?" he can answer "horse," "dog," or "shoe"), and he understands verbs such as "run" and "eat." Then put these words together in simple sentences and describe the action in the picture as you do in real life. Describe, "The horse is running," "The dog is eating the shoe. No, no, dog, don't eat the shoe! The dog is eating the shoe!"

Introduce Stories

When your child is around eight months old, you can introduce a very simple story. The first story should consist of one large, brightly colored picture per page, and one **simple sentence**. Be sure that these first stories contain a significantly different picture on each page. Page after page of only dog pictures will not sustain your eight-month-old son's interest. Stuffed animals representing the characters that appear in the book will help keep him interested. Even though the stories may involve words he doesn't understand initially, with constant repetition he will memorize the words, and the phrases will pick up meaning as he grows. Later he will use these words and phrases creatively in his own speech. As he becomes more and more interested in the pages of books, you may begin to read stories with more prose. In the beginning, one line per page is enough. As his vocabulary increases, look for books that contain two lines per page. As his attention span increases, increase the length of the prose on each page accordingly.

Reading to the Child of Fifteen to Twenty-four Months

Many of the "Beginner Books" or "Bright and Early Books" designed for beginning readers to read alone are excellent for you to read to your child of fifteen to twenty-four months. The simple phrases and repetition of a limited vocabulary are perfect for teaching new phrases and words, and most children love them. Particularly good are *He Bear She Bear* by Stan and Jan Berenstein and *Are You My Mother?* by P.D. Eastman. The constant repetition in these books is useful for the child learning to use certain phrases properly. However, as your child's attention span increases, you may also read more involved stories such as the traditional *Goldilocks and the Three Bears* or *The Three Little Pigs*. Be certain to censor these fairytales for violence, since some of them may be frightening. For example, instead of having any pigs be eaten by the wolf, you can rewrite the story so that the first little pig runs away to the house of the second little pig and then the second little pig runs away to the house of the third.

Repeat the same stories over and over again so that your child can memorize useful phrases. Of course, when your child appears to have lost interest in a particular story, you need some new ones. Let your child choose a book to read at storytime. Try to read to your child every day. A half hour to three-quarters of an hour of reading each day, not necessarily all at one time, is excellent for stimulating language development in a very young child.

Delayed Language Development

The Resistant Child

Some children's language development is delayed because children refuse to imitate as part of being generally noncompliant. Often, a baby who refuses to talk also refuses to do anything else that his parents would like him to do. The problem goes deeper than language and means you must teach him to be more attentive to your requests in general before you will get him to pay attention to your requests to initiate or use speech. Certainly there are other reasons for delayed language, such as articulation problems and hearing problems, etc. It is usually wise to look for the simplest solution first. Get your child's hearing tested, and if he's not talking by three and a half, take him to a speech therapist. But compliance training is important even if there turns out to be other reasons for the language delay.

Sometimes a child's refusal to talk is really a good thing because it indicates problems in a way that is hard to ignore. You know that this development is an important one, and this delay gets your attention. You might not have realized that you were not establishing control over your child's behavior if it weren't reflected in his refusal to speak. You can consider the delay in his language development to be a good thing because it alerts you to your need to take control of your child's behavior. It is very important that your baby learn to comply with your requests right from the beginning. If you teach him the importance of compliance now, you will both have an easier time for the rest of your lives together. The baby must learn to follow rules and submit to authority if he's to be accepted and get along well socially. You are doing him no favors at all if you allow him to do just what he wants to do.

In many cases of delayed language, I noticed that the parents seemed to have an entirely helpless attitude toward their children. One mother would chase her two-and-a-half-year-old son around the house with a diaper and other salves, creams, and powders and try to talk him into getting his diaper changed. If he said no and whined and cried when she tried to pick him up, she would simply stop her efforts and helplessly follow him around, waiting for him to finally decide that he wanted his diaper changed.

When she called him to come at the playground, he ran the other way. She spend a great deal of time chasing him into the street to save him, and he disregarded every request she made to "Stop," "Come here," or "Please give me that." Todd needed compliance training. His mother was helped to make the decision to be *in charge*. We talked about the requests she would make and the way she would handle his behavior. At diaper-changing time, she would say "It's time to change your diaper," and then carry him screaming and kicking to his room. When he calmed down she would hand him a potato chip to eat as she changed him. When she gave a command, such as "Stop" or "Come here," and he failed to comply with the request, he would be put in time-out immediately. After two weeks Todd was significantly more compliant at diaper-changing time and would obey those two requests, "Stop" and "Come here." Then we worked on other behaviors: "Todd, please help me pick up these blocks." "Todd, let's put the pots and pans back in the cupboard." Each time he complied he was praised and given a dried apricot, his favorite. Noncompliance got two-and-a-half minutes in time-out. After a month of compliance training she began to train him to comply with requests to imitate words to get what he wanted. Todd would gesture and whine for a banana, and his mother would say "Todd, say 'banana.'" When Todd made an attempt by saying "nana," he was given the banana with a smile and praise. Todd's language development was rapid from this point on. At age two-and-a-half he said only three words and by three years of age he spoke like the average three-year-old.

Another language-delayed baby I visited at mealtime refused to eat any solid food. Mia insisted on a bottle of milk before breakfast, lunch, and dinner and then couldn't eat her meal. Of course, she needed another bottle of milk soon after. A two-year-old child does not get adequate nutrition from milk alone. At mealtime her mother would offer her food, and Mia would refuse to eat it, screaming and gesturing toward her bottle. If her mother tried to put the food in her mouth Mia would shake her head, seal her lips tightly, and refuse to open her mouth. She continued to refuse and throw food and cry until her mother finally gave her the bottle. Mia had learned to have a tantrum to stop her mother's efforts to obtain control and compliance. It was quite impressive to see the power and control this little creature of two years of age had. She actually controlled the entire family. Clearly, Mia needed to learn to comply with some rules.

Mia needed to be taught that her tantrums and screaming would no longer be effective in dissuading her mother from her requests. I decided to work on Mia's eating first. I asked her mother to refuse to give Mia a bottle before meals, although she would still be allowed to have a bottle at bedtime. At first, I gave Mia foods we knew she especially liked. Of course, Mia had her tantrum, but not nearly to the extent I expected. I think somehow Mia sensed her mother's resolve. Her mother told her "You may eat Cheerios or get down. Bottles are for niteynite time." Mia actually ate Cheerios at the first trial, and her behavior in general changed miraculously. Mia became compliant and willing to attempt to imitate words after only five days of the new program, and her language development progressed rapidly. Certainly not all children will show such immediate change, but many do change as suddenly and completely as did Mia.

There is one decision to be made: just who is in charge in this relationship. Once you decide you are in charge, everything else will follow. You can be kind, you can make it easier for your baby to cooperate and motivate her to want to do what you are asking, and you can be positively reinforcing, complimentary, and pleased when she does as she is asked. But you must be in charge and require compliance. All that is required is that you 1) Do not give in to tantrums or other coercive behavior, 2) Reward compliance and provide consequences for noncompliance such as time-out (see "Decreasing Undesirable Behavior").

Sign Language

A common problem arises with children using sign language. One devoted parent was so empathic that she could understand her daughter's very subtle gestures and behaviors and reliably responded to her needs. The baby, therefore, learned a very complicated sign language and series of gestures to communicate rather than learning to use words. Although this loving mother did lots of well-executed and stimulating language activities with her baby, Jennifer did not use more than four words at two years of age. A home observation revealed that Jennifer had actually learned to use two- and three-sign combinations. She would point to herself, then point to her mother, and then run to the refrigerator and gesture when she wanted to eat. Jennifer was not a resistant child; she was very cooperative in imitating clapping games or playful behaviors with her mother, but used only three or four individual words to communicate. For Jennifer to develop normally, it was absolutely necessary that the mother *stop understanding* the sign language and begin to require her baby to use words. The ability to use words to communicate is an important requirement for much other learning; therefore, it is absolutely necessary that a baby use words in order to advance to the level of which he is capable. Unless your baby can use the words *cow, horse, chicken, duck,* you'll have a hard time talking to him about farm and zoo animals. Words and concepts build, one upon the other, and your child's intellectual growth depends upon his understanding and use of these words to ask questions and acquire new information.

To get Jennifer talking, the first thing I did was to require that she use the words she already knew appropriately. When she was near the dog, I asked her mother to say "What is that, what is that? Say doggie," and, when Jennifer said it, to reward her and give her a hug. When she wanted to get picked up Jennifer would simply hold up her arms. I asked her mother to wait and require Jennifer to say the word "up." She was to ask her, "What do you want, Jennie? Do you want up? Do you want up? Say up, Jennie, say up." When she had said "up," her mother could pick her up. If she said "up" and held up her arms at the same time, that was fine, but she had to make the verbal request before she would get picked up. When she wiggled to get down, her mother was to ask "What do you want, Jennie? Do you want to get down? Say 'down,' say 'down,'" and to hold her until she said "down" or some approximation of it. If she was not able to say "down" perfectly clearly, then we settled for "duh!" Gradually her mother rewarded closer and closer approximations to the well-articulated word. Jennifer was required to make some attempt at verbal communication to get what she wanted.

If, like Jennifer, your baby is not resistant, enjoys imitating, and responds well to your praise, then you'll have an easy time increasing his use of words. You just have to forget all you have learned about his private sign language and teach the words he needs to communicate his wants.

Beginning Language Training Later

For parents who read this chapter later than the suggested time to begin, you are advised to first analyze carefully the level at which your child is communicating. Then, speak to your child at a level slightly beyond the level at which he or she can communicate. For example, if you son is not speaking at all, then speak to him in single words, with frequent repetition and labeling of specific interesting items in his environment. If he is already speaking in individual words, then begin at the next phase and speak to him in three- to four-word sentences. For example, when he can say "horse" and "run," you would say to him, "The horse is running." Link together individual words that he already uses and model sentences for him. The sequence is the same as for parents who begin earlier. You need not pressure him to talk. Simply *provide the input* repeatedly and systematically.

The procedure is the same even for children whose *receptive* language seems to be more advanced (children who can understand a complicated demand and follow directions). You may still talk to such a child at various times in longer sentences to give specific commands, but the emphasis will be on your repetition of individual words and later on the repetition of simple, well-formed sentences.

The same advice is true for children of any age as regards interest. If you speak to your son about something which interests and excites him, he will want to learn to speak about it also.

Long-Term Effects of Language Development

A study by Rosenzweig with gerbils as subjects seems to bear on this question. In a nicely controlled study, Rosenzweig divided gerbils into groups. One group, the experimental group, was given special stimulation in the form of "species-specific" behaviors. This involved equipping their cages with toys and devices for them to climb over, under, around and through, as it is the "nature" of gerbils to do. Other control gertils lived in ordinary laboratory cages and received stimulation, but not of a species-specific type. The control gerbils were handled and given stroking and "love." At the end of thirty days in these different environments, the gerbils raised in the complex species-specific environment performed better on learning tasks than did the gerbils raised in bare cages. At the end of the testing period, the gerbils were dissected, their brains were weighed, and the chemical composition of the brains was analyzed. There were striking differences between the two groups. Those gerbils who had received species-specific stimulation had heavier brains and higher concentrations of chemicals associated with more rapid learning rates. It seemed that species-specific stimulation made a more intelligent gerbil, and actually affected the weight and chemical composition of the brain, whereas general stroking and stimulation did not.

How does this relate to human learning and intelligence? Perhaps there is a "species-specific" behavior in humans that would lead to more rapid learning rates and brain changes. Quite independently of Rosenzweig's research, psycholinguists have suggested that the human language capacity is an inherited species-specific characteristic of humans (Lenneberg, 1967). If it is species-specific stimulation which has the greatest effect on intelligence level, then for human beings the most effective stimulation to promote more rapid learning rates may be language stimulation.

There are a number of studies which have correlated the rate of language acquisition to the general intelligence level of the child.

The children who have been singled out as being bright at school age are often ones who in infancy and toddlerhood acquired speech early, had a higher rate of acquisition of vocabulary words, were early able to use longer and more complex sentences, and whose articulation was superior (Goodenough and Tyler; Cameron, Livson, and Bayley). In another study by William Fowler, children's language development was accelerated by specific language training. Parents used "sentence frames" to encourage language development from the ages of 5.4 months to 12.3 months. One group of three babies used seven words correctly by the age of 10 months and used two words together at 12 months, far ahead of the norm.

We are left with two questions: 1. Does inherited superior intelligence promote more rapid language learning, or 2. Does superior language stimulation produce general intellectual superiority? It may be that *both* questions can be answered affirmatively.

I have research in progress to test the hypothesis that intensive language stimulation can increase a child's level of intellectual functioning. However, to date I have no reliable experimental data to verify this hypothesis.

Although it may be only an educated guess that you can affect the future intellectual functioning of your child through early language stimulation, you may want to conduct yourself as if it were an already proven fact. Commit yourself to stimulating early language development in your child. Many advantages in addition to improving intelligence make such a commitment to communicating worthwhile for both you and your child.

5

Intelligence

Many parents today are aware of the ever-increasing importance of intelligence in their children's adjustment. A bright child with high achievement motivation will be far more likely to survive troubled economic times as an adult. Most parents wish to increase the intellectual potential of their children, teach them the value of learning, and inspire in them the desire to do well in school.

Parents who are convinced that early stimulation will increase the intellectual potential of their children are eager to provide them with appropriate stimulation. Most of these parents ask themselves "What kind of stimulation will increase intelligence?" A number of books suggest ways in which to increase I.Q. and make a brighter child. Some of this advice is supported by research, some is not.

In a course called "The Better Baby" Glenn Doman claims that *any* child can be made a genius through specific teaching techniques. Even after taking the course many parents have questions about the validity of these claims and are interested in how child psychologists evaluate the program. Can every child really be made a genius? Are these early learning experiences meaningful to the child? Isn't this too much pressure? In this chapter, questions such as "What kind of stimulation is best?" "How do I go about it?" and "When do I start?" are answered in the context of relevant research.

Early Stimulation:
What kind? How and When?

A study with gerbils, referred to in the previous chapter on language development, suggested that the kind of stimulation that may be most appropriate for each species is stimulation related to that behavior which distinguishes the species from others: in other words, behavior which is "species specific" (Rosenzweig).

Many psychologists have suggested that the behavior which distinguishes human beings as a species and makes us unique is language. If language is the species-specific behavior of human beings, then intensive stimulation in this particular area would be the most effective kind of stimulation to produce an increase in intellectual ability. It is my belief, as well as that of other psychologists, that language stimulation is the most important kind of stimulation that can be provided for a child in the first eighteen months of life.

Many stimulating experiences will necessarily accompany language development. However, if your purpose is specifically to teach development language, the nature of the experiences may be quite different. If your goal were stimulation in general, you would try to expose your child to as much as possible. For example, you might take a child of eight months to the zoo for the first time to see as many animals as you could in one day. If your reason for taking your child to the zoo is to teach language, you would carefully select five animals and use individual words to label those five animals on that trip to the zoo.

The degree to which your child can attend to, absorb, and incorporate information from the environment is directly related to your child's ability to understand and use language. Therefore, general stimulation often provides a child with ineffective experiences. The child may be so overwhelmed by so much foreign information that none of the information is absorbed.

Research on human learning repeatedly demonstrates that it is far better to present your child with small pieces of new information and to systematically build upon that information. The infant child who makes two trips to the zoo to see the same five animals learns far more than the child who sees fifty animals in two trips.

I am currently conducting a study comparing children whose parents' goal was to "stimulate" them with children of parents whose goal was to provide *language* stimulation. Both groups of parents took their children to the San Diego Zoo and to a park specializing in marine life (Sea World) on a frequent and regular basis. One group of parents received specific instructions in teaching language by way of the chapter in this book and were encouraged to use excursions as an opportunity to teach language. The second group of parents were encouraged only to "stimulate" the child, talk to the child about the things that they were seeing, and to provide excitement and interesting experiences for the child.

Preliminary data indicate significant differences in the children. As was predicted, the group of children whose parents presented the experiences to teach language showed more rapid language development. The language-stimulated children were different in other ways also. They were far more interested in other people and notably less self-centered than the group whose parents were encouraged only to "stimulate." They also seemed to be more responsive to the use of reason as a means of discipline. They asked questions and related to people in ways that inspired an interaction. Not only did they demonstrate a greater measured intelligence on standardized tests of intelligence, but they were also believed to be highly intelligent by those who interacted with them. Even people who ordinarily do not like children found themselves taken in and surprised by the style of communicating of these children. For example, one eighteen-month-old youngster approached an adult saying, "I like your earrings." Another asked the mother of an infant, "Why is your baby crying?"

Teaching a Second Language and the Effect of Bilingualism

Teaching your child a second and even a third language maximizes the effect of language stimulation. I believe it is best to wait until your child is becoming fluent in a first language, then begin a second language at that time, perhaps at eighteen months.

You might worry that learning two languages will be confusing to your child or that it may in some way interfere with your child's achieving real competence in the native language. One study investigated the effects of speaking two languages by following the same children and their intellectual growth over time (Lambert, Tucker). The academic abilities of children who spoke English as the native language and French as the second language were compared with the abilities of children who spoke only French or only English. Contrary to the worries mentioned above, over the seven years of the study it was found that the children who learned both French and English were in no way deficient in their English-language skills when they were compared with the English-only children. However, they didn't speak or write French as well as the children who spoke only French. The bilingual children were not behind in any area tested, either verbal or mathematical, on I.Q. tests. An additional finding of this study was that the bilingual children tended to score better than the monolinguals on tests of creativity.

Other studies on bilingualism find that people who learn a second language in infancy or early childhood do better on certain perceptual tests than children with one language. They are better at tasks involving picking out a figure from a complicated background. Children who learn a second language in infancy seem to develop a special ability to determine which particular rules are required in which situation. They do better on tests which require a change in strategy or rules for solving a problem from question to question.

If it is true that language stimulation is the species-specific stimulation which increases brain growth in humans, then knowing two languages from an early age may be very important in increasing intelligence.

Stimulation: An Attitude

Many ordinary experiences may be stimulating if you take the opportunity to teach your child. A simple trip to the grocery store can be a wonderful learning experience. For your infant son who is learning to talk you can name the foods repeatedly as you shop. Give him choices in the store—"Which shall we buy? Shall we buy some oranges or apples?"—and buy what he chooses. Name each item as you place it in the basket. You may even stop to name items you do not ordinarily purchase.

As his language develops, you can introduce other concepts such as ethnicity by way of the Mexican, Oriental, or Italian food section. Describe the foods eaten by these people and make some yourself. For example, tell your child, "We are going to have Italian food tonight. We are going to the Italian food section to buy pasta and tomatoes for making sauce."

You can teach many math concepts to children two years old or older. When weighing out onions or bananas introduce your son to the concept of weight. Tell him, "These bananas are three pounds for fifty cents today. I am going to buy three pounds." Then allow him to hold three pounds of bananas. Later when you buy a five-pound sack of sugar, allow him to try to lift five pounds of sugar so that he begins to get a concept of various weights. Talk to your two-and-a-half-year-old child about a quart of milk: "We need a quart of milk because we have four people to drink it. There are four glasses of milk in this carton. It is a quart." Teach your child at every available opportunity to increase his general store of information and his intellectual potential.

Teaching children can be a wonderful experience because children love to learn. Tell your daughter everything you know by making your routine duties into learning experiences for her. For example, in caring for the houseplants, let her water the plant as you name it. Help her identify the characteristics of the plant. "This plant is called a coleus. It likes a lot of sun, so we keep it by the window. See how pretty, bright, and red the leaves stay when we keep it by the sun? This plant also likes a lot of water." Do an experiment by making cuttings and showing your child the roots. Plant some cuttings and take some away from the sun. Let her compare the leaves with and without the sun. After she observes the effect of the sun on the greenness of the leaves, you can talk about the whole process of photosynthesis. This kind of biology lesson usually occurs in junior high school or high school, but even children under three years of age really enjoy this kind of learning experience.

When you are preparing a meal, take your son with you and sit him up on the counter. Let him help you pour and measure, discussing quantities of ingredients, three-fourths of a cup of milk, a half cup of flour, and so on. You can easily teach words such as "ingredients" to a two year old by using the word while you are making blueberry muffins together. By the time some children are two and a half years of age, they can accurately describe the entire list of ingredients and the process of making a number of foods such as blueberry muffins, smoothies, roast beef, Ceasar salad dresing, and so on.

The kitchen is also a wonderful place for children to develop their olfactory sense. Let your daughter smell and teach her the name of one spice at a time, then compare two, and then later ask her to guess what spice she is sniffing. When you enjoy teaching your child, she will be more likely to enjoy learning—not only with you, but also later in school.

The Importance of Exploring and Curiosity

From the time children can crawl until they near two years of age they will want to touch, feel, manipulate, and experiment with objects in the environment. This means everything from pots and pans to stereos and radios. It is advisable to move or remove any dangerous or precious objects so that exploration and curiosity can be *encouraged*. Research indicates that children in whom exploring and curiosity are encouraged are inquisitive, independent, and creative in their elementary school years. Children who have been restrained as toddlers and prevented from experimenting with objects in their environment have been described as suffering from poor social relationships and having personality problems in the school years (Hutt and Bhavnani).

Whenever possible, let your son manipulate the forbidden objects he is curious about, under supervision. Show him how the stereo works, let him start a record. Show him your pretty glass vase and let him feel the smooth glass and see the colors while you hold it. Show him the sharp point on the bottle opener and let him carefully touch it. What may at first appear to be mischievousness or defiance is really a burning desire to learn and can be best handled by *teaching,* not scolding.

The "Better Baby" Course

Many parents who are concerned about stimulating their children's intellectual growth have become interested in the "Better Baby" course developed by Glenn Doman. The emphasis on teaching infants to read and do math and other highly academic things usually gets quite a reaction from adults. Some parents are appalled with the idea, seeing it as robbing children of their precious childhood. These parents usually believe that learning is not fun for children, that children would much rather play than learn, or both. Other parents who hear of teaching children such things cannot wait to find out more about it and immediately want to teach their children. Reactions in either direction are usually quite intense.

I was, at first, negative about the entire idea because I believed that children could not have fun learning such things. I also felt that teaching such things as reading to young infants would require entirely external positive reinforcement, and would involve pressure and tension. Additionally, I could see no value in teaching reading or math to children at such a young age when I thought they could easily learn these things later. Because I was in the midst of writing this book, I decided to take the course to find out what it really is about. I am glad I did.

Philosophy and Claims

Glenn Doman and his staff first developed techniques for teaching parents how to teach their brain-injured children. They claim that many children developed academic skills which astounded those who had diagnosed them earlier.

Later, Glenn Doman and his staff started using the same teaching methods with average, normal children and with tiny babies. In his course, Glenn Doman claims that these methods of teaching enabled babies of less than a year to learn facts, some of which not even adults can learn. He believes that the first six years of life are the most important years of a child's life as far as learning is concerned and that our educational system has been doing things entirely backwards. Among his "89 Cardinal Facts" are these:

32. The first six years of life are the genesis of genius.

33. The ability to take in raw facts is an inverse function of age.

34. Tiny kids learn more, fact for fact, prior to six years of age than they learn for the rest of their lives.

35. It is easy to make a baby a genius prior to six years of age.

36. It is extremely difficult to make a child a genius after six years of age.

37. Education begins at six, learning begins at birth or earlier.

39. Function determines structure.

40. The brains grows by use.

41. Intelligence is the result of thinking.

45. All humans are born with a greater potential than Leonardo ever used.

49. The brain is the only container that, the more you put into it, the more it will hold.

50. You can teach a baby anything that you can present in an honest and factual way.

51. It is easier to teach a one year old any set of facts than it is to teach a seven year old.

Teaching Procedures

Reading. He suggests that parents begin by teaching their children to read almost from birth. Using six-by-twenty-four-inch cardboard strips with words in very large red print, the parent teaches the child familiar, enjoyable, and interesting words. The words are in red in the beginning because this color is bright, attractive to infants, and gives a good contrast to the white background. As the child's visual pathway matures, the red is changed to black and the size of the print is gradually reduced.

The words are presented to the child in sets of ten at the rate of one card per second. Glenn Doman agrues that the best way for the tiny child to learn is to see the information for only a brief second, with frequency, rather than to stare at the information. Young children only seem to lack interest in subjects such as reading or other areas of knowledge because adults try to get them to stare at information which is boring to them.

Math. In teaching math to tiny children, Glenn Doman and his staff have decided that the basic honest facts of math are the numbers or quantities which the numerals represent, and not the numerals themselves. They argue that teaching numerals interferes with the child's learning of math. They begin by using dot-cards containing from one to 100 red dots. One card contains one red dot, a second card contains two red dots, a third three red dots, and so on. You present to your child the quantities one to 100 in sets of ten over a prescribed period of time. Then addition is taught. For example, you would say "five plus four is . . . ," then you hold up the nine card and say "nine." Addition, subtraction, multiplication, and division are all taught in the same way and in the prescribed manner. Then equations with mixed functions are taught.

When you have finished with equations, you teach the numerals. By the time the child learns the numeral "9," the child apparently imagines nine dots. Glenn Doman describes the process as he believes it might occur: "It is as if the child has before him a large screen on which he sees dots coming and going." Tiny children are able to arrive immediately at the answer to an equation such as: $30 + 5 \div 7 - 2 + 3 = 6$. Infants are said to be able to point to the correct number of dots even before they can talk.

Information. Parents are encouraged to teach other areas with the same use of cards, called by Doman "bits of intelligence." Using eleven-inch square cards, you present information in categories from all areas of knowledge including geography, history, zoology, botany, fine arts, engineering, anatomy, chemistry, and geometry. Doman argues that the important part of the procedure is to present the information as simple, honest facts. For example, in chemistry the symbols of the chemical elements are simple, honest facts. You write the symbols on large cards and then present them to your child in sets of ten to fifteen, at a rate of one per second, two to three times per day.

According to Doman, presenting bits of intelligence to your infant daughter in categories provides her with "sets of related facts so that she can combine and permutate the facts in the greatest number of useful ways and discover new facts and laws." He states, "If you give the child the facts, she will intuit the laws." For example, if you have presented a category of ten dogs, then when she comes across an eleventh dog she will not only recognize the category to which this animal belongs, but also will recognize that other animals do not belong to this category.

Music. Parents are instructed to present music from birth on. Doman describes a method he claims will teach "perfect pitch" to children under two years of age. Every day for two to three weeks you are to play each of the notes on the scale. For example, you strike a "C" on the xylophone and say, "This is a C," and at other times during the day do the same for D, E, F, G, A, B in random order. According to Doman, after a period of two to three weeks most children under two years of age can name the letter of the note they hear. He argues that although this ability has been believed to be inherited by musical geniuses or people from musical families, it can be taught to anyone under the age of two years.

After the initial two to three weeks, note reading and identification are taught using cards. You hold up a card with a staff, a treble clef and a note on the "E" line and simultaneously strike the corresponding "E" on the xylophone. Before long, your child is supposed to be able to associate the note on a certain line or space with a particular tone. Doman claims that when the musical program is begun before age two, most children have the ability to hear a melody in their head while looking at the notes on the score.

Other areas of emphasis included in the course on which I shall not elaborate include physical development, nutrition, and sensory development.

Positive Characteristics

One positive characteristic of the "Better Baby" program, is that some very sound principles of learning are advocated throughout. Parents are encouraged to always be positive, using only praise. The child is never criticized, coerced, or punished in any way. The parents are encouraged to attend to the moods, needs, and feelings of the infant at all times, and to *always keep the child wanting more.* As any good behaviorist would suggest, the parents are advised never to continue sessions until the child is ready to stop but rather always to stop before the child is ready to stop. This way the child is always left with a very good, positive feeling about the learning sessions.

Another positive characteristic of this program is Glenn Doman's belief that because of the singularly sensitive relationship of the parent and the child, the parent is potentially the best teacher. A parent who is sensitive to the child's moods, facial expressions, way of expressing interest, and so on can use this information to become the best teacher.

The instructors in the "Better Baby" course repeatedly emphasize that the learning process must be an absolutely joyous experience for both the parent and the child. The staff repeat frequently, "So long as the baby is loving it, and the parent is loving it, then the process is exactly right." They discourage the parent from presenting any information when not in the mood or too tired. They also strenuously discourage the parent from becoming a "stage-parent" — putting the child on display for others. Doman and his associates state that children hate to be tested, hate to be put on the spot, and that it is a terrible mistake to try to get them to perform for grandparents, relatives, or friends.

If you and your child enjoy using the methods of the "Better Baby" course, they may help you to maximize your child's intellectual growth. By presenting facts in categories, you help your child to form concepts. This ability to form concepts and think conceptually is one of the abilities included on both of the major standardized tests of intelligence. Another subtest measures the child's store of general information. Because Doman's methods teach concept formation as well as enable you to teach a great number of facts, a child taught in this way may obtain higher scores on the standardized tests of intelligence. If you are truly sensitive to the needs, feelings, moods, and characteristics of your child, and if you keep the learning joyous as recommended, the program might be a good thing for your child.

How Valid Are the Claims
of the "Better Baby" Course?

The validity of the claims regarding instant math, perfect pitch, and creating geniuses has not been demonstrated by research, and most psychologists are quite skeptical. Only one child psychology or developmental psychology textbook out of the one hundred which I reviewed even mentions Glenn Doman.

On a nationally televised special on the "Better Baby" program, babies were pointing to the correct dot-cards when two choices were held up by the mother and she asked "Which one is 7?" Psychologists reviewing the films in slow motion pointed out the obvious clues mothers gave as to the correct choice, such as looking at the right choice and holding it more forward.

Can Any Child Become a Genius?

Doman claims that any child can become a genius. Most psychologists do not believe this to be true, although a controversy continues to rage among psychologists regarding intelligence. Is a child's potential for learning inherited, the result of experience, or both? I will present the arguments for both sides.

The Genetic or Hereditary Position

Those psychologists who argue that intelligence is inherited point to studies which show a very strong relationship between the I.Q.'s of identical twins. Because in identical twins one egg becomes fertilized and then divides, their genetic makeup is exactly the same. The argument is that identical twins' very similar I.Q.s reflect their identical genetic makeup.

Fraternal twins come from separate eggs and have no more genetic similarity than do siblings born at separate times. Therefore, you would expect their I.Q.s or inherited intellectual potential to be no more similar than that of ordinary siblings. This is in fact the case. The correlation between fraternal twins' I.Q. scores and the correlation between ordinary siblings' I.Q. scores is practically the same. Identical twins on the contrary show a high degree of correlation, significantly higher than that of siblings or fraternal twins.

Other data cited by those who argue for a strong genetic influence on intelligence point to the statistics on natural children versus adopted children. Adopted children's I.Q.s tend to be closer to the I.Q.s of their natural parents than they are to the I.Q.s of their adopted parents. This supports the position that a genetic influence does exist. The environmental position would have predicted that the adopted child's I.Q. should be more similar to the adoptive parents than to the natural parents with whom the child does not live.

The Environmental Position

Psychologists who argue that intelligence is a learned function argue that because identical twins are of the same sex and look alike, they will be more likely to be treated the same. Therefore, the environment is far more similar for identical twins than it is for fraternal twins, who are not even of the same sex half the time. This, they say, accounts for the higher degree of correlation of I.Q. for identical twins than for fraternal twins.

Glenn Doman in his "Better Baby" course expresses an extreme environmental position. In his "89 Cardinal Facts" he says:

5. Our individual genetic potential is that of the human race.

6. Our individual genetic potential is that of Leonardo, Shakespeare, Mozart, Michelangelo, Edison, and Einstein.

7. Our individual genetic potential is not that of our parents and grandparents.

9. All intelligence is a product of the environment and our human potential.

10. High intelligence is a product of the environment.

11. Low intelligence is a product of the environment.

12. The wildly wide intellectual differences in us are a result of the wildly wide differences in the environments in which we are raised.

Which Position Is Correct?

We cannot experimentally prove the validity of either position. Most psychologists hold the position that inherited intellectual potential and environment interact.

Research does indicate, however, that the kind, quality, intensity, and timing of stimulation has profound effects on whether or not the individual child reaches anything close to his or her individual potential. One statement of which you can be certain is that what you do with your child in the first three years of life will influence your child's later intellectual abilities.

Can I Make My Child a Genius?

I believe that you can maximize the intellectual potential of your child with early stimulation such as early language training, a broad range of experiences, and perhaps methods of teaching suggested by the "Better Baby" course. However, I do not believe that every child can become a genius.

The available data strongly indicates that there are individual differences in inherited intellectual potential. I believe that you could be very disappointed in yourself and your child if your goal is to make your baby a genius. I believe that it is important to accept your child as he or she is and give all you can to increase your child's own *individual* potential.

Other Problems

Glenn Doman says that children do not need other children or toys. He insists that children always prefer to be with adults and always perfer to be learning rather than playing. He also insists that toys are only a way to get rid of children. I strongly disagree with all of these statements. One important function of other children is that they can inspire in one another a great deal of highly creative and imaginative play. The opportunity and encouragement to engage in imaginative play stimulates the development of creativity. Another important reason for children to play with children is that they enjoy one another. The suggestion that children always prefer to be in the company of an adult rather than to be in the company of children is simply not true. My experience is that children love being with other children as well as loving to be with adults. Sometimes they just want to *play*. Writers on the subject of play emphasize the importance of rehearsing roles and trying out varieties of behavior in play.

The "Better Baby" course neglects the important area of teaching language. Doman believes, as have psychologists in the field, that the opportunity to cry, frequently hearing language, and having parents who talk to a child frequently will be enough to stimulate a child's language development. No specifics are given regarding how, where, or when to talk to a baby. The most extensive specific statement that is given by the Better Baby Institute with regards to developing language is as follows: "The understanding of words provides the information for talking, but speech should not be expected until some ability to understand words is evident. The best incentive for encouragement is an enthusiastic adult who encourages the child's attempts to speak and makes every effort to understand what he/she is trying to say. Avoid trying to make a child talk. It never works."

In my opinion, the most important efforts you can make in the first eighteen months of life are those directed toward your child's acquisition of language. I believe that your child must have real-life experiences with real objects and then learn to relate these to pictures. Pictures on cards of any category will not be meaningful to a baby who has not been given this prior training.

Rather than making a category of fruits and vegetables, it would be better to first work on teaching your child to say the names of the fruits and vegetables. Continuously say the word "peach" as your child eats one. Place a real peach next to the picture of a peach. This procedure gives meaning to pictures. If your time is limited and you must choose which kind of stimulation to emphasize, I urge you to emphasize language teaching in the first eighteen months.

Dangers of the "Better Baby" Course

The real danger with the course is that some parents are so eager for their children to be intelligent that the importance of keeping the learning joyous is forgotten and children are pressured. Love and warmth from some parents are forthcoming only if the child cooperates with the program. Some parents want so desperately for their children to be "geniuses," to do "instant math," and so on that they resort to any number of unrecommended strategies to "motivate" their children to pay attention to the cards. I personally attended several parent meetings of graduates of the "Better Baby" course where parents exchanged ideas on such techniques. They said they withheld desserts or favorite foods, to be delivered only after the child attended to a set of reading or math cards. A child who endures looking at a set of reading cards only so he may be rewarded with a cookie is not "loving" the learning.

Another problem is that the emphasis on learning and intelligence seems to be to the exclusion of teaching children to have a sense of humor and to be imaginative and creative. You need to laugh and be silly with your children. Many children whose parents emphasize intellectual growth and academics are very serious, unable to see a light or humorous side of situations, and missing a whole dimension of life.

Parents who get enthusiastic about a program can forget to take their child places just for fun. Not everything that is good in life is intellectual. Be sure to schedule frequent times for play with age mates. Make excursions to parks, zoos, and amusement parks with fun and relaxation as the goal. If you fail to do this, you'll miss some wonderful times with your child.

6

Creativity

If your daughter obtains a high I.Q. score on a standardized intelligence test, it does not mean that she will be creative. High intelligence does not insure that she will be able to use the knowledge she has in an original way.

A number of research studies on creativity have indicated that intelligence and creativity are different factors (Getzels; Richards; Wallach). A child may be intelligent but not creative, creative but not intelligent, neither, or both.

Most parents prefer that their child be high both in creativity and in intelligence. Research by Wallach and Kogan indicated that children who are characterized as high in both of these areas are usually described as superior children. They are popular with their peers, confident, able to concentrate on the task at hand, and show a great deal of insight.

Creativity Defined

Creativity is involved whether you are referring to scientific advancement, a work of art, or a new mechanical invention. It involves thinking in a novel or unusual way to represent something in a new light and find a solution which has not already been suggested. A certain freedom of thought and lack of inhibition and constraint seem to be prerequisites.

The kind of thinking that is required to be creative has been called "divergent thinking." A question such as "What could we do with this book?" encourages divergent thinking. The quantity and quality of the novel responses which children may give to this kind of question gives us an indication of their ability to think creatively.

This kind of thinking is contrasted with "convergent thinking." Convergent thinking is the mental process that is required when there is one correct answer to a question. Such questions might be, "Who is the current President of the United States?" or "From what animal do we get eggs?" or "How many pennies make a dime?" Most of our traditional formal educational institutions require only convergent thinking and discourage divergent thinking.

Tests of Creativity and Research Findings

Paul Torrance, one of the foremost writers on creativity, believes there are several components to divergent thinking, or creativity. He developed a test of creativity to measure a number of abilities which he calls "components of divergent thinking."

Some tasks which measure the various components of divergent thinking include asking the child to:

1. As fast as possible, name as many words as possible that contain a certain letter.

2. Name words that belong to a particular class. For example, name as many objects as you can that weigh less than one pound.

3. Name words that are associated with other words in some way, such as words that are similar in meaning. An example of this task would be to name as many words as possible that mean "easy."

4. Put words together to meet the requirements of sentence structure. For example, the child may be asked to write as many sentences as possible that have four words starting with the letters "G," "B," "A," "T." A sentence using these letters might be: *Give the baby a toy.*

5. Give a number of new and unique uses for an ordinary item. For example, "What can a paperclip be used for? A brick? A hairpin?"

What is the ability to be creative as it is distinguished from intellectual ability? Wallach and Kogan tried to answer that question by contacting people who are noted for being particularly creative in the arts and sciences and asking them to attempt to verbalize what exactly went on mentally when they produced creative work. When these notably creative people looked inward, two factors emerged: 1. They found that they had an "associative flow"—they can produce a large quantity of associations in an attempt to arrive at a novel solution to a problem, and 2. They felt free to explore a wide variety of possible solutions in a playful manner.

Similarly, Wallach and Kogan also found the same two factors showing up in research involving the Torrance Tests of Creativity. Research with that test found that in people who are highly creative, 1. Ideas will easily flow and continue to be forthcoming, and 2. The flow will be unusual or original because of a feeling of freedom and a lack of restriction on thinking and ideas. The creative child is not afraid to be unusual and is not limited by restrictions on thinking.

Encouraging Creativity

Use Imagery. Teaching children to use imagery in their thought processing may lead to more flexibility and more creativity in thought. Flexibility is considered an important factor in creative thinking. Flexibility refers to the ability to entertain other ideas or views about a problem than those which have been previously believed. The ability to entertain other hypotheses or other possible solutions to a problem is something which seems to be enhanced by the use of imagery. Being able to freely imagine a variety of alternate solutions in a playful manner is related to your child's ability to be flexible in thought and solve problems creatively.

Encourage your son to imagine, to picture, all kinds of events such as having an elephant for a pet. Ask him to picture where the elephant would live, picture it in his room, picture what would happen. Studies have found a relationship between originality and the use of simple images in children's thought.

Act Out Improbabilities. Encourage your daughter to think about improbabilities by acting out things that are highly improbable. For example, play a game such as telling her, "I am tired of you, I'm going to throw you in the trash." Then walk her over to a trash can in the park and put her part way in, feet first. This is a silly and improbable thing which encourages the child to think in the same way. Say to the child, "I'm going to eat your toes for dinner, but they don't taste good. I'm going to put some butter on them." Then actually put a little butter, some salt and pepper, or even some marmalade on her toes. Do the silliest, most improbable things. Hold her up in the air and say, "Come down, come down, what are you doing up there? You're not supposed to float up in the air, you're supposed to be on the ground." Encourage her often to think along improbable lines.

Play with Improbabilities. Torrance suggests "playing with improbabilities" with older children by discussing such topics as:

> What could happen if it always rained on Saturday? What could happen if it were against the law to sing? Just suppose you could enter into the life of a pond and become whatever you wanted to become? (Torrance, 1974, pages 436–437)

For younger children, eighteen months to three years, encourage them to imagine and think about improbable events such as, "What if you floated up in the air and I couldn't get you down?" As your child becomes more verbal and more capable of thinking along the lines of a Torrance-type question, ask your child things such as, "What if all elephants could fly like Dumbo and we had elephants flying all around the sky, what would happen?" When your daughter refuses to eat her lunch ask her, "Should I get Waffle (the dog) and sit him in your chair, and put your bib on him, and let him eat your lunch? Should I give it to Waffle?" These kinds of improbable, absurd suggestions help her to imagine and to think creatively and flexibly along unusual lines. Creating this kind of a playful atmosphere and actually carrying out these crazy ideas will teach her that she can also try out ideas even if the ideas seem crazy.

The Importance of Imaginative Play

Promoting Cognitive Growth. Imaginative play is influential and beneficial to your child's cognitive growth as well as to creativity. When children are pretending, they can pretend something has happened and then reverse it. For example, in play a child might say, "I'm sick" and then in the next breath, "No, I'm not sick, I'm all better."

Reversibility of thought is required to reach the stage of thinking Piaget calls "Concrete Operations." Unless your son can understand reversibility, he makes mistakes in "conservation" tasks. For example, he can not do the conservation of liquid task: first there are two short fat glasses containing equal amounts of a liquid and a third empty tall thin glass. Next the contents of one of the short fat glasses is poured into the tall, thin glass. If your son has not yet achieved the stage of concrete operations or reversibility of thinking, he will believe that the tall thin glass contains more liquid than the remaining short fat glass, even though he *watched* the liquid being poured from a short fat glass into the tall one. He cannot reverse the transformation in his mind and imagine pouring the water back into the short fat glass. He cannot tell himself that even though it looks different, the amount of liquid is the same.

Normally, children become able to solve such tasks as this by the time they are seven years old. Calling attention to the reversibility of thought by asking children questions about their symbolic play has been found to accelerate their attainment of concrete operations. For example:

Parent: "What are you making?"
Child: "We're making tacos. Do you want some salsa?" (indicating pebbles which a moment ago were pretend beans for dinner.)
Parent: "Oh, are these beans or salsa?"
Child: "No, that's salsa. Do you like it?"

If you encourage imaginative play and ask questions about it, your child may develop faster intellectually than children who do not have the opportunity to engage in imaginative play or those in whom imaginative play is discouraged. The opportunity to engage in imaginative play with agemates who are equally in need of and interested in imaginative play is very important for your young child's future intellectual growth.

Promoting Social Competence. Imaginative play is also important in your child's development of social competence, particularly in learning to understand the feelings of others (empathy). Through pretending, children experiment with a variety of roles and positions. At times, your daughter may be the dominant character, a ferocious lion about to eat the hunter. At other times, she may be the hunter about to be eaten, crying and afraid. Experimenting with dominant and submissive roles enriches her understanding of the roles and feelings of others. This results in an improvement in her ability to get along with a group.

Encouraging Imaginative Play

When you sit down to play with your son, encourage him to take on various roles such as the role of the zookeeper with plastic animals, the role of a doctor, or a grocery clerk, or a firefighter. This helps a child under two years of age begin to fantasize.

Once your son is enjoying this kind of fantasy, then you can encourage fantasy play which is even more removed from reality. Create imaginary animals that fly in from some fantasized place to reside at the zoo, surprising the zookeeper. Make up names for people or places rather using real names. Your creation of imaginary creatures, insects, and people different from any he has ever seen encourages him to develop his imagination even further. When he begins to create new words from parts of two words he already is being creative. Children in whom such fantasy is encouraged become very creative in developing their own characters, words, and places in their play.

Research has demonstrated that imaginativeness in play is associated with other desirable characteristics besides creativity. Children whose play was described as imaginative were also described as high in self-control, low in impulsivity, low in aggression, and high in sharing, cooperativeness, and independence (Singer).

Provide toys that allow your child to create and imagine. Some of the more effective toys in promoting imagination are the Lego-Duplo blocks which even young children (eighteen months to two years) can snap together. Another good investment would be some plastic zoo and farm animals. It is worthwhile to spend the extra money to get some very realistic representations of the animals since children really do seem to enjoy playing with the more lifelike versions. They sometimes rapidly lose interest in inferior copies. Dishes, silverware, and play dough together will enable your child to create and imagine a variety of meal situations. A variety of dress-up hats, shoes, and clothes promote imaginative play. More often than not, however, your child will still prefer to be with you than to be alone with toys. The best situation is when you and your child play with the toys together.

Children need some time to play *without* toys. Take your daughter to a place with sticks, leaves, seed pods, and trees and let her imagine, create, and play with whatever she finds. Go to the beach with no buckets or shovels and encourage imaginative and creative play with sand, stones, shells, and seaweed.

The presence of toys in such places inhibits imagination and creativity and their absence inspires creative thought. It is a mistake to give your daughter toys so often that she never experiences all the uses there are for a stick or a leaf.

Your Child's Sense of Humor, Creativity, and Discipline

Some children are by nature very playful, and there are reasons to try to preserve this personality characteristic. At times it may be difficult to decide whether to laugh at or punish certain childish behavior. You will have to make some choices regarding the hoped-for outcome of your child's personality traits, and make some concessions and trade-offs according to your priorities. Do you want your child to be instantly obedient and completely controlled? Can you tolerate less in the way of obedience to promote playfulness and creativity?

For example, if your two-year-old son is creative in his attempt to avoid getting dressed, then you may wish to allow this behavior rather than insist on obedience. For instance, in the morning he may grab his shirt and run in a playful manner and throw it into an unlit fireplace. It may a mistake to discipline him for this behavior, so long as he is being playful and creative in his attempts to avoid getting dressed. You may want to simply be more creative yourself in encouraging him to get dressed.

Not all behavior of children that is frustrating to you should be viewed as behavior to be eliminated. Sometimes your daughter's behavior reflects what she thinks is funny and what she imagines will get a laugh out of you. To her, it may be funny to see an expression of amazement or shock on your face. These behaviors indicate that she is using imagery: imagining the scene and imagining your reaction. Unless the behavior is destructive or dangerous, or in some other way highly undesirable, you may wish to refrain from punishing it. It is especially important that you be sensitive to her mood and emotion at the time. When she does something out of spite or because she is angry at you, it's different from something she does with a smile on her face because she believes that it will be a funny thing to do.

One day my two and a half year old grabbed a handful of freshly laundered clothes and threw them in the toilet as a joke. Because he obviously thought this was very funny, I did not give him any negative consequences, but explained why I did not find this funny and why I would do something serious if he did it again. By explaining to him why certain things are not funny, are dangerous, or unacceptable, his sense of humor will (hopefully) become more sophisticated. To punish playful, joking behavior without explanation may dampen his spirit and interfere with those wonderful traits of originality and flexibility. An over-controlled child who is always obedient and who always does the right thing is not likely to be flexible in thought and capable of original thinking.

To have a child who is creative, playful, and flexible, you may have to settle for a little less instant obedience. When you say to a boy who is creative and enjoys being playful, "Be careful that you don't fall in the mud," he may, with a big grin on his face, lie down flat on his back in the mud and roll in it. When he carries out this ridiculous act, it means that somehow he has actually thought out and imagined himself doing this ridiculous thing and thinks it would be humorous. It means that there is imagery and creative thinking going on which you may really want to encourage, even though it means a mess to clean up. A more controlled child who has been punished or reprimanded for getting dirty or getting wet may never even imagine actually lying flat in the mud and rolling in it.

Find Teachers and Caregivers Who Appreciate Creativity and Humor

If you encourage a playful nature, a sense of humor, and originality, then your child will be likely to be less cooperative in a structured teaching situation. You will have to deal with the problems between the teacher and your child. For example, I brought my eighteen-month-old son to a highly respected swimming class. The program was very well structured and planned around principles of desensitization. Children were gradually introduced to warm water in the presence of toys and play equipment, and most of the children learned to swim very well and very easily. My son loved to swim and was happiest underwater, but he was not always interested in swimming exactly the way the teacher wanted. At times he would do a kind of dolphin kick which he simply enjoyed doing for the feel of it in the water. Sometimes he would spin around making circles in the water. This is a highly original way of swimming and not at all what the teachers had in mind.

I went through three teachers before I found one who would accept his goofy ways in the water and allow him to be his playful self. The first three teachers would tell him no with a very stern voice and stop him in the middle of his dolphin kick or spinning.

I decided that this was a part of his playful nature, part of his enjoyment of the water and his way of doing things differently from everyone else, and a characteristic which I wished to preserve. Therefore, I continued to change teachers until I found one who would allow him to do his goofy things, what she called his "crazy swimming." She would say, "Okay, now you've done your crazy swimming, do you want to swim across the pool with me?" At times she would want him to dive off the side into the water head first. With a gleam in his eye and a great big smile he'd leap off the side, feet first. When he surfaced, she helped him swim across the pool. She would, at the appropriate moment, turn his goofy behavior into something which would be productive for the lesson. But she never told him no, criticized him, or reprimanded him for his original or playful ways. It *is* possible, though difficult, to find teachers who'll do this.

Make certain if you encourage your child to be playful and creative that you realize that a creative way of being is not something that most teachers will appreciate. If a teacher is trying to teach something serious and your child does things differently, asks unusual questions, or gives unusual answers, then your child's behavior may be seen as a nuisance and be punished. If you encourage in your child a creative way of being and personality characteristics that are associated with creativity, then you will have to be very careful to look for teachers, caregivers, and babysitters who will appreciate those characteristics in your child and not punish them.

Caution to Parents Who Value Intelligence

Sometimes parents who are interested in their children learning a great number of facts may neglect to develop creativity. Intelligence alone is not enough to find the cure for cancer or create works of art or even to invent a new type of can opener. The second essential element is creativity.

There is a time for learning facts and for serious study. Clearly, children love to learn, to know the facts, and to understand the world in which they live. However, it is important to save time for play, to promote imagery, humor, and incongruity, and to allow your child to fantasize and create.

Forget the "mistakes" your son makes while he is playing. If he wants a cage for the dogs and cats in the zoo, let him. Don't say, "No, there are no cats and dogs in the zoo. Those are domestic animals, those are at home." If he's making soup on the beach and chooses cloves, hot pepper, and cinnamon for spices, this is *not* the time to tell him that chicken soup doesn't have cloves or cinnamon. Let him be creative and imagine whatever spices he wants to put in the soup. When he picks up a plastic screwdriver and toothbrush to be his violin and bow, don't run to get him something better to be his violin. Let him imagine and use items creatively in his play.

Encourage divergent thinking by allowing your daughter to play with toys in unusual ways rather than telling her how to play with a specific toy. Don't fall into the trap of trying to teach her to play with a toy in the manner in which the toy manufacturer intended. Remember that the ability to think of alternative uses for objects is an important part of creativity. If you fail to develop creativity, imagination, and humor in your child, you may end up with that stereotyped image of the genius that many people possess: the spiritless stuffed shirt whose only interest is in books.

7

Achievement Motivation

As a dedicated parent, you certainly want your child to do well in school, make sensible independent decisions, and develop the general competence to set and achieve goals in later life. There are two things you can do with your child from age one to four that will motivate your child to achieve: encourage independent decision making and promote self-control.

Decision Making

To encourage independent decision making, ask your twelve-month old daughter, "Which do you want to see, the bear or the elephant?" Then take her to see the animal of her choice. To begin with, she may not realize what has happened, but soon she will be aware that her preferences, feelings, and words can have an influence on what happens to her. Repeat such experiences over and over to develop her sense of being able to affect the world.

You can also encourage independent decision making in such matters as choosing clothes to wear, toys to buy, friends to visit, food to eat, and so on. Start early encouraging your son to "do for himself," and later you can with relative peace of mind send him out to buy his lunch or select his own clothes.

On an excursion with your son, let him lead the way. If the trip is for his benefit, let him decide what to look at, even if what interests him most at the zoo is the pigeons wandering freely. Just let him watch the pigeons. As ordinary as they may seem to you, they are exciting to him and the desired effect is achieved: He's interested in what he sees and wishes to pursue it further. When you hurry your child on to see the next thing without attending to his interests, you teach him that he cannot provide himself with any excitement or interesting experiences but must depend upon others who know better.

If what interests your little girl on a trip to the zoo is a bumble bee gathering nectar from the flowers, then regardless of the entry fee to the zoo, your money is best spent by standing with her and talking about what the bee is doing. This becomes easy to do if you try to deeply understand the feelings and motivations of your child and realize that they are far more important than anything you may have hoped she would enjoy.

Attending to the feelings of children is important in promoting their natural curiosity, interest in the world, and belief in themselves as active agents having the ability to seek out interesting experiences. Especially with a very young toddler, try to plan excursions so that you may follow your child. Follow your little boy wherever he leads you, steering him away from dangerous places. If he wishes to study the parrot at the zoo and is very interested in the parrot, then talk to him about its feathers and claws, its colors, and the food in its tray. Study that particular animal as long as your child wants to stay there. This is unusual behavior for a parent at the zoo. On my numerous excursions to the zoo, I see most parents whisking their children away to the next exhibit, the important thing being for the parents to get through and see every animal in the zoo. For a child, this is a most tiresome and unrewarding experience.

If a trip is for you, a perfectly reasonable possibility, then this is entirely a different matter. Children may be hurried from one exhibit to the next, certainly without any psychological harm. However, if your intent is to stimulate your youngster intellectually, then your guide should be the interest and attention of your child.

Self-Control

Besides encouraging independent decision making, you can also help your child achieve by promoting self-control. The best way to do this with young children is to teach them how to wait.

How can these waiting periods be designed? In daily living there will be many occasions when your child will have to wait for you to get a toy which has fallen, to get a glass of juice, to retrieve a ball that has rolled into the street, and so on. In the beginning, say the words, "Wait, just wait a minute," when the delay before your daughter gets what she wants will be just a few seconds. Gradually increase the time between saying, "Wait, just a minute," and her getting what she wants. In early trials you should repeat, "Wait just a minute, wait" several times while something is being done.

Training in self-control can often be combined with training in decision making. The optimum circumstance is where the rules are very clearly specified, clearly understood by your child, and consistently enforced. For example, you might say to your child, "You can play in the yard or the sandbox. But you can't take your trucks into the driveway until later when I come out to watch you."

When researchers look at the attitudes of parents whose children demonstrate high achievement motivation, they find that these parents are:

1. Consistent. The same rules apply today that applied yesterday and the consequences for misbehavior are the same.
2. Warm and Loving.
3. Demanding, in the sense that they require mature behavior and exercise firm discipline.
4. Reasonable, using reason and explanation to exact obedience.
5. Respectful and accepting of their children's decisions even when those decisions do not conform to the preferences of the parents (for example, if their child chooses a blue hat, but the parents prefer red, the child's choice prevails).

Reading Preparation

Cognitive Styles

Before children are able to learn to read, they must be able to pay attention to small details and respond slowly and carefully. You can predict how well they might learn to read by asking them to match familiar figures such as the teddy bears below. Children are shown the top teddy bear and then asked to find one exactly like it from among the other six teddy bears.

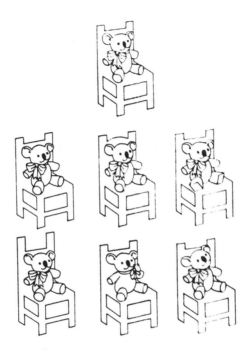

There are two extremes of behavior revealed by this test. A child who is described as "reflective" looks at the standard and then at each of the six pictures and continues to check back and forth between the standard and each picture before making a response. The reflective child looks at more parts of each of the pictures: the eyes, the arms, the legs, and so on. The reflective child more often has a particular strategy or plan for studying the standard and each of the other figures in the stimulus array.

The "impulsive" child, on the other hand, frequently may not even look at all the alternatives in the array before answering. The impulsive child checks back and forth between the array and the standard much less often, and makes many fewer comparisons. For example, the impulsive child may not look at the feet and arms, but only at the head and bow. As a result, the impulsive child often does not attend to the particular area where the significant difference between the standard and the other figures occurs.

As you'd expect, impulsive children don't read as well as reflective children. Children who are not promoted in the first grade are often more impulsive than their classmates who are promoted, but are not different in intelligence tests scores (Messer). In other words, it is not lower intelligence which holds them back, but the impulsive cognitive style. Other studies also indicate that a reflective cognitive style results in superior performance on tests of discrimination learning, reasoning, memory, and conservation (Neimark; Pascual-Leone).

Teaching the Reflective Cognitive Style

You will want to be sure that your child approaches academic tasks with a reflective cognitive style. You can help her to do so by teaching certain strategies: (1) To look at all of the possible choices in a task before she makes a decision, and (2) To break the various choices down into parts (for example, comparing the Teddy bears' arms, legs, body, bow) and to consider all the parts, and (3) To look for similarities and differences and eliminate choices until there is only the correct one left. Teaching her the specific response strategies is much better than simply saying "take your time and think," which doesn't really tell her what to *do* when she does a matching task.

You can teach the strategies of reflection using coloring books to make your own matching tests. Find a good coloring book, with simple and uncomplicated pictures for young children and more complicated ones for older children. Then make four photocopies of a picture interesting to your child. For example, photocopy a picture of a duck and, on the standard to be matched, draw and color a bow. Then color it in slightly differently on three of the copies and exactly the same on the fourth. For the young child between three and four, start with a difference that is pronounced, perhaps a simple color difference. You might have a red bow on the standard and the correct choice and different colored bows on the other three choices. As your child matures and gets better at detecting similarities and differences, you can make the differences smaller and less obvious.

Using Puzzles

Puzzles are very useful for teaching an impulsive child to be more reflective. For your eighteen-month-old daughter, a good simple puzzle might be a beach scene with a child figure, a ball, and a bucket. Left alone, your girl would be likely to pick up a puzzle piece, try to put it in any one of the three holes without looking, and attempt to force that piece to fit. You can help her by coaching her through a reflective strategy.

Encourage her to first check the orientation of a piece (top vs. bottom), then look for the appropriate space on the board, and then focus on the various parts of the piece and the parts of the board.

Say to her as she picks up the first puzzle piece, "Look at the shape of the puzzle piece. What is it that you have?" After she responds that it is a girl, ask her, "What goes up, what part goes up? Now look for a place on the board the same as the shape of this girl. Look at the shape of the girl. Now look at the shapes on the board to see if you can find one like this girl. Is this the shape of the girl? Is this the shape of the girl? Now where is her head on the shape? Look at her head. Now where is her head on the board? Where are feet on the board? Put the head where the head goes, and put the feet where the feet go. Look at the head and at the feet and put them where they go."

Model the reflective style by saying, "Now I will put in a piece. This is the bucket. The handle goes up and the bottom goes down. Now, let me find a shape on the board that looks like this bucket. Is this the bucket shape? Now, let me look at my shape again. This is the shape I'm looking for. Is this the bucket? Yes, this is the bucket, it goes here. Here is the handle and here is the bottom on my shape. Let me find the handle and the bottom on the form board. Here is the handle, the handle goes in here and the bottom in here."

When your child imitates any of these behaviors say, "Good, you looked at the shape and you looked for the shape in the board. See how nicely it goes in place when you look for all the little parts of the piece."

The most important part of this procedure is that your child is taught a deliberate strategy which may be successfully applied to more and more complex puzzles. Begin with a puzzle well within your child's capabilities. Once the response strategies have been mastered on an easy puzzle, you can introduce a slightly more difficult puzzle. Proceed in small steps.

Teaching Reading Readiness

When you sit down with your son to play with him, you do more than play. Your being there helps him to sit down and pay attention to an ongoing activity for an extended period of time. This increases his attention span, which is very important in preparing him to read. Particularly if your son is active and tends to move quickly from one activity to another, your time will be very well spent sitting down with him and helping him keep his attention on one activity for a longer period of time. It is not necessary for you to force him to stay with an activity. Your being involved will be enough to keep him interested in that activity longer than he would have been alone. Gradually he will sit still with activities longer and longer and his attention span will increase.

One of the things that kindergarten teachers test for to determine whether or not a child is ready to read is the child's understanding of positions in space. Children usually learn these through speech but you can deliberately teach them to make certain your child understands the subtle differences. One activity which is very useful for teaching positions in space is setting the table. Show and describe to your daughter how she must put the fork *beside* the plate *on top* of the napkin. Then ask her to put the glass *above* the plate. There is an important but subtle difference between *on top of* and *above* and many children have trouble with this one. Be careful to use prepositions such as *between, below, above, beside,* regularly as you talk to your child. Some parents use the preposition *by* when they mean *on top of, beside, above, between,* or *below,* and do not differentiate. They say, "Go put your shoes by the door" when they could very easily say, "Go put your shoes *on top of* the rug *beside* the door." Instead of saying, "You sit by Nancy," it would be better to say, "You sit *between* Nancy and David."

Another important readiness skill is knowing the colors. You can actually teach your son to know his colors as young as seventeen or eighteen months if you make the discrimination easy for him. The problem for children in learning their colors is that first you call an item a truck, and then you call it red. Then you call another item a shirt and later you call it red. It is usually a long time before your son will notice the similarity between the truck you called red and the shirt you called red and attend to the dimension of color. To make it easier for him to pay attention to that stimulus dimension, you should begin with only two colors. Collect a variety of small objects in each of two colors, for example yellow and blue. You might have blue and yellow blocks, plastic animals, crayons, cups, pencils, doll dishes, cars, and so on. Then get two clear containers or two wide boxes and sort the toys by color, naming the color while you do it: "All the yellow ones go in this box. This is yellow, this goes in this box. This is yellow, it goes in here." Then put a blue one in the yellow box and become very silly about it: "Hey, what are you doing in here, you're not yellow," and flip it out of the box up into the air. Continue to sort them, labeling each item yellow or blue as you put it in each container.

When your son is clearly able to discriminate blue and yellow, then you can add another color. Now you will separate blue and red into two piles. Later on you can separate three colors into three piles, introduce a fourth color, and so on. When this is done systematically many children know all the primary and secondary colors by the time they are eighteen months old. By the time they are two, they can talk about beige, aqua, and magenta.

Top to bottom and left to right are both concepts that your child will need to know when he begins to write. Teach top to bottom with paints and an easel with children as young as two and a half years old. Help your son start at the top of the page and make a line all the way to the bottom. Then go back up to the top and make another. Hold his hand and help him make the first couple of stripes and then gradually fade out your help and let him make stripes all over the page from top to bottom. Teach him on another piece of paper to go from left to right. Start at one side of the page where his left hand is and go all the way over to the other side of the page. Later use crayons and pencils and smaller pieces of paper.

A fun way to teach left to right sequencing is to take pictures on an excursion to the zoo. Take a picture of the entrance, then take pictures all along the way of the animals that you visit. Take pictures of your daughter as she eats her lunch and then take pictures as you leave the zoo. When you get the pictures developed you can paste them in a scrapbook and make your own book and call it "A Trip to the Zoo." Together you and your daughter can arrange the pictures from the beginning of the trip to the end. Instruct and help your daughter to begin on the left (locating her left hand) and line them up in sequence from left to right, then down to the next line, from left to right. Then you can follow your trip to the zoo from left to right.

Another way to teach your child essential sequencing skills is by helping him to think about the order in which he does things.

For example, take three pictures of him as he prepares to feed the cat: one picture of him getting food from the cupboard, another of him opening the can, and a third of him putting the food in a bowl. Then ask him to put these pictures in order on one page of a scrapbook. Think about taking pictures whenever he does something that can be put in sequential order. Household tasks such as making a bed, setting the table, and feeding animals make good subjects for sequencing and also will be very good for his socialization, encouraging and motivating him to be helpful around the house.

Another discrimination that you can teach to children as young as three years of age is the difference between left hand and right hand. There is an easy way for your little one to learn this discrimination. First, look for some beauty spot, scar, freckle, or other permanent mark on one of your daughter's hands. Tell her, "Your right hand is the one with the freckle, your right hand has a freckle on it." Then ask her, "Which one is your right hand? Look for the freckle." Eventually she will automatically lift her right hand to look at the freckle when you ask for her right hand. Finally, she will not have to look at the freckle at all. If she has no permanent mark on either hand, then you might consider putting nail polish on the thumbnail of just the right hand for a long period of time until she doesn't need that clue any longer.

Another important readiness skill is sorting and classifying. Ask your child to help you sort out common household items. You can, for example, ask your son to help you put away the silverware. Show him where the forks go, where the spoons go, and where the knives go. Let him separate them into their appropriate piles. When you are sorting laundry, you can ask him to put all the underwear into one basket and all the socks into another basket. Another time ask him to separate dark and light clothes. Ask him to put all the vegetables in one drawer of the refrigerator and the fruits in another.

It is most important that your child learn to follow directions. Give your daughter simple directions to begin with and then gradually make them more and more complex. First get her ready to hear the instructions. To your two and a half year old you might say, "Betty, I want you to do two things. First, close the door, then bring me your socks and shoes that are beside the door." Gradually make your directions more complicated and add on a third direction.

You will want to teach your child the shapes, particularly the circle, triangle, square, oval, and diamond. It is especially helpful to teach the shapes two at a time and then look for the shapes in your environment. Look for the shapes on signs and buildings as you walk. This will be helpful not only to your child's reading and perceptual skills, but also in the many art programs that rely on young children being able to see basic forms in nature.

In your speech to your child use as many descriptive words as you can. Try to use words such as "couple," "few," "many," and "several" and explain the meaning of these terms. Use phrases such as "more than" and "less than" in everyday conversations with your daughter. Then they won't appear strange to her when she starts her schooling. For example, when someone gives her a new matchbox car you can say, "Now you have five matchbox cars. You used to have four. Now you have one more than four. Five is one more than four."

Continue to read interesting stories aloud to your child every day. Research has found that children who are read to are themselves superior readers. When you read a story to your daughter and she gets to see the pictures that accompany that story, the words have a great deal of meaning to her. Later when she reads a story which has few or no pictures, she will be able to imagine the scenes as she reads and her comprehension will be enhanced.

Beginning Reading

Many teachers believe that the best way to teach reading is through phonics or sounding out words. There has been a controversy for years, and both sight reading and phonics have been tried. Currently most school systems favor the phonics method. Phonics is necessary to develop good independent reading skills.

Teaching Reading by Phonics

When you seriously set out to teach reading, you want to be certain your child knows all the alphabet sounds. Begin by systematically going through the alphabet teaching letter sounds. Show your little one the letter *a,* work only with that letter and words that begin with that letter. Tell her the sound that *a* makes (short vowel sound) and talk about words that begin with *a,* such as *ant, alligator, apples,* and so forth. Play games with the letter *a* using plastic letters and words that begin with *a.*

One helpful tool that I strongly recommend is the Play Skool desk which contains magnetic letters. Little children seem to enjoy sitting down at this desk and playing with the letters. The letters that come with the desk are too curvy for the beginner, but others are available (Fisher Price for capital letters and Child Guidance for lowercase letters.)

You can play alphabet games while you are riding in the car. Start by saying, "I'm going to say some *a* words: a, a, apple . . . a, a, ants . . . alligator." Then ask your daughter what letter she wants to do and let her take her turn. If she cannot think of one, then you begin the next one.

When your child can pick out an *a* among three other letters and name words that begin with *a,* move on to the letter *b.* Play games naming words beginning with *b,* such as *baby, box, ball, busy.* Show him the letter *b* and teach him to find it among three other letters. When he can name words beginning with *b* and find *b* among letters he knows, you can move on. Go through the entire alphabet this way and keep reviewing sounds until, when you say a word such as baby or ball, he can pick out the letter that begins that word.

When he knows all the beginning letter sounds, teach him how they sound at the end of a word. Focus on ending consonant sounds, exaggerating them so that he can hear the ending sounds clearly: "catttt." After some repetition, ask him to show you the letter that ends the words *hat, cat, mat, sit.* When he can clearly identify that sound, then move on to another consonant, such as the *d* sound.

When he can identify beginning and ending sounds, it is time to teach him to hear the short vowel sounds in three-letter words. Remind him of each of the short vowel sounds and elongate the vowel in three-letter words, such as *caaaat.*

An activity that will help your child to be ready for a phonetic approach to reading is to play rhyming games and sing rhyming songs. Being able to hear the similarities in words is necessary to reading phonetically. Play records with nursery rhymes and read poems with frequent rhymes. This will help your daughter develop her ear so she is able to discriminate the sounds in the words she will need to write and read.

Some of the Dr. Seuss beginner books are excellent to read aloud to your child. Although these books are designed for beginning readers to read alone, hearing the short, rhyming words will help your daughter develop the ability to hear the similarities in words long before she can read them. Some of the books that are excellent for this purpose are *Hop on Pop, Great Day for Up,* and *The Cat in the Hat.*

Teaching Words

Once your child can successfully identify all the individual letter sounds, then you can help him learn to put them together to
read short words. Begin with the short vowel *a*. Select a variety of
items whose names contain the short vowel sound *a* and put them
in a box. For example, you might have a man, a cat, and a fan.
On three-by-five-inch cards clearly print the corresponding names
(*man, cat, fan*). The vowel should always be in red to call the child's
attention to the sound in the middle. Now encourage him to elongate
each letter's sound in each word so that he is saying "mmmmmmmm
aaaaaaaa nnnnnnnn" and eventually gets the word *man*. Then he
can take the little man out of the box and put it on the card that
says *man*. Then he repeats the sequence with *cat* and *fan*. The use
of concrete objects helps to keep your child's attention and also helps
to give meaning to the words he is learning, which is very important for his comprehension. Teach one vowel at a time in short sessions so that your child enjoys them and learns the basic phonics
method of sounding out three-letter words with short vowel sounds.

After you go through each of the vowels separately, use items
and three-by-five-inch cards with a mix of short vowel sounds. Now
the task is more difficult; since it could be any one of the five vowels,
the child sounds out the word on the card without knowing which
vowel sound it is. If your child makes errors, you may be going
too fast. Slow down and spend more time on the letter sounds.
Remember, she must master the individual components of the task
of reading before she can read. Each basic skill is necessary for the
next one; they build upon one another.

When she can sound out three-letter words in the mixed box
then you can make her a simple book to read. Use words and sentences that appeal to your child's interests. Take pictures of her doing
things she likes to do. Think of things that she likes that can be
stated in three-letter words with short vowel sounds. For example,
take pictures of her swimming, running, petting her dog, looking
at her dog or cat. Use words that she likes and that she will successfully be able to sound out. This will give her the exciting experience of reading a book all by herself. You will probably want
to teach some individual words such as *the, this, is, my,* and *we,*
because these will be needed in any little story. So teach these individual words before you use them in the story she will read. Keep
the story simple: My pet dog. We run. My big cat. My cat in my bed.

Once you have taught your child these basics, she should be able to continue her reading instruction in school with few problems. Or you may decide to go on and teach her further. If your child is young then you may want to begin your collection of little objects ahead of time. Below is a list of some things that you might want to look for in preparing your collection of short-vowel items.

a: pan
   man
   fan
   can (a can)
   cat
   bat (baseball)
   hat
   mat (little doll rug)
   ham (little food)
   bag

o: cow
   pot
   mop
   top
   box
   fox

e: jet
   pen
   hen
   red
   bed
   net
   ten

u: cup
   rug
   mug
   pup
   bug
   bun (hot dog or hamburger bun)
   nut (walnut or other one she knows)

i: kit (mini first aid kit)
   pin
   fin
   mit (catcher's)
   pit
   pig

Teaching Blends

Once your child can hear the blends at the beginning of words, teach him to hear the sound of the ending blends and then to visually identify those letters in combination. When he sees *sh* and knows the sound it makes at the beginning and end of words he is ready to sound out words beginning with and ending with blends. Start with short vowel sounds such as those in *ship, fish, shop,* and *wish.* When he can sound out words with blends and short vowel sounds, add words with blends and long vowel sounds, such as *shape.* Include these blends in a new storybook about him with interesting pictures. Help him sound out the individual letter components and put them together by exaggerating the sound of each letter as he sounds it out.

Remember that one of the most important things in teaching your child to read is that you *don't let him guess* impulsively. Help him sound out the letters carefully. If he has trouble doing it, help him, give him the answer. Prompt him and then as soon as you finish prompting him, *let him practice right away without the prompt.* This is so you can be certain that he encounters the difficult word again and has paid attention to your hints. You never want to let your child just guess impulsively — "red, rug, run" — until he finally hits upon the right word. This does not teach him to *decode,* it teaches him to respond impulsively to the first letter sound without concentrating on the rest of the word. You want to help your child to learn a reflective cognitive style, to analyze each letter and consider the *whole word,* not to become impulsive.

Always be certain that the child knows all of the individual components before you put them together in words. As you introduce words with double letters, such as *food* or *feet,* make sure you teach the sound of this letter combination before you put it into a word or into a book. Remember the rule: *He must know the individual components before he can read a word containing those individual components.*

Teaching Action Words

Print the following words individually on pieces of cardboard: *jump, eat, tickle, walk, run, turn.* Help him to sound out the words, then randomly hold them and ask him to do the particular action when the word comes up. Games like this make reading fun, a pleasant interaction between you and your child. It is better to have short, successful sessions that you both enjoy than to have long ones that frustrate you or make you angry. Remember, those five-minute sessions add up to be highly productive hours of quality learning time.

Math Readiness

If you prepare your child for numbers and math with the idea that numbers are fun and that he will enjoy learning about them, then he will approach math in school with enthusiasm instead of fear.

There are a number of activities that you can do with your three and four year old to prepare her for the math she will do when she enters school. Let her do activities involving grouping things such as the silverware in the drawers. "Will you put the spoons where the spoons go, forks where the forks go, and knives in their own space, Suzie?" Ask her to put things in order in terms of their size, from biggest to smallest. You might ask your youngster to help you in the kitchen cupboard to put all the tall things in the back, the medium ones in front of them, and then the short cans up front so that they can all be seen.

Every trip to the grocery store can be a good experience in classifying or grouping. Ask your child to put all the vegetables in one pile and all the fruits in another pile. Then ask him to separate the produce by color, all the green vegetables in one pile and all the orange or yellow vegetables in other groups. Teach him the four food groups, and then ask him to group the things that are made from flour, and all the things that are considered to be meat. Teach him to change from one classification scheme to another and learn to say the reason one item goes into one category or another. When he gets the idea, give him the instruction "Show me how many different ways you can group these things."

Allow your three-to-six-year old to set the table for dinner. This is a very good learning experience. She has to think about five people being at the dinner table. She needs five place mats, five forks, and five napkins, and she needs to pour five glasses of water. This helps her not only with her mathematical concepts but also with her feeling of being a participating member of the family.

Concrete items and objects help children to understand the mathematical concepts that they are expected to learn. Use blocks and beads, apples and oranges, trucks and tools to teach your child to group and classify, count, add, subtract, divide, and measure. This helps your child to be able to understand the *meaning* of these mathematical concepts.

There is a great deal of opportunity to teach your child as young as two and a half years old the basics of dividing and fractions. For example, you can teach dividing and multiplying when you have six cookies and three children. Tell your son "We have six cookies here so that means each person will get two cookies. Two, plus two, plus two makes six." Count them out. "One, two for Peter, one, two for Paul, and one, two for Zachary. One two, three four, five six."

Fractions, too, appear frequently in everyday life. Each time you give your daughter an apple you can sit her down at her place with her favorite stuffed toy beside her and say "Here, I have a whole apple, but let's give half to your friend. Here's half an apple for you and a half an apple for your teddy bear." Later graduate to thirds. When your child has two friends or two stuffed toys, say "Oh, we have three people who need some apple today so we have to cut it in thirds. One third for you, one third for the teddy bear and one third for the puppy." Call attention to the fact that the higher the *number* in the fraction, the smaller the piece each person receives. Show her the apple cut in half and in thirds and ask her which she would rather have. Let her compare the sizes as you say the quantities. Later do other comparisons the same way "Would you rather have a fourth of an apple or half of an apple?"

I used to play "the pie game" with my son several times a week from the time he was two and a half to about four and a half. He begged to play it! We used Lauri's "Fita Fraction Circles," which are different colored foam-rubber circles cut in halves, thirds, fourths, fifths, sixths, sevenths, eighths, ninths, elevenths, and twelfths, representing pies. The red circle was cut in half, and that was the strawberry pie. The white was cut in sixths, and that was the vanilla pie. The pieces are fun to handle. We used stuffed animals and teacups to play "pie." The problem was always to figure what pie to serve and how many animals we could invite for the party. We'd say, "What pie shall we serve? Shall we serve mint?" "Well, let's see, the mint pie is cut into thirds, that means we can only have one visitor come. Three pieces means three people. Who should we invite? Oh, you want the rabbit. Here's a piece for the rabbit and a piece for Ian and a piece for mommy." Then Ian would decide on five little animals that would all come to the party. We might have the kangaroo and the rabbit and the stuffed bear and the hippopotamus and the elephant and me and Ian. Then our job would be to find a pie that was cut into the right number of pieces. If we got the wrong number, some one was left with no pie and cried. All this was very amusing to Ian. He'd say "Don't cry, don't cry, we'll get another piece of pie for you." And then everyone would complain "He has a bigger piece, he has a third of a piece, we only have a sixth of a piece, that's not fair." Then we would have to look for the pie that was cut into the right number of pieces so everyone got exactly the same size. Ian absolutely loved the game, and it gave him a concept of fractions that is clear and firmly based in concrete understanding of the actual meaning of fifths, sixths, sevenths, and so on. Fractions are now very, very simple for him. So be creative, think mathematically and have fun while you make everyday activities into math lessons. The more you think about it, the easier it becomes, and the more fun you'll both have.

Conservation

Children's Thinking

Children think differently than adults, and their thinking changes in characteristic ways as they get older. The child from two to about six thinks quite differently from the school-aged child. The two to six year old's thinking is called *preoperational* and the seven to eleven year old's thinking is called *concrete operational*. It is easiest to understand the way preschoolers think by looking at the mistakes they make on specific *conservation tasks* when they are *preoperational*. Generally children will not understand these conservation tasks until the ages given above, but some will progress faster and understand the logic of the concrete operations tasks at a younger age. These children usually do better in school. Those who progress more slowly and understand concrete operations tasks later may have difficulty in school.

Conservation of Number

If you make a row of eight M & M's and a row of eight pennies and line them up in one-to-one correspondence, your four or five year old will probably be able to count to eight and tell you that there are the same number of M & M's as there are pennies. But if you spread out the M & M's so that they take up more space on the table and the row is longer, she will tell you that there are more M & M's. Even if you ask her to count the M & M's and the pennies again, she will still insist there are more M & M's than there are pennies when they take up more space on the table. This tells you that your preschooler does not really have a concept of numbers even though she can count. The reason the preschooler makes this mistake is that she responds to the question on the basis of her perception: it looks like more. In order to be correct she has to base her judgment on *logic*. Usually by the time the child is six years old she can reason that the rows contain the same number of objects, that they were the same to begin with, and that you moved the M & M's but did not change the number. The preschooler has not yet developed an understanding of "Conservation of Number." The preschooler has not developed concrete operations or the ability to think logically about concrete things she sees.

There are other kinds of conservation tasks that develop later for most children.

Conservation of Liquid

Show a four or five year old two identical cups of juice filled up to the *one cup* line. Then pour one cup into a tall thin glass and the other in a short fat glass. Even if your child watches you pour the cups directly into the glasses in front of him, he will not know that there is the same amount of juice in each glass. He will be overcome by his perception of the height of the juice in the tall glass, and he will tell you that there is more juice in the tall thin glass. Occasionally a child will say that the short fat glass has more. In that case he is responding to the width of the glass. The important thing is that the preschooler can only focus on one dimension at a time: he either focuses on the height of the glass or the width of the glass but cannot pay attention to both dimensions at the same time. His reason is unable to outweigh his impressions. He can't say to himself that the amount of juice hasn't changed, that only the way it looks has changed. Not until around age seven do most children have the logic to understand conservation of liquid.

Conservation of Mass

Make two round balls of clay of equal size so that your child agrees that they are equal. Right before her eyes either roll one of the balls into a hot dog shape or flatten it into a pancake shape.

Then ask her if the new shape has the same amount of clay, more clay, or less clay than the ball does. The preschooler will either say that the sausage shape has more clay than the ball or that the ball has more than the sausage. The reason for the mistake is that your child is attending to the dimension that strikes her first and most impressively. She is only able to focus on one dimension at a time. Sometime between the ages of six and seven most children understand conservation of mass. As with drinks, you can't expect your little one to accept a shorter, wider piece of cake when you give her brother a long thin piece until she understands the logic of this task.

Conservation of Length

Show your child two sticks of equal length such that he agrees that they are of equal length. Then move one stick further over to the right so that it now projects over the one below it. The preschooler will say that one of the sticks is longer. Not until age six or seven does the average child get this one right.

Conservation of Area

Present your child with two identical sheets of 8½ by 11 paper with four wooden blocks placed in one corner of each of them in identical positions. Your child will admit that there is the same amount of space on each piece of paper. Then scatter the four wooden blocks on one of the pieces of paper. The preoperational child will say that the paper with the scattered blocks has less space. When she reaches seven and has concrete operations, she will say that both pieces have the same amount of open space. Again, the preoperational child is overwhelmed by her impressions; it looks like there is less space.

Her understanding of weight and volume will develop even later because these are even more abstract. When a child of seven has the concept of conservation of mass, she will tell you that the sausage-shaped and ball-shaped pieces of clay are composed of the same amount of clay even though they look different. But if you put two balls of clay on a balance scale—even if she sees that the two balls weigh the same—she will say that they don't weigh the same when you roll one into a sausage. Not until she is about nine will she understand that they weigh the same.

However, at nine, although she knows there is the same amount of clay, and that they weigh the same, she will make mistakes in conservation of volume. Even when you show her that the two round balls displace the same amount of water, she will say that the water level will not go up to that same level when one is in a sausage shape. This understanding of conservation is quite abstract, and most children don't understand it until they are eleven years old.

For the purposes of this book, I will not focus on conservation of weight or volume but on the simpler types of conservation tasks.

Why Teach Conservation

What are the applications of the logical abilities used in conservation tasks? The logic involved in conservation is the same logic that your child needs to be able to do simple arithmetic. The preoperational child cannot understand that $1 + 2 = 3$ and therefore $3 - 2 = 1$. He is unable to reverse his thinking. Until your child is able to understand the logic involved in these conservation tasks, he will be unable to do many arithmetic problems involved in concrete operations. Once he understands them, he will be able to do mathematical operations and think logically. He'll be able to understand that if 1 foot is equal to 12 inches then 12 inches is equal to 1 foot. When he can think logically he'll be able to reason deductively, i.e., Spot is a dog. All dogs are animals. Therefore, Spot is an animal. This kind of thinking is particularly important in school.

Ways to Teach Conservation

A number of studies indicate that you can advance your child's abilities to conserve or to develop concrete operations by certain training. One study by D. Field pretested three and four-year-olds and found that they did not understand any kind of conservation problems, number, liquid, mass, or weight. During the study, the children were trained in number and length conservation problems only. The training took place during three different sessions for a total of one and a half hours. In the conservation of number training, the child was given two rows of five checkers and one row of three checkers, and his job was to pick out the two rows that had the same number of checkers. The problems were then repeated with different items, such as two rows of five squares and one row of three squares, two rows of five wrapped candies and one row of three candies. The task again was for the child to pick the two rows that had the same number. Every time the child picked his answer, the teacher stated a rule that explained how to solve the problem. "No matter where you put them, the number of candies is just the same." This rule taught the child the reasoning to use in the concrete operations tasks.

This training in conservation of number emphasized the *reason* why the two rows were the same. Conservation of length was taught by presenting the child with two objects of the same length and one that was shorter and then varying the sets of objects which were used. There would be, for example, two brown sticks of equal lengths and one shorter brown stick, two equal yellow ribbons and one short yellow ribbon, one short pink rod and two pink rods of equal length. Each time the child was to pick out the two equal-length objects. Again, each time the child made a choice the teacher stated a rule that explained how to solve the problem. The rule stressed the same kind of logic that has to be used to solve the concrete operations task of conservation of length. "Look, you just have to put the sticks back together to see that they are still the same length."

What was the effect of training? When the trained children were compared to three and four year olds who did not receive the training, the effect was clear. The children who had received the training did better not only on the conservation of length and conservation of number tasks but on the conservation of liquid, mass, and weight problems as well. In this study almost 40 percent of the children who had received the training were able to solve at least one other type of conservation problem on which they had never been trained. When the chldren were tested again several months later it was clear that the effect of the training lasted. Of those children who had been able to do the conservation tasks they'd never been trained on right after testing, 79 percent of them were still able to conserve better than they had at pretesting. The four year olds profited more from the training than the three year olds. Even those three year olds who were able to do the conservation tasks right after the training were not able to do them three months later. It seems that there is a limit as to how much you can advance a child's cognitive development, but training for a four year old can have a positive effect. Why not try this training with your four or five year old?

In another study by Sigel, Roper, and Hooper, children were trained by calling their attention to the dimensions of pairs of objects. For example, they were given an orange and a banana and asked to describe how they were the same and how they were different. The adults called attention to the length and height of the banana and pointed out that the orange is taller and higher up but not as long. After training the children's performance on conservation of mass and conservation of liquid tasks was improved. You can do this kind of training on your own with many pairs of objects: a gum ball and a stick of gum, a cupcake and a pancake, an ice cream cone and an ice cream bar—just use your imagination.

Teaching Sorting and Classification

Concrete operational children are able to sort objects and then regroup them another way. For example, they can sort flowers into classes of flowers such as roses, tulips and daisies and regroup the flowers by color, red, yellow, and pink. To help your child develop this ability, do sorting games with all kinds of objects. In addition to advancing his vocabulary, these classification games help him develop the logic of concrete operations and prepare him for school.

Conservation Tasks

1. Conservation of Numbers

average age: 6

- Show your child two rows of checkers, bears, candies, buttons in one-to-one correspondence. He counts and agrees there is the same number in each row.
- Spread out one row, then ask your child "Do both rows still have the same number or does one have more?"

2. Conservation of Liquid

average age: 7

- Fill two identical cups to same level with juice (colored so he can see it) so he agrees they are equal.
- Pour the liquid from one cup into a tall thin glass or container. Ask your child "Do these glasses have the same amount of juice?" "Does one have more?" "Which one?"

3. Conservation of Mass

average age: 7

- Give your child two identical clay balls so he agrees they have the same amount of clay.
- Roll out one ball as your child watches. Ask "Do they still have the same amount of clay?"

4. Conservation of Length

average age: 7

- Line up two pencils or sticks in front of your child. He agrees they are equal in length.
- Move one stick to the right. Ask your child "Are they still the same length? Is one longer?"

5. Conservation of Area

average age: 7

- On two identical sheets of paper, place the blocks in identical positions. Ask your child if there is the same amount of space on each paper.
- Scatter the blocks over one of the papers. Ask your child "Do both pieces of paper still have the same amount of space?" "Which one has more?"

6. Conservation of Weight

average age: 9

- Present equal clay balls on balance scale. Ask child if they weigh the same.
- Roll out one ball and ask your child "Will they still weigh the same?" "Which one will weigh more?"

7. Conservation of Volume

average age: 11

- Show your child two equal balls of clay. Then drop them into two equal beakers of colored water. Show him that the water level rises to an equal height.
- Remove one clay ball and roll it into a sausage shape. As your child watches ask your child "Will the water rise to the same level when I drop this sausage in?" "Which one will be higher?"

Developmental Irregularities

Parents and teachers usually have a general idea as to the age at which children should have certain skills. You expect that by the time a child is in first grade she will be able to recognize and print the letters of the alphabet and the numbers. You also expect that she will easily learn or already know letter sounds, and that she will have the necessary prerequisite skills to be able to learn the complicated process of reading and to understand the basic concepts of math. Most children *do* acquire all these skills by the expected time, but some do not. Many children arrive at the age of six unable to do the kinds of things that are asked of them in academic tasks in the first grade.

A child who is unable to learn to read, to do math, or to write at the same rate as his average classmate may be called learning disabled. A child who has average intelligence, knows about the same amount of information as his peers, and reasons and uses words like his agemates but is significantly behind his agemates in academic skills may be called learning disabled. Researchers have looked for explanations for this inability to do reading, math, or writing at grade level. They have looked for signs of minimal brain damage, some sort of brain wave pattern differences, and other physiological explanations.

About the only characteristic that the "learning disabled" share is that their performance in school is poor. What ends up being called a learning disability can be the result of a child failing to learn a number of behaviors that are required for success in reading, writing, and math. Behaviorally oriented psychologists believe that labeling a child as "learning disabled" does nothing to help the child. A label tells you nothing about what to *do* about the problem. References to brain dysfunction only complicate the matter even further.

The behavioral approach focuses instead on finding the *particular* kind of instruction that the child needs to learn the skills he is missing. When certain fundamental skills and abilities have simply not been acquired through casual play and experience, you have to use methods of instruction to teach them.

Reading Problems: Prevention and Treatment

When a child is not learning to read at the same rate as the average child his age he may be called dyslexic. The term *dyslexia* appears to have more meaning to most people than it deserves. They suspect that it is a disease, that something identifiable is *wrong* with the child. Nothing could be further from the truth. A review of the research on dyslexia shows that all it *really* means is the child is not learning to read. Explanations involving brain damage are just speculation. There has never been any clear underlying brain impairment substantiated as causing dyslexia.

All the symptoms of dyslexia, such as reversing letters and reading backwards, are mistakes that younger children make when learning to read. Looking at it in this way, reading disability can be viewed as a developmental problem, that is, that the child is functioning at the level of a chronologically younger child.

To prevent the kinds of developmental problems that can result in your child being labeled "learning disabled" or "dyslexic," you can work on developing the specific abilities your child will need when she begins her reading instruction.

One of the most frequent reasons for a child being delayed in her reading is that she has not yet developed her ability to selectively attend to details. To be able to read, she has to be able to pay attention for a sustained period of time to very small differences in letters. A seven year old who is unable to make important discriminations such as between a *b* and a *d* may be called dyslexic. I prefer to see this child's difficulty in learning as the particular problem to be solved.

Teaching Attention to Small Differences

To teach a difficult discrimination, such as that between *b* and *d,* print *b*'s and *d*'s randomly on a large sheet of paper. Then make a colored transparent plastic b and a different colored transparent plastic d. Now ask your child to go through all the letters, find all of the *b*'s, and go over them with a marker. Then he can color all of the *d*'s a different color. He should place the plastic letter over the letters to see if they are the same. This task forces him to pay attention to the important detail; that is, which side of the line the loop is on. Another method to help increase selective attention is to at first exaggerate the differences between the two details that he is confusing. For example, in your work with him exaggerate the curves on the *b*'s and the *d*'s in words which contain the letters and then gradually reduce the size of the curves. To maintain your child's interest, try to use a great deal of variety in presenting the letters to be discriminated. You can use different-sized letters, different colors, lights, and letters in the sand.

Research in teaching children to make these discriminations shows that if the discrimination is visual, then the best practice is for a child to make that discrimination visually, using plastic overlays, lights, or other things that he can see. A motor response is not necessary for him to learn a visual discrimination, but sometimes having him make a motor response as well will help him to maintain his interest and pay close attention. A fun motor activity is to have him practice making *b*'s and *d*'s with a large piece of butcher paper and his favorite flavor pudding instead of finger paint. Smear his favorite flavor pudding on the paper and then have him make *b*'s and *d*'s and lick his finger after each one.

Teaching Your Child to Pay Attention

Another way children who are called learning disabled differ from their peers is that they are often labeled hyperactive. This simply means that the child has not learned to stay attentive to an academic task. A child can be highly active and need to run the equivalent of two or three miles a day to be able to sleep at night and still not be called hyperactive. As long as this child is able to sit down, concentrate, and selectively pay attention to the details that are required in learning to read, he is not hyperactive. However, there really is an interaction between so-called hyperactivity and failure to pay attention. What a hyperactive child needs is something interesting to entice him to pay attention, and then to receive positive reinforcement and encouragement for doing so.

In order to train your child to be able to pay attention to the task at hand, you want to 1) Make the task as interesting as possible, using a variety of materials, colors, shapes, and sizes, 2) Be certain that he can be successful, and 3) Keep the learning sessions short. Sit down and work with your child for *five good minutes* when he is paying attention and successfully completing the tasks. Then you can praise him and perhaps give him something special to reward his attention. *Only gradually* increase the length of your sessions, but don't make it longer than he can tolerate the session and maintain his attention. Start out with five-minute sessions with interesting materials and leave him wanting more. If your child is still interested and wanting to continue after five minutes, say, "not today, but we can do some more tomorrow." Then try six minutes the next day. Over time you can increase the length of time he works, up to twenty-minute learning sessions.

There are two important strategies for teaching children: 1) *Never give them a task involving parts which they cannot do.* Make sure that they can do all of the individual components of a task. It doesn't make any sense to give the child words to read when she doesn't yet know the individual letter sounds. Once she knows all the individual letter sounds, then you can give words. 2) *Never let your child practice mistakes.* As soon as you find that she is making a mistake, show her the right way and make certain that she learns the right way. If she is calling a *b* a *d,* then you need to teach her the difference between a *b* and a *d* right away. The more often you let her make the mistake the more difficult it will be for her to learn the right way. Another mistake you will not want to allow is *guessing* based on the context, rather than *decoding* or sounding out the word. When children who are called dyslexic are faced with a word they don't know, they just think about the context and say *something* instead of paying attention to detail. When your child makes a mistake, assume that she is trying and *don't ask her to try again.* Teach her the right one by *telling her*—give her the word. Rather than encouraging her to try again, *encourage her to sound out a word.* Help her to sound it out to decode by using her understanding of individual letters.

Writing Problems

It isn't surprising that in most studies of learning disabilities, boys outnumber girls about six to one. One reason for this is that boys tend to be interested in large motor activity in their play. Girls' small motor development is more advanced than boys', and they tend to be more interested in small motor activities. They are much more likely to sit down at a table and color and draw for extended periods of time. They are exposed to letters, words, and sentences on the pages of their coloring books. Girls are much more likely to practice writing letters, and their perceptual-motor development and ability to write is superior to that of most boys by the time they are school age.

Little boys are more interested in large muscle activity than this small muscle activity. While little girls are coloring and drawing and practicing writing their names, the boys are outside running and screaming and jumping off balconies. Many little boys almost never pick up a pencil until they get to school. Boys who do not draw or color are at a distinct disadvantage when it comes time to make letters, because they have not had the hundreds of hours of practice holding a pencil, drawing shapes and forms, and looking at pictures. When a boy arrives at first grade without this background he may be unable to form letters correctly, unable to print by the end of the year, and be diagnosed as having a writing disorder.

My own son was thought by his teacher to have a writing disorder when he was in kindergarten. Although he was only five years old, his teacher felt that his letter formation was unusually poor, and it was. But I knew that with Ian's background, he could not be expected to be able to form letters very well. Ian was an exceptionally active boy. In fact, he was so active I had to take him to the beach to run at least a mile each night before bed. If not, he would run the mile he needed around the living room, risking his life at every turn. Because he was such an active child he never had any practice at sitting down to writing or coloring activities. Regularly, I would offer him artistic materials, crayons and pencils of every color and variety. He was absolutely uninterested in any activity involving such small motor movement. As a result, by kindergarten age he had not even had the practice in writing and drawing that the average boy gets, and his letter formation was very much behind that of his classmates. Should this be called a writing disorder? I think that perhaps it is better to say that Ian did not have the necessary prerequisite skills to be able to formulate letters. He had an inadequate reinforcement history for those behaviors that are necessary for forming letters promptly. It was necessary to reinforce those specific individual abilities that add up to being able to form letters. To give him the specific practice that he needed, we worked on one letter at a time. We spread chocolate pudding on a large piece of butcher paper. Then I would ask him to close his eyes, and I would move his finger to make a letter with a large movement so that the letter was about five inches high. The large movement helps him focus on the kinesthetic cues or muscle patterns to learn the movement. As the muscles learned the moves, I could take away my help. First I would help him make the letter with my hand on top of his. Gradually, I would move his hand more lightly, and then take my hand away and have him make the letter by himself. We also used *verbal cues* such as "around, around, up, down" as we made the *a* together. Repeating "around, around, up, down" each time he made an *a* helped Ian remember the moves he would have to make to form the letter.

Research shows that it is best to have the child make big letters, five inches or more in size, *with his eyes closed* so that he can concentrate on the muscle patterns. When he can make the big letter with closed eyes alone (usually after at least five to ten trials) then he can open his eyes and do it. Next, help him make a big letter with a pencil, then smaller and smaller letters. With the pudding, he was able to lick his finger after every letter; this was his reinforcement for progressing. To help him make the discrimination between similar letters we made the *b*'s in the brown chocolate pudding and the *d*'s in the vanilla pudding. It is good to have the child learn to make these discriminations with a little reward at first.

After Ian was successfully forming each of the letters with pudding and then pencil and paper, he needed to practice placing his letters on a straight line and spacing them properly to form separate words. To help him do that I made boxes on lines with tracing paper and gave him colored pencils to keep him interested. We practiced only five minutes every day, tracing and spacing letters to make words and sentences. With a few minutes practice every day, his handwriting improved dramatically. What a teacher was ready to call a writing disorder was very easily remedied with the proper instruction. Also important to note is that his writing difficulties had nothing to do with intelligence or other abilities. Ian is a bright boy; I had taught him to read at age five by teaching him to recognize letter sounds visually and to sound out words using the methods I have described. He could read the letters although he could not form them! Each skill, reading, arithmetic, writing, has its own set of prerequisite skills that build upon one another. Ian did not have the reinforcement history necessary to do the writing.

I suspect that it is common for children who have had inadequate training in the necessary prerequisites for reading, writing, or arithmetic to end up being labeled "learning disabled." Unfortunately, with eighteen to thirty students in a classroom, teachers cannot provide the time and attention to an individual child who is missing the prerequisites for reading and writing behaviors. Therefore, you want to be certain that you teach and reinforce the skills that will be required when your child's teachers ask her to read and write in the classroom.

If you find that your child is not progressing at the level of his agemates, that her abilities are irregular, you may want to consider placing her in a school system where children move according to their own rates. I am an advocate of the Montessori method, which allows children to progress at their own rate rather than requiring all children to do the same work at the same time. Particularly if your child seems to be uneven in her abilities, you may want to consider a Montessori school. If your child is reading at the third-grade level but is writing like a four year old, she will be able to progress in her reading instead of being held back because of her writing. A good Montessori teacher will allow for these developmental irregularities as Ian's teacher did. In the first grade, Ian's teacher allowed Ian to use plastic letters on a magnetic board to do most of his writing work because forming the letters was painful in the beginning. By end of year, he was able to write like the rest of the children were. Teachers of the Montessori method are usually more aware of the development irregularities in children. They understand that they don't all develop all abilities at the same time and at the same rate and allow a great deal of individual flexibility.

Of course, there may be some problems you won't be able to treat at home alone. You certainly want to get professional help and evaluation if the problems are not responding to your treatment, and, of course, you want to get your child's eyes and ears checked. But before you spend time and money and put your child through testing and labels, I would recommend that you do a thorough analysis of your child's learning history to see if she has learned the prerequisite skills for the complicated tasks that will be asked of her in the first grade. If your child is in school and having problems, you would be wise to go back to the individual letter sounds and evaluate which of those letters she knows and doesn't know and work on the individual letters she needs to learn. Then make certain that she has the basic phonics skills to sound out simple words.

III
Socialization

8

Disobedience
and Temper Tantrums

Socialization is a complex process which involves teaching your child to inhibit certain impulses which our society defines as antisocial and to develop alternative behaviors which our society defines as prosocial. Although you may be fairly clear about the kind of person you want your child to become, the way to teach your child the necessary self-control and appropriate behavior may be far less clear.

Common questions you may ask yourself are: How do I deal with tantrums? Should I spank? If I don't spank, how can I punish disobedience? How can I stop my baby from hitting, pushing, or biting? Should I bite my son when he bites me? How can I teach my child to share and play cooperatively? How can I teach my child to make friends? How will my style of discipline affect my child's adult personality?

Like many parents, you may find that the answers to these questions found in basic childcare books seem superficial and do not really provide you with constructive ways to deal with the problems. You may also be unsatisfied by dismissing undesirable behaviors as "normal," as many books do. If you intuitively believe that your way of dealing with these child behaviors is of great importance, you are right. The research on child development indicates that the way you handle these matters has effects on children that reach into adulthood. For example, the regular use of reasoning as a means of control has a very different effect on children's moral development than the regular use of physical punishment. Whether your approach to child behavior is characteristically "permissive," "moderately restrictive," or "authoritarian" has lasting effects on your child's development of self-control.

Unfortunately, most parents treat undesirable behavior and desirable prosocial behaviors as if they were unrelated matters. The focus in this chapter and the next is on *preventing undesirable behaviors* while they are in the making and *teaching alternative, prosocial behaviors* at the same moment. The approach is discipline with the intent to teach.

Younger Children

During a baby's first year of life, most parents are unconcerned with discipline and are quite permissive and accepting of their baby's behavior. Very few parents are concerned when the child of less than twelve months pulls hair or bites, or when the newly mobile crawler empties the contents of cupboards or drawers. Most people are aware that these behaviors are exploratory and innocent and understand that the baby has no concept of good or bad, harmful or hurtful behavior, or self-control.

However, sometime after your son's first birthday you will probably become concerned about discipline. He may be developing communicative speech. By fifteen months he may understand simple commands. Because he seems to understand so much, you may begin to expect him to understand the consequences of his behavior and to exhibit self-control.

Probably the easiest and most successful way to deal with unacceptable behavior in the period of twelve to eighteen months is distraction. Most childrearing books take into consideration the innocence of children and suggest to parents of toddlers that they must redirect their child to another suitable activity when removing their child from some unacceptable activity. For example, parents are encouraged to say, "No, we don't write on the wall, we write on the paper," or "No, we can't touch that, it's dangerous. Let's play here with these toys." This tactic tends to work very well for children from twelve months to somewhere between fifteen and eighteen months.

There comes a time, usually around eighteen months, when your child will no longer be so easily diverted. When you remove her from an undesirable activity, she will immediately run back to it and, in what may seem to be a defiant manner, repeat over and over again the same behavior. For example, if she is pulling leaves from a plant and is reprimanded, "No, let's not pull leaves off the plant, let's go play with the toys," she may, even while you're playing with her and the toys, immediately return to pulling leaves off the plant. There may even be days when she will run from one prohibited behavior to another. She'll go from pulling the leaves off a plant to turning the knobs on the stereo, to trying to remove the caps from the electrical outlets. On these days you may wonder what is wrong with your child. In most cases, when these things happen there is something very right with your child. She is attempting to determine the rules which govern the household.

Your child merely wants to learn the rules. He wants to hear you state the rules over and over again. In a highly verbal child this process can be understood more fully. For example, when he returns to the plant for the tenth time in two days to pull more leaves, and you say, "No, don't pull the leaves off the plant," he may himself complete the rest of your previous speech if you fail to do so: "I like that plant—don't hurt it." As he bangs the glass table and you admonish, "Stop doing that," he may complete the chastisement by saying, "You might break it." Your child's behavior may be more tolerable if you can try to adopt the attitude that he is, in these cases, asking for another explanation. If he could, he might ask you in words what he asks by his behavior: "Tell me about this plant again, why I can't hit it," or "Tell me again about the electrical outlets and what happens if you stick something in them."

Of course, there will be behavior such as playing in the toilet that seems to be repeated randomly just because your child enjoys water play. It is usually not these behaviors that you will find troublesome but those which seem willful, deliberate, and defiant. You should be assured that these "willful" behaviors are a result of your daughter's attempts to determine some consistency and incorporate the rules, and are not evidence of a defiant attitude. In fact, it seems that the brighter the child, the more scientific her approach to the situation will be, and the more likely it is that she will carry the experiment further.

Strategies for Handling Disobedience

During this difficult period, there are a number of things you can do. First, your explanations should be clearly stated and frequently repeated. Second, you should provide your child with as much stimulation outside the home as possible. If you take your daughter out in the morning on a nature walk to look at bushes, rocks, bugs, pinecones, and leaves, she will be less likely to pull the leaves off your plants when you come home. Her curiosity and interest in the world is intense. The more you satisfy her intellectual curiosity, either outdoors or at indoor museums or stores, the less desire she will have to hear your explanations repeated.

You should also reduce the number of rules she has to learn. Before you prohibit a certain behavior, ask yourself if it is necessary, important, or desirable to prohibit this particular behavior.

Make transgressions unlikely to occur by moving things, locking cupboards, and rearranging furniture. Teaching your daughter to stay away from certain items will be much easier when she is three years old and more reasonable and capable of self-control.

Those behaviors which are prohibited should be prohibited every day. The rules should not depend upon your mood. If there is any variation in whether a behavior is allowed or not allowed on alternating days, then your daughter should not be reprimanded. For example, if you decide that because today is hot and sunny, she can hose off the dog to cool him down, then expect her to do it again! Do not expect that telling her not to water the dog will have any effect on her behavior tomorrow. Once you have permitted that behavior in fairness to your daughter, all you should do to dissuade her from it is to help her redirect the hose somewhere else or remove the dog. It is unrealistic to expect her to listen when you say, "Don't water the dog," and unfair to turn off the hose or take it away if she does water the dog. The young child simply has no awareness of weather conditions or the reason why this exciting and fun behavior is prohibited today. Likewise, if you let her squirt you with the hose when you have your bathing suit on, don't be angry if she does it when you are dressed to go out.

It would be difficult to overemphasize the importance of consistency in parental discipline at this time, because there is so much apparent inconsistency with which your child will already be having difficulty. For example, most children are encouraged to pour water from one container into another container in the bathtub and they delight in water play. Therefore, children who have previously been drinking from a cup in a very civilized manner may suddenly begin to experiment by pouring the contents of their cup all over the highchair tray, or in their dinner plate, or on the floor. The rule regarding water play must be very carefully spelled out for them repeatedly before they will be able to assimilate the differences between the occasions when pouring liquid is permissible and the occasions when pouring liquid is not permissible.

If you allow your son to pour his water at the high chair in the kitchen but not his juice in the dining room, the discrimination is too difficult. At this point it is better to figure out what is the simplest rule and abide by it. For example, tell him, "You may play with water in the bathtub but not anywhere else in the house." To impress him with the importance of following the rules, try to prevent the pouring by anticipating the behavior and taking the cup away just as he is about to pour, repeating the rules over and over again: "You may pour in the tub." If he cannot follow the rule, then you may say, "I have to hold the cup to help you not spill it. You can't pour milk in the house, so I will help you with the cup."

Temper Tantrums in the First Two Years

From the time your daughter is eleven months of age, you and she will have differences of opinion. At this early age, she knows when she wants to get down, get up, or have something, but will not yet have developed the method of using her voice or behavior to try to get her way. So she squirms, kicks, and screams. By age two, many children will have learned to have full-blown tantrums to protest when things don't go their way.

There are a number of causes of tantrum behavior in the two year old. Sometimes a tantrum is merely a response to overwhelming frustration and tension. It is the same as an adult kicking a door or using profanity when exceptionally frustrated. This usually happens when your daughter is trying to become more independent and to do more things on her own than are possible. She may become exhausted from the tension of trying to put on her shoe, or buckle her seat belt, or put butter on her bread without breaking it. If you offer your help at the wrong time, or don't offer it at the right time, or frustrate her by refusing her something when she is already frustrated, she may explode in tears and screams and kicks in an attempt to release some of the overwhelming tension.

Another reason for tantrums at age two is that your daughter is beginning to really feel and experience herself as a separate individual with ideas and feelings of her own. She will become very interested and involved in her activities. She will therefore resent having to leave something in which she is highly involved to go home, to get ready for bed, or to go shopping.

Sometimes she will simply feel that certain things are not as important as you think they are. She may be inclined to tantrum behavior to prevent you from imposing your needs on her. One common area of conflict concerns grooming and dressing. Most children are unconcerned about their hair being combed or their clothes being handsome or pretty. If you interrupt something your daughter is doing to focus on dressing or washing, she will be most unhappy about it and may let you know with a tantrum.

Sometimes children of this age will become very concerned about what they wear and insist on wearing only one or two items. When these are dirty or in the wash, they will have a tantrum, insisting on wearing the item that is filthy.

By your reactions when your daughter is as young as ten or eleven months old you can either begin to train her to use civilized means of persuasion or tantrum behavior. If she wants to get down, *screams,* and you put her down, then you are teaching "beginning tantrum behavior." If she wiggles, squirms, and kicks, and you put her down, you are teaching the same.

Even though your daughter may be unable to tell you what she wants, you can teach her to do something other than scream or cry to communicate her needs. By paying attention to and rewarding other sounds or gestures you can prevent her from learning to scream to get what she wants.

Wait until she is still for a second and look for a more civilized gesture such as reaching toward the ground or saying "down." Then, if you are willing to let her down, say, "You want to get down?" and put her down *immediately.* The behavior you are reinforcing may not be apparent to anyone else but you, because the screams may precede the gesture of saying "down" very closely in time. However, it is what *immediately* precedes her getting what she wants that she will learn to do the next time. After several reinforcements, she will omit the screams and get right to saying "down," since the screams only delay her getting what she wants.

If you have scooped her up to leave a place and you cannot stay any longer, or if you definitely do not want her to have another cookie, then ignore the screams and the thrashing about. If you have a change of heart, and decide that she can stay a few minutes more, or have another cookie, or stay a little longer in the tub, make certain that she has quieted down and is not screaming or thrashing about before you tell her you've changed your mind. If you change your mind and put her back into the bathtub, back down on the beach, or give her a cookie while she is screaming, then she will have learned that screaming works to get her what she wants. She will scream louder and longer the next time you disagree. Once she has accepted the "no," or the removal from the play situation, and is quiet, then you may say, "Do you really want to play some more? Okay, we can stay a little while longer," or "Okay, you can have another cookie."

Older Children

Reinforce Asking Nicely

Once your son has acquired sufficient language, you can help him learn to ask rather than scream by telling him, "I can never give you another cookie if you scream for it. You have to tell me what you want, say, 'Please, more cookies, Mommy.'"

If he has asked nicely to "stay on the beach some more," then whenever possible, try to reinforce asking nicely and bend to his wishes. This will firmly establish habits of asking nicely. If you see that he is sunburned, you may tell him, "Look, Alan, your arms and back are all red. If you stay in the sun anymore it will hurt you very badly tonight. I can't let you stay. We'll come back again. Do you want to come back?" Give him the *reason* why you have to leave and talk about some desirable upcoming event: "Let's go buy some popcorn for the ride home."

The single rule to follow is to never, under any circumstances, give him what he wants in response to his tantrums. Even if you have decided that it was a mistake to say "no" to begin with, you have to stick to your first decision. After that, the way you handle the tantrum depends both upon your feelings about the tantrum and your child's response to you during tantrum. Some parents can hold a child lovingly while the child screams it out. Others become too angry and are better off leaving the room or the immediate vicinity while the child screams it out. Some children do not want to be touched during a tantrum.

Avoid Reinforcing a Chain of Behavior

There should be a difference in the way you handle screaming in an eleven month old and tantrums in an older child who already knows another gesture or word to communicate needs or wants. To initially establish a response in the young baby of asking or pointing to get something, you will look for a civilized gesture among whines or screams. But once your child has learned the desired response, you need to avoid reinforcing a chain of behavior. Once your child has been positively reinforced many times for using words or gestures instead of screaming, you will want to reinforce "asking nicely" only.

When your daughter who is old enough to know better begins to scream and cry and thrash about to get her way, this should be a guarantee to her that she will not get what she desires. Even if she quiets down, do not give her what she wants. If you do, she may learn this chain of behavior: "First I have a tantrum and scream and cry, then when I quiet down I get what I want." If she screams and cries and thrashes about to stay at a friend's house you can tell her, "I cannot let you stay now even if I would have changed my mind. When you cry and scream to get what you want, you can never, never have it." Then go home. Even if she calms down and says nicely, "Please can we stay at Polly's house some more?" You must insist, "No, not today. Maybe another time when you can ask me nicely. Today we have to go home because you screamed and cried. I cannot change my mind when you scream and cry."

Make It Easy to Cooperate

In this section I will describe a number of strategies for avoiding conflict in circumstances which commonly lead to tantrums in children. To come up with these methods I asked myself, "How can I make it more likely that my son will want to cooperate?" When you must be inventive in situations I have not dealt with, ask youself, "How can I make it easier for my child to do the necessary or appropriate thing?"

You will want to think seriously about your child's needs, interests, feelings, moods, and desires in order to make the appropriate behavior less likely to occur. For example, if you know that your son has difficulty sitting in one place, either the high chair, the car seat, or the shopping cart at the store, then try to think of some circumstances in which he is happy to sit still for a while. If it turns out that he doesn't mind sitting while eating grapes, while looking at pictures of himself, or while playing with a favorite toy, then provide him with those things when he is required to sit. This may mean that you save his daily portion of grapes for the trip in the car and present the grapes to him as soon as you buckle him in the seat belt. If you know that he finds it hardest to sit in the car seat when he is tired, then save the popcorn or his favorite treat for the trip home.

It is of great importance that you recognize that your son is becoming a person with his own interests and ideas. You wouldn't consider saying to an adult friend at the instant you are ready to leave, "Let's go to the store," and expect your friend to jump up in the middle of an ongoing activity. You should not expect your two year old to do so either. There are ways to prevent conflict. First of all, you can try giving him sufficient notice that you will be having to leave in a little while. Many parents find setting a timer to be effective. Tell your son, "We have to leave in five minutes. I will set the timer so we know when it is five minutes. When the timer rings that means we have to go." Many children accept this as a fair method.

When visiting a playmate whom your son has a very difficult time leaving, you would be wise to do a great deal of planning for departure time. Make sure he has had enough time to play. If this is a favorite friend and he finds leaving very difficult, then don't drop in for fifteen minutes and expect him to be able to leave gracefully. It may be better to wait until you can spend a good two hours. When the time comes to leave, rather than talking about leaving, try talking about something else: "We have to go to the store and buy some groceries. Let's buy something special for your dinner. What should we buy?" Try to interest him in the upcoming events rather than focusing on leaving.

Similarly when you must wash, change, or dress him it is better to just continue your conversation about other things. Pick him up and carry him to the bathroom to wash his hands and face, never mentioning the washing. You can avoid the whole confrontation by just keeping his attention on other things.

If he cannot feel the importance of washing his face, combing hair, and changing clothes while he is at home, take him as he is and dress him when you arrive at your destination. For example, take him as he is to the party house, then wash his face with a washcloth and dress him in the car when you arrive. When he sees the party house and wants to go in, he will be better able to feel the importance of looking nice.

If your son is one who hates to be dressed, then try to think of ways to make getting dressed more fun and less disturbing. Some ways to minimize the battle would be to take him to the store to choose some fun clothing. Let him help to pick out a shirt with a hippopotamus or rabbit on it, or a certain kind or color of shoes, or some pajamas with a particular pattern he likes. When it is time to get dressed, he may find it easier to put on an article of clothing which he has chosen. You can ask, "Would you like to wear your bunny shirt or your hippo shirt?" When he selects one you can talk about the character on the shirt. Talk to him about how nice it will look and stand him in front of a mirror so he can see how nice the hippo shirt looks on him. Sometimes it is helpful to put on each article of clothing in a different room. Put on his shirt in the bathroom, his pants in your bedroom, and then take him into the kitchen to put on his socks and shoes.

If he is reluctant to put on a bathing suit at home when you are trying to get him ready for swimming lessons, then take him in the car with his pajamas on and put on his bathing suit at the pool. When he sees the water and wants to go in, he will be more likely to cooperate. Always ask yourself, "What would make him want to do what I want?" As much as possible, make the required activity something he will enjoy or something he will find pleasurable.

Some of the difficulties are a result of your child's limited cognitive abilities. Children in their twos and under live in the immediate present and do not think in terms of future or past. Your arguments about needing to be dressed to go to the party or needing a bathing suit on to go into the pool have no real meaning to your son until he sees the party house or the pool. By the time most children are three years old they have a better sense of the future and will be able to understand terms related to the past and future. Then when you tell your son that it is time to get dressed for Kelly's party he will be much more interested in dressing for the upcoming event.

When you see that the tantrums are becoming more likely as your son is trying to become more independent and do new things on his own, you can help by trying to avoid having many frustrating situations in a day. Be certain to set up stress-free times such as a relaxing hour in the tub or an hour of quiet time. However, even when you know that a tantrum is a result of frustration, you cannot give him what he wants following the tantrum or to quiet the tantrum, or you will be teaching him to scream for what he wants in the future.

When You Cannot Avoid the Tantrum

Even if you have been extremely careful never to reinforce tantrum behavior, have always given your daughter advance warning, and have tried to keep her attention on other things, she may still have a tantrum when it's time to get ready for bed. The problem may not even be that she does not want to go to bed, but that she does not want to put up with being washed and dressed appropriately for bed. However, it is necessary that she be washed, wear a diaper and pajamas, and so on. She may scream and thrash about the whole time you are trying to dress her. If you allow her to kick and thrash about and avoid getting dressed, then she has won through the tantrum. You must not allow this behavior to succeed. In such cases it is desirable to forcibly restrain her from kicking and to tell her that she can never get her way by this behavior. Sometimes it helps to use a very stern tone of voice and say such things as, "Stop it! You just stop this! You can never get your way by kicking like this. This will never work. I know you are tired, but you don't have to do this. You don't have to kick and scream. If you cooperate with me it's over faster. I can get your diaper and your pants on fast if you cooperate with me. If you kick and scream it just takes longer."

You can do your best to keep her favorite clothes available, but when it is impossible you may have to deal with the tantrum. She may refuse to cooperate with dressing and continue to cry while insisting on wearing a certain item. If possible, let her experience the natural consequences of refusing to select some other piece of clothing. Tell her, "No you can't wear the gray pants. They are dirty. You can wear these pants or these pants and that is all. When you decide what you want to wear you tell me." Then you can say, "Since you have no clothes on and its cold outside, you'll just have to stay in bed under the covers." When she comes to you to say, "I want to wear these pants," and selects another item, then you can dress her.

Teaching Your Child To Be Reasonable

Reasoning as a Means of Discipline

The use of reasoning involves giving your child explanations for your behavioral requirements. Sometimes the explanations include your feelings and wants. For example, when you ask your son to help pick up his toys you may say, "I don't like to be tripping over toys" or "I don't like seeing toys all over the floor. The living room doesn't look pretty this way." Giving explanations which involve your feelings is quite different from the authoritarian statement, "because I said you have to."

Authoritarian parents expect obedience because "they are the parents." They are nonaccepting of their child's arguments, will not negotiate, and do not give reasons for their behavioral requirements. They want their child to have respect for adults and authority. Additionally, authoritarian parents are likely to use physical punishment as a means of control.

Children of authoritarian parents are usually very well behaved at home and exhibit no aggressive behavior with their parents. They do what is asked of them instantly and they do not answer back. Unfortunately, many of the same children are behavior problems away from home. It seems that the behavior that is demanded at home is exhibited because of fear of punishment. When the fear of punishment is absent, the reasons for the behavior are not clear or meaningful to the children and do not control their behavior.

Serious problems may emerge in adolescence because such children have little practice in thinking through the reasons for behavioral requirements or prohibitions. It is more difficult for children who are raised in an authoritarian way to arrive at independent moral decisions when faced with peer pressure to use drugs, drink, vandalize, and so on.

Democratic or authoritative parents use reasoning and explanation as a means of control. Note the distinction between authoritative and authoritarian. Authoritative parents are affectionate and loving towards their children and are described as "warm." If you are this type of parent, you will have a great deal of empathy — understanding of your child's needs, feelings, and point of view. However, you will also know that your child's limited experience requires you to make certain decisions about what kind of behavior will and will not be permitted. You will give your son considerable freedom but will impose restrictions or make demands on his behavior when his limited cognitive or emotional development would lead to undesirable behavior. You will clearly and consistently enforce the limits on behavior. In summary, the democratic or authorita*tive* parent is warm, empathetic, moderately restrictive, consistent, and uses reasoning and explanations as a means of control.

A considerable body of data indicates that children of democratic or authoritative parents have a higher level of self-control, self-esteem, competence, adaptability, and popularity with peers. When an empathetic parent uses reasoning and is consistent, then the child's attachment to the parent and the use of reasoning work together to promote the child's development of self-control and internalization of social standards. The child's attachment results in strong identification with the values of the parents. The use of reasoning teaches the child to think and to arrive at independent moral decisions in the absence of the parents. Even as toddlers these children exhibit more self-control when they are away from their parents.

With reasoning and explanation, behavioral expectations make more sense to children than rules presented without explanation. Children are much more likely to follow a rule if they can understand the reason for it. A review of the research on discipline indicates that the use of reasoning and explanation as a means of control, with an emphasis on the needs and feelings of others in the explanation, is associated with the highest degree of self-control and the most mature moral decisions.

As behavioral norms change from generation to generation, you cannot expect to provide a complete list of appropriate ways to behave in each situation. Your child must be able to *reason* in the face of peer pressure and pressure from sometimes-incorrect authority. Practice in thinking about behavior and why it is necessary, appropriate, or inappropriate should begin in toddlerhood. The short-term drawbacks are that your child will be more argumentative and may at times appear disrespectful to adults. You may be extremely frustrated when your child's arguments are unreasonable and persistent. The long-term advantages are that you can expect your child to exhibit a high degree of self-control away from home. Your child will be able to make independent moral decisions as an adolescent and an adult.

Teaching Moral Principles

There is a great deal of moral learning to be accomplished. Consider the fact that your baby, in a very short span of time, will be expected to incorporate rules of civilization which have taken centuries to develop. Children have no idea of these rules until you interpret them and provide the information.

Learning rules of behavior can be made much easier for children if you treat it like any other learning experience. Make the rules as simple and straightforward as possible. Provide exceptions to the rules only after they have been thoroughly learned.

It is valuable to ask yourself, "What is it that I am trying to teach?" If you are trying to teach respect for property, then it is important to remember the *principle* when your youngster brings home a piece of broken toy or a worn and torn book from a friend's house. I remember a twelve-year-old boy who was brought to me for therapy by his parents after he stole $500 from his grandmother's purse. Upon questioning the parents, I discovered that they had permitted the child to come home with small items from friends' homes for years. The parents reasoned that, "The book was old and not worth more than 25¢ to begin with," and used similar reasoning for permitting other, similar behaviors. In the child's mind there was no difference between taking a worn book from a friend's home and taking $500 from his grandmother's purse. He wanted both the book and the money, and both belonged to someone else. The notion of "value" is not something a child considers when he is allowed to take things that don't belong to him.

Similarly, when you are attempting to teach respect for other people's gardens and flowers, it is best not to allow your son to pick flowers from people's gardens even if there are thousands of blooms. Make a simple rule: "We can't pick these flowers, they are not ours. They belong to someone else." Teach him to ask permission of the owner to pick a flower or play with someone's toy to develop a respect for other people's property.

There is logical progression in giving rules to children based on their ability to understand them. First you teach the simplest form of the rule. Then you introduce the exceptions. For example, depending on your son's level of conceptualization, you may introduce the notion of "wild" flowers and "garden" flowers, permitting him to pick those that no one planted and not those which belong to someone. If he can understand one aspect of a rule, then exceptions may be given. For example, once he has learned that he cannot hit people because hard things hurt, and he seems to understand which items are hard and which are soft, then you may introduce an exception such as a pillow or a sponge ball, stating simply, "We can hit each other with this ball because it is soft. We can't hit with the truck because it is hard and it hurts." It is important that he first has a basic understanding of which toys hurt before you begin to introduce the exceptions.

Another way to help your daughter acquire rules of behavior in places outside the home is to let her know that authority can come from someone else. For example, when she wants to get inside the cage with the ducks, you can say, "No, the zookeeper does not want us to get in with the ducks. The zookeeper says, 'No, no people in with the ducks.'" When she wants to rearrange the shelves in a department store, tell her, "No, no the storekeeper says we have to leave them here. The storekeeper does not want us to move them." Giving children a reason having to do with someone else's property and someone else's feelings seems to exercise more control over their behavior than an arbitrary, "No, don't touch that."

Building a Relationship Based on Reasoning

Some of the conditions which will make your reasoning and explanations effective include an empathetic attitude toward your son and an appreciation of his need to explore and experiment. This attitude will lead you to prohibit only what is necessary for his safety or for the needs of others. When you appreciate his needs you will say no only when necessary. Your empathy tells your son that you really care about how he feels. As a consequence he will become strongly attached to you, and your smiling face and warm feelings toward him will be very important to him. Because of his attachment to you, he will really try to keep you happy. By the time he reaches the age of three, if you have a warm and loving relationship and discipline him with the intent to teach, he will be likely to cooperate with you simply because he wants to please you. He will not want to see you upset or angry and will often modify his own behavior just to keep you happy.

Reasoning with Young Children: It May Not Be Enough

Although you hope that reasoning alone will eventually be enough to control your child's behavior, you should realize that before age three the effects of reasoning and explanation are limited by your child's cognitive abilities. The effect of explaining your rules may also be overshadowed by the enjoyment your child experiences in hearing the explanation. For example, your two-year-old daughter may be learning that it hurts other children when she scratches them. But she may so enjoy hearing your explanation of the no-scratching rule or the cries of the hurt child that she will increase the frequency of her aggressive behavior. Therefore, it is often necessary to supplement your explanation with a consequence that she experiences as negative, such as her immediate removal from a play situation. Your explanations of the consequences should be clearly and simply stated: "You can't scratch children. It hurts them. If you scratch children, you can't play with them. You have to go home now." Following your explanation, take her home immediately.

There are individual differences in the age and degree to which children are controlled easily by reason and explanation alone. Some differences are a result of temperamental and personality characteristics. Differences in rates of language development and the degree of attachment to you also influence the effectiveness of reasoning. Factors such as other family members will also exert an influence. Older siblings may be inconsistent and therefore interfere with your use of reasoning. The amount of time you have available to teach your child, explain rules, prevent misbehavior, structure the environment, and promote desirable behavior all influence how soon your child will respond to reason alone.

Providing Natural, Logical Consequences to Undesirable Behavior

Often before your child reaches age three you will find that there are situations in which reason and explanations alone may not be enough to exact desirable behavior. Other methods such as punishment or negative reinforcement may be required (see the chapter on Decreasing Undesirable Behavior for definitions of punishment and negative reinforcement). However, punishment or negative reinforcement need not be either physical or arbitrary.

The most reasonable form of punishment or negative reinforcement is to allow your child to experience the logical or natural negative consequences of his behavior. At times natural consequences are programmed into the environment: Your son refuses to wear a coat, you let him experience the consequence of the cold, and he asks to have his coat to avoid being cold (negative reinforcement). If he refuses to wear his shoes in the summer, the experience of hot pavement will prompt him to wear his shoes (negative reinforcement).

For the eighteen-month-old child who scratches her playmate's face, a logical consequence for his behavior would be to withdraw her from the play situation saying, "You cannot play with children if you scratch them, you have to go home now." (Punishment). If your daughter will not share her toys with her friends but proceeds to grab everything anyone touches, it is logical to tell her, "Your friend has to go home now because he wants to play with some toys, and you won't let him have any. He's going home to play with his own toys." (Punishment). When your three year old fails to pick up her toys when it is time to go to the park you may say, "Oh, I see the toys are not picked up. I guess we will have to stay home and pick them up. I'll call Suzie and tell her we do not have time to go to the park today." (Punishment).

The single most frequent problem is that parents are very reluctant to allow their children to experience the negative consequences resulting from their behavior. It is wise to remember that a few experiences of the logical or natural negative consequences may prevent many more negative encounters between you and your child. Ultimately these consequences will not have a harmful effect on your child.

Many parents ask with astonishment, "You mean I should let her go barefoot in the snow?" or "I should let her go outside without a coat?" The answer is yes. Once your daughter experiences the cold on her body or her feet, she will ask for her coat or her shoes. Your concern for her health is unwarranted (of course, you must bring her coat or shoes along with you).

A mother once complained to me that her three-year-old son dawdled in the morning to such an extent that he was rarely dressed for nursery school when the driver in a car pool arrived to pick him up. She would send the driver on, angrily throw on her son's clothes, take him and her infant child in the car, and then drive him to nursery school. Repeatedly the child dawdled, the mother became very frustrated and angry, and drove him to nursery school. When

I suggested that she keep him home if he were not dressed in time, she replied that the nursery school was paid for, that she needed the time to get her household chores done, and that the school provided time for her to spend with her newly arrived baby. Though understandable, this reasoning was very short-sighted. Because her son truly loved nursery school, the natural consequence of missing a day or two would have prompted him to dress himself more quickly to avoid this loss on another occasion. Even if he had to miss nursery school on several successive days, in the long run he would learn that to get to nursery school he would have to dress himself more quickly in the morning.

One real advantage to allowing your son to experience logical consequences is that you are not personally responsible for the pain or emotional discomfort he experiences, so he won't hold it against you. If you warn him of the consequences, then let him experience them, you are on his side. Having warned him, you have tried to help him. For example, tell him, "If you throw your book out the window it will be all gone. I won't be able to get it for you on the road and you won't have it anymore." Then, when he throws it out and starts crying, you can sympathize with him. "I'm sorry you threw your book away. You liked your book, and now it's all gone." The next time you are in the car and you see he's thinking about throwing his toy, you remind him. "Remember how sad you were when you threw your book out the window? If you throw your toy out the window you will be very sad!"

Consistency

When words come to exercise control over your child's behavior, your child will be far more easily managed. To teach your child to respond to your words is a simple matter. Let your words become a consistent signal that consequences will follow a transgression. If you say, "Do not push children" and then do nothing when he pushes, your words will be meaningless to him the next time. If you say, "Do not push," and provide a consequence immediately (go home or ask your visitor to leave), then the next time you repeat these words they will be more likely to control his behavior. If you provide consequences consistently, every time you prohibit a behavior, then with time your words alone will be enough to cause him to inhibit his unacceptable behaviors.

By the time your daughter is two years old, her growing feelings of competence in dealing with the world will give her increased feelings of independence. She feels brave enough to do some serious testing of the rules and consequences to determine your degree of commitment to these consequences. This is an important time to have carefully considered consequences for specific behaviors.

Occasionally there is no way to prevent a transgression and you can neither physically remove your child from the situation nor provide some logical or natural consequence. When the behavior is *intolerable,* particularly when it is destructive or injurious to your child or others, "time out" should be considered. Time out is explained at length in the chapter on Decreasing Undesirable Behavior.

9

Aggression, Empathy, Sharing, and Cooperation

If you realize the advantage of exposing children at an early age to play with other children, you also realize the importance of teaching your child to share, to play cooperatively, and to inhibit aggressive behavior. However, you may be uncertain about how to teach these social skills or what degree of self-control and social sophistication you can develop in your child in the early years. Research in psychology has discovered principles of learning which you can easily apply to teaching the social skills of sharing, generosity, sensitivity to the feelings of others, and initiating play.

It is true that many children eventually learn to play cooperatively, are peaceful and nonaggressive, and share with their friends in the absence of specific training. However, there are those who do not learn the appropriate social skills and who are therefore unpopular with their peers and even adults. Rather than leave such important matters to chance, you can teach your child some specific behaviors which will make positive social experiences possible for many years.

With a great deal of attention, even a child under two years of age can learn to ask for something rather than grab from an agemate, to ask nicely rather than scream for things, to wait patiently when needs cannot immediately be met, to take turns, to play cooperatively, and to share.

Aggression

From twelve to eighteen months, all youngsters occasionally strike or step on one another, and this behavior does not seem to have any particular motive. Your daughter may be attempting to obtain possession of a toy and may not seem angry as she hits a friend. She seems to be treating her friend as an object, another toy, regardless of her playmate's feelings or experience of pain. The abusive behavior seems absentminded and may remind you of the way she handles a doll, dragging it along by its foot. Because prior to eighteen months of age she does not understand the difference between an inanimate doll and a living human being, you should expect her way of treating her friends to be insensitive. You will have to repeatedly tell her not to step on her friends and help her walk around them. You will have to help her find something else to bang her truck on besides her friend's head.

By eighteen months of age many children seem to be able to use the word "hurt" appropriately when they have been hurt. Because your daughter seems to understand the word, you might be led to believe that she can comprehend that her biting, hair pulling, or slapping have a hurtful effect on you or a playmate. This is incorrect. At this age a child may be expected to use many words appropriately and yet have an understanding of the words only in a particular situation. She may understand the word "hurt," but only as it pertains to her. She does not yet understand that this word describes similar feelings in other people.

Definition of Aggression

Let us define aggressive behavior as behavior which intentionally causes distress in another individual — behavior with the intent of inflicting pain or hurt upon another person. With this definition in mind, a close look at the characteristics of a child's thinking between the ages of eighteen months and two years will show that a child is not capable of performing a true aggressive act at this time.

In order for your daughter to perform a true aggressive act she must be able to understand that her behavior can inflict pain on another. This understanding requires a great deal of thinking which is not possible for her before age two. For her to understand that others feel hurt requires that she learn at least three discriminations.

First, she must learn the difference between living and nonliving things. This alone is a difficult conceptual task and is not fully accomplished in most children until they are close to two years of age. It is for this reason that your daughter treats her cat or dog as if it were just another stuffed toy and her friends as if they were dolls.

Once she begins to realize that another individual may be hurt, she then needs to discriminate between which of her actions are hurtful and which are not. How hard can she hit before Mommy becomes angry? What kind of grabbing does Mommy call a hug? How hard can she pinch before Mommy says NO!

Third, she must learn what kind of actions hurt which particular people. For example, Daddy laughs when she pushes, but her little friend cries. Her friends don't want to be hugged. This learning requires a considerable quantity of thought which becomes more and more available to her as she matures and develops. As she approaches two years of age, this kind of thinking becomes more likely to occur, but not much before.

Aggression as Claiming Ownership. To what do we attribute the increase in assaultive behaviors between the ages of eighteen months to two years? One reason for increased assaultive behavior involves a child's relationship to toys. Especially towards the end of the second year, there is an increasing interest in toys and objects in the environment, and an increasing involvement with the function of toys. Additionally, your daughter will have an increasing awareness of the concept of ownership. What this means is that: 1. She will become increasingly upset when a toy is taken from her, and 2. Her own toys will become far more difficult to share than toys belonging to a nursery or friend.

Most of the behaviors that appear to be aggressive in children of this age are emitted when they are attempting to obtain possession of a toy or when there is some disagreement over a toy. The behavior seems to be directed more toward obtaining the toy than towards a particular person. The victim is really treated as an object in the way rather than as an individual on whom the assaultive child would like to inflict pain or hurt. Once the toy is obtained, the aggressive behavior ceases.

Aggression as an Experiment: Another reason for an increase in seemingly aggressive behavior in the period from eighteen months to two years is a consequence of your child's advancing cognitive ability. At this time, your child is in the process of testing similarities and differences in behaviors and their consequences. Your child may, therefore, resume behaviors which had been eliminated previously in order to further test the rules and the consequences.

For example, your nursing son, when his first teeth begin to emerge, will be easily dissuaded from biting by abruptly removing the nipple from his mouth and simultaneously saying NO! in a loud voice. If you choose to nurse your toddler, then at around eighteen months he may once again start biting. This time he will not be easily dissuaded from biting by a couple of nipple withdrawals and loud nos. *He wants to hear the reason* and will want to hear the reason over and over again. When you withdraw the nipple and say, "Don't bite Mommy, it hurts, it makes the nipple sore," it seems that he begins to think about the difference between nursing and biting and wants to experiment further.

What often happens is that the toddler will bite the nipple, be reprimanded, then bite his mother's shirt, then bite his own finger. He seems to be experimenting to determine when biting causes hurt and does not cause hurt. He is learning something about the difference between animate and inanimate objects, things which live and feel and things which do not live and feel. These are difficult concepts for the young child to acquire, and many repetitions of the undesirable behavior may be expected in this stage of experimentation.

Unfortunately, the consequences of your son's behavior may be damaging and therefore cannot be tolerated. If he persists in biting, then you may simply have to withdraw the nipple altogether for that feeding in order to emphasize the importance of not biting. After missing a feeding or at least having it delayed for some minutes, the toddler may be impressed with the consequence of biting the nipple.

In many children between eighteen months and two years there will be a sudden increase in assaultive behavior. Your daughter who has been for months playing nicely with children may suddenly begin to push, bite, pull hair, or slap other children and do the same to you or the babysitter, without any apparent provocation. This too is part of the toddler's developing ability to think about cause and effect, animate and inanimate objects. Your toddler wants to assault the other person for a number of reasons: 1. She wants to see whether this child will cry like the last child did. Do all children cry when they are hit? Does Mommy do the same thing Grandma does? 2. Does hitting with all things hurt? She may experiment by hitting with trucks, with cups, and with balls. 3. Does hitting the wall and other things have the same consequences as hitting children and parents? For her to understand explanations such as "That hurts . . . it is hard," requires that she know that her behavior hurts the other person, and that she understand the difference between hard and soft. This is a very difficult conceptual task for a toddler.

What parents usually do in these circumstances is to tell their child that the behavior is hurting the other, point out the other child's tears, and attempt to teach their child about the feelings of the other child. The hope is that feelings of affection for the friend will prevent further attack. Sometimes this is effective, and sometimes it isn't. Most of the time you should expect the assault to be repeated, since limited cognitive abilities make your child incapable of compassion for the hurt child at this time.

At times, with a verbally advanced child, you can gain insight into the experimental nature of the assaultive behavior. I recall sitting in the bathtub with my nineteen-month-old son who asked me questions: "Bang Mommy with the sponge? Bang Mommy with the cup? Bang the wall with the cup? Bang the wall with the sponge?" It was clear that my son was experimenting with hard objects and soft objects, living things and inanimate objects, and attempting to determine some consistent rules for himself.

Preventing and Eliminating Aggressive Behavior

Pay Close Attention to Play Behavior. For your young son (under three years) to be able to be in the company of agemates, he requires *constant close supervision*. Although children differ, nearly all of them will exhibit some undesirable behaviors which you will not wish to be further developed. If your son hits, bites, scratches, pushes, grabs toys, or in any way exhibits unsocial behavior, the best procedure is to *stay by his side* when he is with peers. Pay close attention to signs that the undesirable behavior is in the making, and prevent it from occurring. Then take the opportunity to teach him the appropriate alternative behavior for that occasion. For example, if he wants a bean bag from a child who has several, tell him, "No, Ian, you can't take that toy away. You have to ask him for a bean bag. Say, 'May I have a bean bag?'" Before he becomes verbal, help him make a gesture such as holding out his hand while you ask the other child for the bean bag.

Data on play behavior of children indicates that the more socially active child not only has more positive social encounters, but also has more aggressive or negative incidents. If your child is highly active socially, your attention, teaching, and involvement will have to be more intense than that of a parent of a less socially active child.

Many books suggest you let children teach each other about sharing. I am suggesting that children are inadequate teachers and that you can far more skillfully teach such appropriate behaviors as trading. These behaviors will accelerate your child's ability to play cooperatively and to enjoy the friendship of peers.

Research indicates that the best approach to undesirable behavior is to prevent it from occurring and to reinforce alternative behaviors. This is far more effective than trying to punish the undesirable behavior *after* it occurs. Therefore, when you see your child about to grab a toy from another, run to her saying, "No, Lucy, Roy is playing with that truck. Let's find one for you, let's find Lucy a truck." If she really wants *that* truck, help her try to make a trade. Take her by the hand to Roy, help her hold out a truck and say, "Do you want this one, Roy?" If Roy agrees, the trade is easy. If not, then you must help her to become interested in something else or wait for Roy to finish with the desired toy. It is far easier to *prevent grabbing* and teach finding another toy, trading, or waiting for the toy, than to try to eliminate excessive grabbing behavior once it's established. Once the grabbing occurs and is naturally reinforced many times by gaining possession of the toy, the habit is quite difficult to break. Such behaviors will not make your daughter a desirable playmate either to the children she grabs from or to their parents.

If you maintain constant vigilance in the earliest part of your child's socialization from thirteen months to two years, and watch her for undesirable behavior, you may be able to prevent the further development and elaboration of these behaviors. After age two, there may be only particular behaviors or situations for which you need be so alert, and you may be able to relax a little more while she plays.

Redirect High-Frequency Problem Behaviors. Certain toddler behaviors occur with a very high frequency. Rather than try to eliminate them altogether, a more effective approach is to redirect the behavior. For example, "banging" is a high-frequency behavior. When your son bangs a friend with a stick tell him, "Bang the floor. Don't bang David, it hurts him."

Provide Consequences. Sometimes the cries of the victim or the reasoning and explanations you give your son will actually be reinforcing to him and in fact increase the frequency of the attacks on other children. In this case, the consequences of the assault must be more impressive than merely stopping the behavior and explaining the hurtful nature of that behavior. For example, if your son is in a playgroup and grabs and scratches other children, you should immediately run over to him and tell him what he has done: "You scratched Emily's face. That hurts. I can't let you do that. You have to go home now. You can't play with other children if you scratch them. You have to go home."

This consequence is often very difficult to use because it spoils a nice time for everyone. You may have scurried around in the morning to get yourself and your son ready to spend the morning playing with a group that meets only once a week. The group may provide *you* with a rare and needed opportunity for companionship, as well as providing socialization for your child. To abruptly leave this fun time and go home to an isolated and boring household is very punishing to you as well as your child. However, nothing could be more worth the brief period of unhappiness. If you immediately and consistently respond to your son's assaultive behavior by removing him from the play situation, then he will learn a very important message: "If I want to stay and play with my friends and my toys, then I cannot scratch." This will promote the beginning of his development of self-control—thinking about behaving in a certain way to be able to participate in social living.

Teach Assertive Skills. Many times children's aggressive behavior represents an attempt at self-protection rather than being an attack on another child. In this case, to effectively eliminate the aggressive behavior you must teach an appropriate assertive behavior. For example, if your daughter is having a toy forcibly taken from her and her response to this assault is to bite, push, hit, or otherwise retaliate against the attacker, then to merely provide some consequence to her aggressive act is not sufficient to eliminate the behavior. If she has no other behavior in her repertoire with which she can defend herself, then you must teach her one, or next time she will again resort to aggression.

To solve the problem you must be alert for the situation in which your daughter is trying to prevent another from forcibly taking possession of a toy. *Before* your daughter strikes, stop her in the

act and say, "No Rachel, don't hit—tell Judy, 'No, that's mine.'"
At the same time help her hold the toy behind her back or move
away from the attacker.

Similar lessons are called for if your daughter's response to an
assault is passive. As soon as she is capable of the verbalizations,
try to teach her to assert herself with statements such as, "No, that's
mine," "Don't push me," "It's my turn." It is surprising the degree
to which children nearing two years of age and older will modify
or cease their assaultive behavior when the victim verbally asserts
himself. The most effective way for you to teach an assertive statement to your daughter is to immediately run to her and *model* the
statement. Say to her, "Tell Danny, 'No Danny, it's my turn on
the slide.'" If someone pushes her and he responds with tears and
screaming, say to her, "Tell Ariel, 'No Ariel, don't push me!'" (See
the chapter on Modeling Behavior for a detailed description of this
technique.)

Why Not Spank

Spanking your son or using other forms of physical punishment to punish his aggressive behavior is not recommended because
you want to teach self-control, not aggression. Children learn a great
deal about how to behave from you as a model. When you spank
for aggressive behavior you are in the peculiar situation of modeling
the precise behavior you are trying to eliminate. There is a considerable body of data studying imitative behavior which demonstrates
that children imitate adults, especially those to whom they are attached. Children of parents who engage in aggressive behavior or
who discipline them with physical punishment are themselves more
aggressive than children of parents who use other methods of discipline (Bandura).

Some parents do to their offending son what he has done to
another, such as pulling his hair, or biting him, or hitting him with
a toy. This is certainly a mistake because he will make no connection between what he has done and the feelings that they have caused
in him.

Be Consistent. When your son tries to forcibly take possession of
a toy, and the second child does not object, the temptation is to
allow that forcible behavior to occur, since the second child does
not seem to care. The problem is that your son had no way of know-

ing whether the second child had any real interest in the toy until he forcibly grabbed it. The rule must be: "We don't just take things from other children. We have to ask, or we have to trade, or we have to wait until they put it down." You cannot allow the grabbing to go unchecked and then be rewarded by obtaining the toys.

At times you may have to be a wet blanket when your son is having a wonderful time playing with older children who enjoy roughhousing. If they fall over with a big crash when your son hits at them, or if gales of laughter follow his striking at them, then your toddler will be learning some behaviors which will not be well received in other playgroups. It is better to caution the older children that your son will not be appreciated on the playground if he does that to children his age, and encourage them to play with him in another way. The same advice is certainly indicated for dads who enjoy rough-and-tumble play and may encourage hitting or striking. Your son will be more likely to get into aggressive encounters after you roughhouse, so you may want to play some other way.

Empathy

A considerable body of research data indicates that empathy, or the ability to be sensitive to the feelings of others, plays an important role in self-control of aggressive behavior. A high degree of empathy is also associated with altruism (helpful behaviors) and, in later years, more mature moral decisions. When cooperation is encouraged as an alternative to incompatible behavior, the frequency of aggressive behavior in children decreases.

Definition of Empathy

Empathy is the ability to be aware of the emotions, thoughts, and sensations of another. Piaget suggested that the capacity for empathy develops at age seven or eight. However, other data indicates that at six or seven years of age children inhibit their aggression in response to the pain of a hurt child (Feshback). On the contrary, in young children, viewing the pain and suffering of an attacked child may even increase their aggressive behavior (Patterson, Littman, and Bricker). Therefore, with young children there often must be some negative consequence to aggression, such as being taken home immediately or having the friend go home immediately.

The ability to be sensitively aware of the feelings of others seems to develop first toward people to whom children are intensely attached, particularly their mothers and fathers. Even as young as twenty months of age, your son may express distress to the point of tears when you stub your toe and express pain. He may ask, "Did you hurt yourself?" and cry. These early expressions of understanding for the feelings of another are usually quite specific, involving situations in which your child can recognize the cues or behaviors associated with pain.

Another characteristic of these early signs of empathy is that your son usually has no need or feeling which is in conflict with your needs or feelings at that time. Expressions of understanding of the needs or feelings of others when they conflict with his will develop much later. For example, a boy younger than six years will not be able to inhibit his voice or play behavior when he is told, "Mommy has a headache." The ability to understand "My head hurts," perceive a frown and a depressed attitude, and remember the pain he felt in similar circumstances requires years of experience. Secondly, your son's need to run and shout in play are predominant. It is only when he gets closer to six years old that he will both conceptually and emotionally understand that your head hurts. Then, because of his attachment, he may find these feelings so important that he will control himself by repeatedly reminding himself to keep his voice down and play quietly.

Similarly, a girl under six to eight years of age will not generalize the experience of being shut out by two friends to her doing the same to another child. You can remind her how she felt, but full appreciation of the point of view and emotions of another child will be highly unlikely to occur before age six, and therefore will be unlikely to change the excluding behavior. You will have to demand fair behavior and provide consequences to unfair behavior until that time.

Although your three-year-old daughter cannot fully appreciate the feelings of another, when she sees how important her behavior is to you, she may inhibit her aggressive behavior or include a third child in her play. With years of repetition, the explanations will take on meaning and significance. When she becomes capable of empathy, somewhere betweeen ages six and seven, her own decisions about her behavior will then reflect the degree to which she has identified with you and incorporated your morals and values.

Teaching Generosity and Empathy

You can begin to teach generosity and empathy long before your son can really interact with others. Usually children enjoy giving food to animals. The sight of animals eating is so entertaining that many children would give their lunches to them. If you make a *daily* habit from the time your daughter is nine months old of taking her to feed the birds, the squirrels, the ducks in a nearby pond, or your dog or cat, then you can begin to develop habits of generosity and the ability to understand the feelings of others. As you feed the birds you can talk about their feelings: "The birds are hungry. Look at how they all fly to us. We're making them happy." If you have a pet dog or cat, point out the puppy's or kitty's crying: "The kitty is crying because he is hungry. He wants some food. Let's get some food for the kitty." Let your daughter be the one to throw the bread or birdseed to the birds or to give the catfood to the cat. Later, the "generous" behavior may generalize so that she may enjoying sharing with a friend.

Model Empathy. Empathy is a skill which is learned, and one which you can teach your son by your empathetic responses to him, as well as to others. You model empathy when you consistently respond to your son's needs and feelings. Reflect his feelings for him: "You are very tired, aren't you?" or "You didn't like the bus ride?" or "You don't want Michael to go home, do you?" or "Maggie made you happy by sharing her apple." When you are sensitive to your son's point of view, feelings, and needs and let him know that he is understood, you will be teaching him how to do the same with others. His capacity to understand someone else's feelings, especially when different from his own, will not really develop until he's at least six, but the training can begin in infancy.

Point Out Similar Feelings in Others. Another way to help your child recognize someone else's feelings is to point out the behaviors reflecting those feelings when your child simultaneously feels the same. When your son does not want to leave a playgroup, say, "Look, Michele doesn't want to go home either. She is sad, too. She is crying, too." When your child and another are both cold, point out the other's blue lips and shivering and say, "Look, Joel is cold, too. He's shivering and wants a towel." In this way, the development of empathy may be accelerated by making the behavioral signs of the feelings of others meaningful to your son. Otherwise, his attention to these fine discriminations and subtleties of behavior may require more time. If you deliberately teach the skill, empathy in certain specific, simple situations may even appear before age two. A well developed ability to be empathetic in complex situations may be accelerated so that the skill appears at age six rather than at age eight.

Sharing

At less than one year of age, children enjoy sharing experiences with others. They point to interesting events in the environment to elicit your comments and exclamations and the smiles of an agemate. Some children as young as eighteen months will hold out items for another child to see. Many children are ready at eighteen months for training in the social skills of sharing.

To begin with, encourage your daughter in her attempts to share with you. It is easier for her to share with you than anyone else, so accept her soggy toast saying, "You are sharing with Mommy— thank you!" It is also easier for a child to share with another child to whom she is attached. To foster attachment to another child, try to make regular excursions with another child. Arrange to meet biweekly at a park, the zoo, or the beach. Children, like adults, prefer to relate to someone with whom there have been many pleasant shared experiences and whose behavior they can predict.

At eighteen months, you may begin preparing your daughter for more advanced social interaction by using the word "sharing" repeatedly and making the experience associated with the word very pleasurable. For example, give her a cookie for her and also one to share, saying, "Here is one for you and one to share with Joyce." Sit down with the two children on the floor and encourage your daughter to share her toys when there are many toys from which to choose. It is easier to share two trucks from ten than to sacrifice one's favorite truck. It is best to begin your daughter's lessons in sharing when it is the least difficult for her to give up the particular item. After she has offered a toy to her playmate, then you will want to give her a hug or other sign of affection and verbally label what she has done: "That's very nice—you are sharing with your friend. That's very nice to share. Joyce is very happy because you are sharing your cars with her."

For young children who are just learning to share, try to prevent situations in which there is one toy that both children want. When there is one item that both children want, it is best to physically remove that item. Put it away in a closet out of sight rather than allowing the hostile behaviors between the two children to develop. Later on it will become easier to allow a favorite toy to be enjoyed by a friend. For some children, there may be one special toy which you will agree they don't have to share. Between eighteen months and two years it should be put away when visitors come. However, by age two many visiting children will understand and accept your saying, "David does not share this toy — this one is his special one."

Cooperation

Teaching Cooperative Play

By the time your child is nearing two years of age, you may begin specific training in cooperative play. It is helpful to have a large toy wherein the activity can be broken down into specific "jobs." For example, with a large toy garage, you can tell the children, "Let's work together and cooperate. It is hard work to run this garage. George, your job is to be the elevator man. You take the cars up the elevator. Paula, you fill up the cars with gas when they come down the ramp." Children are less likely to infringe on the other's play territory if tasks are delineated in terms of jobs. Similar lessons in cooperation may include one child being the cup holder while the other is the juice pourer, or one child adding the ingredients to the batter, the other child stirring, and so on. Repeatedly use the word "cooperating."

Teaching Your Child to Initiate Play

As early as eighteen months of age you may begin to teach specific behaviors for entering a play situation. There are certain behaviors that characterize children who successfully join ongoing play. Help your daughter stand by and look for awhile, until she understands what the children are doing. Say to her, "Let's see what they are doing. Oh, they are making a castle!" Then, help her add something to the process, like an additional rock, or block, or handful of sand. Children who do this are more likely to be welcomed into the ongoing play.

Another successful behavior is for your child to offer something to the other child, such as a shovel or another block, accompanied by, "Do you want this?" Even at eighteen months many children can be taught to offer a toy as an initial gesture of friendship. Help your daughter hold out her hand and tell her to say, "Do you want the shovel?" As she becomes more verbal, teach her to ask a child, "What are you making?" and "Do you want to play with me?"

If children do not acquire the appropriate behaviors necessary for them to initiate play, undesirable consequences may occur. Some children will knock over a block structure, kick a sand castle, or otherwise disturb other children in an attempt to get their attention. These children may be ostracized by the other children, and in some cases may even be victimized. Rather than leave such matters to chance, you should teach your child some specific social skills for joining others in play.

Teaching Cooperation to Older Children

Cooperation and Family Participation

From the time your child is two or three years old, she may begin to express the desire to help with chores. In the beginning, washing dishes can be fun, setting the table looks like a good time, and running the vacuum cleaner seems like something special. If you are wise, you will "capture" these behaviors, letting her help and positively reinforcing her helpfulness when she shows an interest. When the motivation for these activities comes from within your child, when it is not something you are demanding of her, you can easily teach the importance of cooperative behaviors in a family. This takes a great deal of patience and certainly makes every job take longer, but her early willingness to contribute to family life gives you a wonderful opportunity to show your appreciation of your child's participation.

For example, you can use some plastic dishes and stand your two year old on a stool before the sink to let her wash the dishes. As she does it, express your appreciation for her help, "You are helping to do the dishes like a big girl. It makes Mommy very happy you are helping. That means I don't have so much work to do." When she runs the vacuum cleaner and picks up a few pieces of visible paper or dirt, you can comment, "You made the rug look so nice for all of us. Now we can all see a nice clean rug because you vacuumed it." When she wants to water the lawn or the flowers, let her have the hose and express your appreciation again, "Thank you for giving these thirsty flowers a drink. They were all really thirsty. Now they will be healthy and stay pretty for a long time. The grass is going to be nice and green for us all to look at because you helped to water it." Allow your child to participate in the activities of family life and seize these opportunities to reward habits of cooperation and helpfulness.

It is much more difficult to demand these helpful behaviors from a seven year old when it hasn't been his idea to start with. If you don't want his help as a two, three, and four year old and discourage him from participating in family life, he will not be likely to be cheerfully helpful when you ask him to drop all his activities and do dishes or take out trash at age seven or eight.

If you have failed to take advantage of your little one's natural desires to be helpful and participate, and you now have a four or five year old who is reluctant to pick up his toys or unwilling to clear his plate, you might want to provide some motivation from the outside temporarily. You may want to start by shaping cooperation with an edible or tangible positive reinforcer just to get the behavior going so that you can have a chance to show your appreciation.

Promoting Cooperative Behavior

Children respond best to positive reinforcement and to expressions of appreciation; you are much more likely to be successful using this approach than nagging or criticizing or punishing. However, if your daughter does nothing that can be appreciated, it is hard to be positive. Ask yourself the question, "What can I ask my son or daughter to do that she would be *most willing* to do?" Then ask her to do one of these things so you can reward her cooperation. "Cindy will you help me to give some food and water to the cat? You know how to use the can opener and you can reach the water with your stool. I think that you are big enough to be able to feed the cat." When she has fed the cat, give her a positive reinforcer (a handful of chips, a cookie, a trinket you already know she would like). Say "Thank you Cindy, you made the cat happy! Listen to her purr!" If Cindy would be willing to play with the dog, then make that request: "Cindy, will you take Gretle out to play ball in the yard?" When she willingly does so, bring her a glass of her favorite juice you rarely buy, or the bowl of fresh raspberries she didn't know you had and verbally reinforce her by saying "It's very helpful to mommy when you take the dog out and play ball with him. This way he can get some exercise and doesn't feel so lonely in the yard. Now that I don't have to take him for a walk tonight I think I have time for a game of checkers!"

Always remember that your goal is to *motivate* your child to be cooperative and helpful so that you can honestly appreciate her cooperative and helpful behavior. Once you have rewarded these well-liked cooperative tasks you can begin to ask your child to do some less well-liked tasks and reward her for doing them.

By the time your daughter is five or six years old you may decide she is able to have certain *jobs*. Suppose you decide her responsibilities include feeding the cat, playing ball with the dog every day, and emptying the trash. You may want to put these three jobs on a chart so she can check them off as she does them. Research shows that often just putting a check mark on a chart makes children feel good about themselves and is rewarding. The chart should be placed in a prominent place such as on the refrigerator or on the bulletin board in the kitchen so that it is easy for your child to reach and also so that you will be likely to pass it many times during the day. As you notice your child doing one of the jobs, or as you notice something checked off on the chart, pay attention to her. "Oh, I see you are feeding the cat. She looks very hungry. I bet she is going to be happy to see you." Or "Oh, look, the dog is very happy that you are coming to play with him. Look at his tail wagging. He really is happy that you are going to play ball with him." "Boy, it sure is nice to go to the trash can and find it empty instead of spilling all over the place. I sure do like that." These comments and statements of appreciation regularly and repeatedly will reward your child's cooperative behavior.

Be certain that your requests are reasonable to your child and discuss his feelings about certain jobs. Everyone dislikes certain tasks and prefers others. Your son deserves the same consideration you would like. If he would rather take out the trash can than clear the table, then allow the trash removal to be his job.

Remember that your goal is to reward a spirit of cooperation and working together as a family and not to get unpleasant jobs done. It is not a good idea to ask a six year old to clean up animal feces or change a litter box daily. It would be better for family members to take turns with those fairly unpleasant activities that no one really wants to do. You want to make it likely that your child develops a spirit of willingness and cooperation.

It will seem logical to your child that if she participates in the responsibilities of running the house, taking care of the animals, and so on, that you will have more free time to play with her. If you reward her participation with interaction with you, by playing board games or baking in the kitchen or some craft activity, then the relationship between the reward and the behaviors you're asking for will be logically connected and far less artificial and contrived. When she willingly does her jobs, be certain to interact with her in a special way: "Gosh, we got the kitchen cleaned up so fast and the table is all nice and clean! Let's play a game of checkers there now."

Am I in a Power Struggle?

The parents who have the most difficulty with eliciting cooperative behavior from their children are those who are in a power struggle with their children. When parents complain that the child is disobedient, uncooperative, or undisciplined, there is often a very maladaptive interaction between parents and child. If you have been trying to control your child's behavior by using criticism, physical punishment, or power, you probably have had a lot of negative response. The more you intensify your attempts at punishment or coercive control, the more negative his behavior becomes. The solution is, of course, to change the interaction between you and your child so that it becomes a positive one. If your youngster is presently unwilling to participate and contribute to the family, then instead of feeling angry, a soul-searching is probably in order. Have you been giving orders and expecting that your child will obey immediately? Is your reaction one of anger when you don't get instant obedience? If you answer yes to these questions, you are probably in a power struggle with your child. It would be a good idea for you to take a close look at your own feelings and ask yourself "What is it that I am trying to accomplish? Am I after obedience or am I after a spirit of cooperation? How can I best get the spirit of cooperation?"

Remember, your goal is *not* to make him do something that he doesn't want to do, but to be a responsible family member. You can teach your child to be responsible and contribute to a family in a way appropriate to his age and abilities. Don't be hard on yourself if you haven't taught your child this lesson yet. As much as you love your children, with the busy life you lead, the real nature of the problem can sometimes escape you. Be guided by the question "How can I make it more likely that my child will want to do what I would like him to do?" If your son enjoys using the can opener, then buy canned cat food. That way feeding the cat is something he can look forward to. If your son would be more willing to empty the trash if you had special trash-can liners with colored twistees, then consider investing in these special trash-can liners. Then watch your son, try to catch him in the act of doing what you would like him to do. Notice him when he does what you ask and is participating in family life. Remember Grandma's axiom: "you catch more flies with honey than you do with vinegar."

Sometimes a parent and child will be at such odds with each other that a more structured reward system is necessary to get cooperative behaviors going initially. If these methods don't seem to be enough, consider using charts and stars or points as a solution (see Chapter 14, "Behavior Modification Techniques for Older Children").

IV
Behavior Modification

10

Increasing Desirable Behavior

You are constantly affected by the consequences of your behavior. If you wear something and receive many compliments you are likely to wear it again. When you tell a joke that gets a good laugh you repeat it; if you tell a joke and nobody laughs you are less likely to repeat it. When you touch an electrical appliance and get an electrick shock you are much less likely to touch it again. Children are even more influenced by the consequences of their behavior because they are less able to reason things through or to discount other people's moods or feelings.

You may have some negative feelings about the idea of using behavior modification with your children. To many people, using such techniques seems mechanical and insensitive. It is important to recognize that whether you *intend* to use behavior modification or not, all parents do. Whenever you react to your child and even when you don't react, your child's behavior is being influenced by your reaction or lack of it. Becoming aware of the principles of behavior modification will make you a more effective parent by helping you to recognize the ways you are influencing your child's behavior.

Behavior modification teaches you to carefully analyze patterns of behavior to determine the conditions that promote either a desirable or an undesirable behavior and the consequences that reward it. For example, if your son were doing some unnecessarily destructive things you would ask yourself the question "Under what conditions or what circumstances does he do these destructive things?"

You may then notice that he tends to do the worst things when you are nursing the baby or when you are on the telephone. Next you would think about the consequences the behavior usually gets: what you do when your son acts this way. You might find your typical reaction is to stop nursing the baby or get off the telephone to verbally reprimand him. As we will discuss later, when you stop what you are doing to pay attention to your child, even though you are angry and your words are critical, your attention can actually *reward* your son's destructive behavior.

Some patterns of behavior are very clear and easy to see, but at other times the patterns are not so apparent. Unless you are in the habit of thinking through sequences of behavior you may actually teach your child some very undesirable behaviors, and you may not teach some very desirable ones by not responding to them at all. Once you are convinced that your child's behavior is influenced by the consequences it receives, you will want to look for patterns of behavior and always be asking yourself, *"If I do this now, what will I teach my baby?"*

Consider the following examples to see if you can analyze the patterns. One mother complained to me that her children whined and cried excessively. I asked her what she did when they cried and she said, "When I can't stand it anymore, I give them candy, and they stop crying. Then I get a few minutes' peace." The pattern of behavior here is probably clear to you: the mother is unknowingly teaching her children to cry more frequently by rewarding crying with candy.

Another mother described this situation: "If my baby wants something, and I have told him no, I try to keep it from him. If he gets really upset and cries a lot, then of course I will give it to him. It is not *that* important to keep most things from him." Again, you may already understand that this pattern of behavior teaches the baby to cry longer and louder to finally get what he wants.

Research in child psychology has found that this kind of learning becomes especially important in infants three months of age or older. By the time your daughter is three months old, she will have learned to cry so that you will pick her up and to laugh at you so you will continue to make your funny faces. From then on the consequences of her behavior are increasingly important in influencing what she does.

In this and the next three chapters I will carefully illustrate through a variety of examples each of the specific principles of behavior modification. You'll see how you can consciously and carefully apply these to the behavior of your own child to increase desirable behaviors and decrease undesirable ones. I hope that after reading this section you will make behavior modification a way of life. You don't need graphs, charts, or lists—just an awareness of the effect you have on your child's behavior. Being thoroughly familiar with these principles will allow you to be far more consistent in your discipline, something recommended in every childrearing book.

A consistent approach to behavior modification is important with all children but is especially important with children of a difficult temperament. In fact, several organizations that have been formed to help parents deal with difficult children teach the parents to use the principles of behavior modification.

Thinking in terms of behavior modification is a way of becoming clear in your own mind about your requirements for your child's behavior. You will want to be acutely sensitive to your son's individual personality and very sensitive to his individual needs. Then when you maximize the circumstances that help him behave appropriately and minimize the circumstances that promote undesirable behavior, you can be confidently consistent in your reactions to his behavior.

Positive Reinforcement Procedure

The most effective way of teaching any behavior is through positive reinforcement. Very simply stated this procedure involves rewarding behavior that you want to increase. The basic steps are simple:

1. Define the desired behavior.
2. Choose an appropriate reward.
3. Wait for or promote the behavior.
4. Present the reward.
5. Continue to reward the behavior.
6. Gradually phase out the reward.

Define the Desired Behavior

First you must decide exactly what behavior you want to increase. When parents complain to me about their children's behavior, often the description of the behavior is very vague. For example, a mother might say that her child is uncooperative and that she wants to increase cooperative behavior. This definition is too general. You need to be more specific in defining what it means to be cooperative in order to use these methods successfully. For example, you might decide that being cooperative for your three-year-old girl means that she would pick up her toys and put them in their proper place, that she would come to you when you call her rather than running in the opposite direction, or that she would sit still and allow you to bathe and dress her or comb her hair.

Choose an Appropriate Reward

Once you have defined the behaviors that you would like to see more of, the second step is to figure out what will be an effective positive reinforcer or a reward for your child. Most psychology textbooks define a positive reinforcer as "anything which increases the frequency of a response which it follows."

What this means is that if the reward you have chosen has no effect on the behavior that you are trying to increase, then it is not a good reward and you must find another. You cannot assume that because your child seems to like cookies or candy that this will be an effective positive reinforcer. It may not be. If you give your son a cookie after each time he uses the potty, and he doesn't seem to be using it more frequently, then the most likely problem is that you don't have an effective reward. Cookies might be for him what celery is for you. You eat it when it's on an appetizer tray, you wouldn't walk across the room to get a piece. Celery probably would not be a very good reward for you and a cookie may not be a very good reward for your son. Ask yourself, "Would he walk half a mile to get this reward?"

What are some possible rewards for your child? Try foods or drinks that your daughter particularly enjoys, toys she wants, fun clothing, books or records she would enjoy hearing, the opportunity to play with a favorite friend, being able to talk with somebody special on the telephone, or your attention and approval.

When you are not getting results, the first thing you should try is changing your reward. If your son will not sit on the potty for a cookie, then try three potato chips or reading to him from his favorite book while he is on the potty.

Children are highly social creatures and find the *attention* or the approval of their parents very rewarding. Your praise and appreciation may be all that you need to encourage your child to continue some behaviors. For example, when your little girl begins to pick up her toys to put them away you should tell her, "Thank you for putting away your toys, that helps me so much. I like it very much that you helped me." When she remembers to throw her gum wrapper in the trash, you can say, "What a big girl! I'm so proud of you, you remembered to put your paper in the trash can." And when she answers you or comes to you the first time you call her, you can tell her, "You looked at me to see what I wanted the first time I called you and that makes me very happy." When she waits patiently for you to finish a conversation or a phone call, you can tell her, "That was terrific the way you waited so patiently for me to finish my conversation and you didn't interrupt me." Then give her a big hug. Most children really want to please their parents and your child will try very hard to repeat those behaviors which she sees please you very much.

When you're teaching a behavior that is especially important to you and you aren't getting results with lots of praise and approval, then you should think about using a primary reinforcer—food. For example, in the early stages of toilet training many parents find it necessary to reward using the potty by giving a special food item that they do not allow their child to have very often. The younger your baby is and the more difficult the behavior is for your baby to accomplish, then the more you need to think about using primary rewards such as foods or drinks.

Something else that may be used to reward your boy's good behavior is an opportunity to do something he likes to do a lot. For example, if he likes to run and scream but you don't let him do it in the house, then when he does something that you would like to reward you might say to him, "You've been sharing your toys so nicely with your friend that I want to take you outside to run and scream. Let's go to the park and we will run and scream in the park." If your daughter loves to take things out of your jewelry box and line them up, then when she does something you like you can tell her, "You've been playing by yourself so nicely this morning. You didn't whine at me or bother me or keep asking me to do things for you. So now, I'm going to let you play with all my jewelry for fifteen minutes."

Wait for or Promote the Behavior

In order to be able to reward a behavior, the behavior has to occur. If you want your little boy to learn to share his toys you have to make certain that some sharing takes place so that you can reward it. If you merely turn him loose in a play situation and hope that some "sharing behavior" occurs, it may not. It is much better to structure the situation to promote the sharing behavior so that you can reward it. For example, give your son two cookies and say, "Bring one to your friend, give him a cookie," and then when he does so, smile and say to him, "That's very nice. You are sharing with your friend." This way he learns what the word sharing means and that you appreciate it.

When he is first learning to share it is helpful if you take your baby and a playmate to a play situation such as a park with a sandbox, away from home, where neither child will feel possessive. Bring along two of everything of the same color (two shovels, two buckets, and so on). When he willingly allows his playmate to use a shovel or a bucket you can reward him by saying, "You are sharing with David so nicely, thank you! That makes David happy." You may even reward the behavior with a primary reinforcer: "It makes me so happy to see you sharing. I have some raisins for each of you!"

Gradually you can move into more difficult situations such as having David come to your home and share your child's toys. In the beginning, suggest that David bring something to share so that your child is not the only one doing the sharing. Your child can also have something to share and they can make a trade. Again, it is very important to get any particularly unique and interesting items out of the way so that the children do not argue about them. If you can have two or more of every desirable item you can promote friendship and play behavior rather than fighting and possessiveness. Every time your son does anything that resembles sharing, you should comment on it and reward him by telling him how much you appreciate his sharing. In the beginning, you will have to stay very close to him to make sure that other kinds of behavior do not develop. The more efforts you make toward structuring the situation so that you promote sharing in the beginning, the more likely it will be that your child will learn at a very early age to enjoy the company of his peers and to share well.

Sometimes you will want to reward a particular behavior and yet your child will show no signs of making that response at all.

For example, you may have to wait years for your child to voluntarily sit down to use the potty so that you can reward it. The method of *shaping* helps you to teach your child a new behavior by first rewarding behaviors that are only remotely related to the behavior you are hoping to teach.

Many parents intuitively use this shaping procedure with their infants in teaching them to talk. When your daughter is near the dog and says, "da," you smile at her and say, "That's right, dog." You are rewarding an approximation of the word, "dog." In the beginning you don't ask your baby to have perfect articulation and to say all of the beginning and ending sounds of words. Rather, you reward and respond positively to anything that comes close to the word you're hoping she will say. As she improves in her ability to say these words correctly, you stop rewarding her early, more primitive approximations and only reward her better ones. This is what the shaping or successive approximations procedure is all about. When there is some behavior that you would like to develop in your child and she either cannot do it yet or is not inclined to do it, then you can reward successively closer and closer approximations to the goal behavior.

Present the Reward

To be effective, your reward must be given *immediately* following the behavior that you would like to increase. This means that when your son does something that you would like to see him continue doing, you should reward him within seconds. For example, you should say to your two year old, "You just looked at my plants and you touched the leaves so nicely and you didn't break one leaf. That makes me so happy that I want to give you a special surprise. Would you like to have a fig cookie?" For a young child it is ineffective to say, "You didn't break the leaves on my plant, so I'm going to take you to get an ice-cream cone later this evening." Your son won't even have a very well developed sense of the future until he gets closer to age three. By the time he is three and a half or four, you may be able to give him some verbal praise and a promise of something special later on in the day if you have no immediate reward.

Be sure to reward small bits of behavior as well as offering a large reward for continued good behavior over an extended period of time. For example, when your son is first learning to stay dry at night you should give him a special reward in the morning when you see that his bed is dry. As a next step you might say to him, "If you can stay dry for a whole week (showing him how many days make a week), we will do something extra special for you." In southern California, we go to Disneyland. Even though you've made this special promise for a whole week of being dry, it's best to continue a lesser reward each day that he wakes up dry in order to keep the response going.

Continue to Reward the Behavior

"Do I have to reward every response? What happens if I reinforce only some responses?" These questions refer to the schedule of reinforcement. There are some very clear findings about the effect of rewarding behavior on various time schedules or response schedules.

When you are trying to teach a new response or behavior it is best to reinforce every instance of the behavior for some time. When you are trying to teach your little girl new behaviors such as picking up her toys, sharing, or using the toilet, you will want to reward her each time she picks up a toy and returns it to its place, every time she shares, or each time she uses the toilet. This is a continuous reinforcement schedule. Once the behavior is learned and is a clear habit, then you can change your schedule of reinforcement so that only some responses get rewarded.

In daily life with your child, you probably will not reward many behaviors on a continuous schedule of reinforcement. Most of the time you will be rewarding an occasional response, rather than every single response. Even if you *want* to use a continuous reinforcement schedule it is difficult to be so attentive to your child that you catch each response to reward it. Rewarding only *some* responses is an intermittent schedule. An important result of using an intermittent schedule of reinforcement is that behaviors that are rewarded in this way tend to be very strong habits. They will drop out (extinguish) much more slowly when they are no longer rewarded. When you reward some, but not all, of the times your child puts something in its proper place, your child's neatness habit will persist much longer when you stop rewarding it.

Gradually Phase Out the Reward

You may worry about the results of using positive reinforcement on your child's adjustment in the future. Will your son always think that there must be some reward for everything he does? You needn't worry. In time you can phase out primary reinforcers and let natural reinforcers maintain the desirable behavior. For example, it may take a spoonful of ice cream to get your son to use the potty at first. But as he starts to consistently use the potty, you can gradually decrease the frequency that you give the ice cream until finally you give it no longer. Ultimately your son will continue to use the potty because of the rewards of having dry pants, not having to wear uncomfortable diapers, and not having to be taken away from playtime to get cleaned up.

Helping your child learn to share presents a similar set of considerations. In the beginning your little girl will have no experience with friendship or the joys of sharing, and will probably be very greedy and possessive of her toys. If you repeatedly reward her sharing with praise and treats, then eventually her playmates' positive reactions toward her and the joy of sharing a toy or an experience will become effective in keeping her sharing behavior going.

Psychologists like to think about the use of arbitrary reinforcers such as food, drink, or special prizes as "priming the pump" to get a response going in the beginning. When you see that the behavior you've been working on has become a fairly strong habit you can begin to "fade out" your primary reinforcer. Food and drink will not be given every time but only every second or third time, until at last the food or drink will be completely withdrawn. Fading out the primary reward is usually quite simple because as your child's behavior becomes a stronger habit, both of you will probably forget about it and your child's behavior will be maintained by the natural reinforcers of dry pants, returned friendship and sharing, and your smiles of appreciation.

Toilet Training—The Prime Example

Behavior modification, especially with the successive approximations procedure, can be very effective in teaching the use of the toilet. Because this is such an important event for both parents and children, I will take the time to discuss and describe the use of shaping in toilet training thoroughly.

When to Begin

You will want to consider both your son's physical readiness and his individual personality when you are deciding when to begin toilet training. Your baby will be physically ready to begin when he can stop urine at midflow and when you find there are longer and longer periods of dryness. This usually happens by the time a child is about eighteen months old. Emotionally your baby may not be ready until some time later. It is best not to begin toilet training when your baby is in a contrary frame of mind. If he is determined to express his independence and individuality and his favorite word is no, then wait a few months until he becomes eager to please before you start toilet training.

Setting the Stage

You really want to begin toilet training only when you will be able to stay around home for most of the day for at least two weeks. If you are working and a babysitter will do the toilet training then the babysitter must be able to stay around home for most of two weeks. This means that if you have to spend a lot of time in the car or visiting in other people's homes or running errands, it's not a good time for training.

Once you begin toilet training you should not put your baby in diapers during the day while you are at home. For most children having the diaper on is strongly associated with urinating or defecating whenever the urge strikes. Wearing no diaper helps them to remember that something is different now and to learn to do something *else* when they feel the urge to eliminate, although at first they do wet the floor. Because it is best to have your baby barebottomed, you might want to wait for warmer weather to begin this training. If you begin in winter and your house is too cold for a bare bottom you should expect as many wet pants as you had wet diapers in the beginning.

Most children are bowel-trained before they are bladder-trained, but there are exceptions. You can work on both at once. Keep the potty chair in *one place* and teach your baby how to get there from various locations. Take your daughter by the hand and practice running to the potty from three or four places she might be when she feels the urge to eliminate. Say to her, "Let's practice running to the potty so you'll know where it is when you have to go." Take her to the kitchen and say, "If you are in the kitchen, and you feel you have to go potty, you run, run, run to the potty like this." Hold her hand and run with her to the potty. Do the same from several other locations of your house. Although she will not be likely to run to the potty alone for some time, this practice prepares her for what is to come when you prompt her the first time to use the potty.

Select a Positive Reinforcer

If you wait until age two, your child may be one of those children who practically potty train themselves with only verbal praise as a reward. If you would like to begin potty training earlier, you will probably need to use some tangible, positive reinforcer such as food or trinkets to teach the toilet habit. Even after two years of age, some children consider learning to use a toilet rather unimportant. Many children are unbothered by messy diapers and will have very little of their own motivation to use the potty.

It is a good idea to have several rewards available and to vary them. Save some favorite food or drinks for when your child uses the potty. Collect a variety of trinkets or small toys for rewards. Sometimes a piggyback ride or being spun around like an airplane will be an effective reward.

It is most important that whatever you use as a reward not be accessible to your child at other times during the day. Otherwise, it will not be effective as a reward for using the toilet. If your son is going to get three potato chips every time he uses the potty, he should not have potato chips any other time during the day.

Make certain that what you think is a reward for your son really is rewarding. If you see that it is having no effect on his behavior, you should try something else. If you use food, be careful to use small enough quantities so that your child does not tire of them or become full. For example, it is better to give him a tablespoon of ice cream rather than a bowlful and a small cookie rather than a large one.

Some children are motivated to continue using the potty by your telling other parents or friends who come to visit about their achievements. It may be helpful to announce to your son's friends and their parents that he is wearing big boy pants and keeping them dry. Sometimes it is helpful to take children to the store to pick out some special pants which they won't want to wet or soil.

Shaping Potty Behavior

Many children find it upsetting to sit on the potty and simply refuse to do so. They may become very aggravated and angry if you try to force them to sit there. Shaping can help you get your daughter to sit on the potty, a necessary prerequisite for toileting. In the beginning ask her only to sit on the potty for a second or two, and reward it. You may even need to give her a bite of a cookie and tell her she can have the rest if she sits on the potty just one second. Then as soon as she sits down, give her the cookie. Require nothing more than sitting at first. Several times a day ask her to sit on the potty for you just a few seconds. Gradually increase the number of seconds you ask her to sit there before you reward her. Be careful to increase the time you require gradually enough so that she never refuses. If you increase your time requirements for her too fast you will lose the response and she will refuse to sit there at all. Increase your requirements from two seconds to five seconds, to ten seconds, to twenty seconds, to thirty seconds, to one full minute, continuing the process until she is sitting on the potty for two to three full minutes at a time. As you increase the time be sure to fill in the time with verbal praise to help her stay seated: "You are sitting there like such a big girl!" Judge the length of time that you ask her to sit on the potty by her response to being asked to sit there. If she is cooperative and undisturbed then you can increase your requirement by greater amounts of time. If she begins to balk at sitting there, drop the time requirement down to ten seconds or even less until she is once again willingly and happily cooperating. Then gradually increase your time requirements, but more slowly. The sequence should be that your daughter sits for some period of time, you praise and positively reward her sitting behavior, and after being rewarded she gets up.

On each new day you should ask a little less of her than you asked the night before. For example, if the last time she sat on the potty before bed the night before she sat for thirty-five seconds then the following morning you should not ask her to sit for more than twenty-five seconds on the first try.

Catch Him in the Act

Once your child is willing to sit on the potty, then you may shape running to the potty and using it at the right time. In the beginning you will want to prompt your little boy's running to the potty when you can tell that he feels the urge. Look for specific behaviors which usually indicate when he needs to have a bowel movement. Some children will run back and forth across the room, other children stop and stand still in one place, others may go to a corner by themselves. Be on the lookout for these behaviors around the time he usually defecates, and when you see the signs, run to him saying, "You have to poop? Let me help you run to the potty." Then grab him by the hand, run with him to the potty, and help him to sit down. When he leaves something in the potty, give him his reward. In the initial stages of potty training you should have a big celebration when he leaves something in the potty, with lots of praise and attention in addition to the usual reward.

Teach Her to Signal

The next step is to teach your daughter to tell you when she has to use the potty. To begin, when you notice those behaviors which tell you she has to use the potty, *prompt* her to tell you. When you notice her running back and forth across the floor or standing in the corner, say to her, "Tell me when you have to go potty! You tell me when you have to go potty, and I'll take you." On subsequent days, continue to remind her to tell you when she has to use the potty each time you notice the behaviors that indicate that she has to go.

At first, reward her for even the smallest indication that she has to use the potty. Even if all she does is to answer yes when you ask her if she has to use the potty, reward her, saying, "Good girl! You told me you had to go potty. That's very good!" Sometimes in the beginning a child will give you some signal indicating that she has to go potty, and you will miss it. For example, a child in the habit of running back and forth across the room before she poops may run to her mom and touch her but say nothing. If you miss her signal and as a result she has an accident, reward her for telling you anyway. Say to her, "You tried to tell me you had to go potty. You came running to me to try to tell me. That is so good you tried to tell me!" Give her something special for trying to tell you so you can keep the signal going.

Teach Him What to Say

In order to be sure that you will understand when your son is trying to tell you that he has to use the potty, help him practice some signal or special word. It helps to model a statement or word that he could say: "When you have to go potty, you say 'Poopie, Poopie,' and I will take you." Then help him rehearse his word by asking him, "What are you going to say to me when you have to go potty? Tell me what you are going to say." If he can't answer you, then tell him what he is going to say and ask him to repeat it after you: "You're going to say, 'Poopie, Mommy, Poopie.' Tell me what you are going to say." When he answers, "Poopie," then you say, "That's right! You're going to say 'Poopie,' and I will help you run to the potty."

Fade Out Your Assistance

Once he is reliably running to tell you that he has to use the potty, you may gradually fade out your help. In the beginning you might say, "Oh, you have to go potty! Where are you going now? Where are you going to go? Show me where you go!" If necessary, remind him where he would like to go, prompt him to go there, but don't take him yourself. Prompt him by saying, "Okay, run to the potty! Run to the potty!" Eventually when you ask him, "Where do you want to go?" he will remember to run to the potty. When his habit is stronger, you will say nothing and let him run to the potty himself when he has to go.

Generalize the Training

Once your child is consistently using the potty at home you will want to teach your child to use the potty at other places. For example, take your daughter to play at her friend's home in her pants instead of a diaper. Remind her that she is not wearing a diaper. Show her where her friend's potty chair is located and help her practice running to the chair from several places just as you did at home. Repeatedly reinforce her dry pants by saying, "I see your pants are still dry. That's good! You are remembering to keep your pants dry and use the potty here at Beth's house." At first, help her as you did at home by looking for signs that she needs to use the potty and helping her get there. Gradually fade out your reminders.

Once she is successful in using the potty at her friend's home, take her on an excursion to a park with a restroom nearby. Show her where the restroom is and tell her that you will take her there when she has to go. Remind her that she has pants on and no diaper and verbally reward her for dry pants. When you see the signs that she has to use the potty say, "Don't forget to tell me when you have to go potty." In the beginning you should expect some wet pants and bring along some extras. Also remember to bring along your food rewards or toys and reward her using the toilet.

Loss of Behavior Once It Is Established

Sometimes a child is fairly easily trained with shaping and positive reinforcement. You confidently fade out the rewards. Then a month later you find that accidents are becoming more and more frequent until now you have as many wet pants as you once had diapers. This probably means that you have been premature in fading out the positive reinforcement. Immediately start rewarding the potty response every time. Once your child is again in the habit of using the toilet you may gradually fade out the rewards.

To maintain using the potty it is necessary to reward some children at least once every day for up to a year! Problems in toilet training merely reflect the fact that toilet habits are not particularly important to some children. To develop a strong habit of using the potty you must provide added motivation in the way of rewards for a year or more. For most parents having to occasionally reward a child for using the toilet is preferable to having the child in diapers past age three.

A Case Study

A mother consulted me about her two-and-a-half-year-old daughter who refused to defecate in the toilet. She was completely bladder-trained, but when she felt the urge to defecate she asked her mother to put a diaper on her and she would defecate in the diaper. Attempts to force her to sit on the potty resulted in tantrums, and it was simply impossible to hold her there.

In treatment we used a shaping procedure. At first when the girl asked for the diaper her mother would put the diaper on her within two feet of the potty. When she defecated in her diaper near the potty she would be rewarded for "being near the potty." Gradually over many trials her mother was advised to bring her closer and closer to the potty until finally she was asked to sit on the potty with her diaper on and was rewarded for doing so. On later trials the mother put her on the potty with the diaper fastened on one side and her mother holding it closed on the other side. Next, her mother merely held the diaper in place with no pins. Eventually, the diaper was not placed over her anus but only covered her pelvic area while she eliminated in the potty. Each successive step her mother rewarded with lavish praise and a food treat. For a time the child merely held the diaper on her lap and finally did not even ask for the diaper while she eliminated on the potty.

Teaching Waking to a Full Bladder

Most children will begin to be dry at night with no training. Sometimes after the age of two, or when they are day-trained, they will simply not urinate when they are asleep. Other children will not be able to make it through the night without urinating. This means either a wet bed or getting up during the night to use the bathroom. Some of these children will not wake up, and so the bed will be wet.

You might try waking your son to use the bathroom to avoid the problem. But this rarely works. He must learn to wake up himself when his bladder is full.

If he is nearly four years old with no signs of night dryness, it is likely that he will need to wake up to use the bathroom. What you want to teach him is to wake up to the sensation of a full bladder. A very effective device for this teaching is the Mowrer Bell and Pad. This device includes a pad which is placed in the child's bed. The child is placed in bed with no diaper or clothing. The pad is wired to a bell which will ring with the first drops of urine. After several pairings of the full bladder sensations and then the bell sounding, the child will be conditioned to awaken to the sensations of a full bladder without having to hear the bell ring.

It is also very helpful to follow nights with a dry bed with a special treat or special event. Tell him in the morning, "you got up to go potty during the night. I'm so proud of you! I have a special present for you because I'm so happy your bed is dry."

Accidental Reinforcement of Undesirable Behavior

Attention as a Reward — Be Careful

If you are a warm and loving parent, then your smiles and expressions of appreciation will be very rewarding for your baby. When you smile and say, "I like the way you touched the kitty so nicely," your baby will much more likely pet the kitty softly the next time. If you repeatedly tell your son, "You are eating so nicely with a fork," or "I like the way you asked me to go outside like a big boy. You didn't even whine. You just said, 'go outside'," he will continue to do these things for you.

Unfortunately both for parents and children, many people are not at all aware of how powerfully rewarding adult attention is for a child. Many times what happens is that when a girl pets the kitty nicely nobody notices, but when she picks it up by the fur or the tail, some adult comes running. This teaches her that to get your attention she must behave in this undesirable way. This is certainly not your intent, but it is the effect nevertheless.

Your attention as a parent may be so powerful a reward to your child's behavior that it won't even matter what you are saying or how you are saying it. Even though you believe you are punishing your son by reprimanding him, telling him how much you dislike a certain behavior of his, and how angry or upset it makes you, the *content* of your statements may have no effect whatsoever on his behavior. What will affect his behavior is the *attention* you have given him. You may actually reward some very undesirable behavior while trying to reprimand him.

Your feelings or intentions are not what determines whether your reactions to your daughter's behavior are rewarding or punishing. It is the effect on her behavior which will tell you whether or not what you have done is a reward. You might correct her in what you think is a very punishing way and she will think that what you said and did was very funny. You may have an angry look on your face and with an angry tone of voice be telling her, "I don't like it when you throw food all over the floor. Look at the mess you made. Now I have to clean this all up." She may think sudden jerky movements and this tone of voice are just hilarious. As a result, she will make a bigger mess the next time.

In babies between fifteen to eighteen months old this happens very clearly as they begin to experiment with slapping faces, pulling hair, and scratching. Many times the adult who is holding the child will react with a painful or surprised expression, draw back his or her face and scream "Ouch!" Then you might explain, "Don't hit, that hurts." You then find that the baby continues to scratch, pull hair, or slap even more often. The only conclusion is that your reaction to your child's slapping, scratching, or pulling hair is rewarding that behavior. The fact that you are explaining that it hurts you is having no effect, while the expression on your face and your screaming in pain is very interesting and therefore rewards the behavior.

Repeatedly, parents of children of this age ask me to explain this sudden outburst of aggressive behavior in their previously darling infants, never dreaming that they may be rewarding the aggressive behavior themselves. In order to eliminate this kind of behavior all you have to do is put your little girl down on the floor the instant she slaps you or pulls your hair and leave her down a minute or so. If she gets put down on the floor every time she slaps you, scratches you, or pulls your hair, this won't be fun for her to do anymore and she will stop.

You can reward many other undesirable behaviors with your attention to that behavior as you reprimand your daughter. You may feel angry and believe that you are punishing her as you run over to her saying, "Don't you pull those leaves off my plant, I like that plant, you just stop that, you're making me really mad." But she may think that it is terrific to see you drop whatever you are doing and come running over in the middle of a phone call, doing dishes, or feeding the baby. It may be very rewarding to her to get your attention, to see you run to her, and hear your exasperated voice. To teach her not to pull leaves off your plant you need consequences other than a verbal reprimand. These other techniques will be explained in the chapter on decreasing undesirable behavior.

A Case Study

A very intelligent and devoted couple came to see me about their three-year-old boy. They complained that soon after his new baby brother was brought home, Matthew began to have many behavior problems. Particularly upsetting to the parents were the things that he would do at dinner time. At every meal, Matthew would end up kicking the table, screaming, and throwing food. This was the pattern of behavior:

Matthew would begin to kick the table and whine. His parents would then go through a series of what they thought were punishing consequences. First, they would stop their conversation or feeding the new baby or whatever else they happened to be doing and ask Matthew to stop. When Matthew did not stop with the polite request, the parents would then scream at him. Finally, in desperation, one of the parents would stop dinner and spank Matthew. After he was spanked, Matthew would run into his room and begin throwing his bedding and toys on the floor. By this time, his parents were usually worn out and would sink into a depression and do nothing more.

Obviously, what the parents thought was punishing was not punishing since it did not decrease his rotten behavior. In fact, the attention he got by kicking and whining at the table actually rewarded those behaviors, and so he repeated them daily. My advice to the parents was that they pay a lot of attention to Matthew when he was behaving positively at the table, because Matthew obviously was influenced by their attention. From the moment Matthew sat down at the table and as long as he was behaving and eating nicely his parents were asked to talk with him, to comment on how nicely he was eating, and to keep up the flow of conversation with him at dinner.

This procedure was immediately effective. Matthew's parents realized how important their attention was to the boy and that he had been kicking and whining in order to get it. They vowed to pay attention to his desirable behaviors in other situations and solved many similar situations by themselves. Certainly not all cases will be so easily treated, or respond as quickly and immediately. However, when you shift from paying attention to something bad to paying attention to something positive, you will see an increase in the good behavior and a decrease in the bad behavior.

Once you become aware of the powerful effects of your attention, you will certainly want to pay attention to more behaviors that you would like to encourage in your child. Simple comments like, "Oh, you put your train back on the shelf, thank you," or giving your son a big smile and saying, "Oh, that's so nice" when he does something you like can help you to teach him to behave appropriately.

The Variable Ratio Schedule

You can accidently teach your child some highly undesirable behaviors through unknowingly rewarding these behaviors on an intermittent schedule. For example, if when you are talking on the telephone you ignore your girl's polite requests for help until she has whined the same request four or five times, you teach her to whine and be persistent to get your attention. From her point of view, she never knows when the next request will be the one that gets rewarded. If she has asked you five times, maybe the sixth time she asks you to help her you will finally say yes. By rewarding her behavior on this intermittent schedule you teach her to be very persistent.

It is not uncommon for parents to become controlled by their children after teaching them that if they persist in whining or pestering them that they will eventually get what they want. Whenever you fail to stick to a no and give in after your son makes a number of whining demands, you teach him to whine longer and longer. If you resist until he whines or begs even louder and more annoyingly before you do what he wants, you shape his whining behavior to be more intense. I have known mothers who dread being at home for a day alone with their children. They feel that their only choice is to give their children their undivided attention or listen to very unpleasant nagging and whining.

To avoid such accidental training, you must pay attention to your daughter when she asks you something politely the *first* time. Carefully consider your answer before you say yes or no. If you need time to think, tell her so: "I need to think a minute, but if you keep asking me I won't be able to say yes." It is also very important that you be able to stick to your answer when you say no. If after you have said no, she pleads and whines and then you change your mind, you teach her to beg. She learns that if she persists and asks you a few more times then you will probably give in. She will have no way of knowing which times you are committed to your answer of no. You will become angry when she begs and she will be frustrated and angry when her begging doesn't pay off.

The Variable Interval Schedule

Parents often accidently use the variable interval schedule with their babies in their handling of bedtime. You might, as many parents do, reason to yourself, "I will let Suzie cry for about five minutes, and then if she is still crying, I will know that she is not tired and pick her up." What you teach your baby when you return to the room after five minutes of crying is: "If I persist in crying for at least five minutes, then I will get picked up." Then on the night when you decide "This is bedtime, whether she cries or not," she will still expect you to pick her up when she cries, and she will probably cry much longer.

11

Modeling Behavior

Do As I Say, Not As I Do

Much to the chagrin of parents, children do as their parents do rather than as they say. Because of the effects of modeling or imitative learning, children or parents who smoke, swear, eat sweets, drink, and even abuse them are likely to do the same themselves when they grow up. No matter how frequently parents warn their children of the dangers of smoking or of the negative effects of eating sugar, children tend to imitate their parents.

There is also a great deal of positive behavior that children can learn by observing their parents. If you become familiar with the way modeling works and how to use it most effectively, you can maximize your child's learning of desirable behaviors and minimize your tendency to model undesirable ones.

Research clearly shows the factors which make a model attractive to children. Children are more likely to imitate an adult who is warm and nurturant, one who is competent or powerful, and one whom they see as similar to themselves. If your son views you as warm, competent, and similar to himself, he will be more likely to imitate your behaviors, and the behaviors which you model for him will be of great significance.

Children imitate both parents, but by the time they are three years old they tend to imitate more the parent they perceive as similar to themselves. Therefore, boys imitate their fathers and girls imitate their mothers. If you are the same sex as your child it is particularly important for you to model behaviors that you hope your child will acquire. If you don't want your child to become a tele-vision addict, then you would be wise to model another use of leisure time, such as reading, while your child is awake. If you hope that your child will ask for milk instead of soda at a restaurant, then you have to order milk. If you drink soda with your meals but in-sist that your child drink milk, then when your child is away from you he will probably choose soda.

Children learn to speak to others the way you speak to them. Sometimes you may be horrified to hear your children speaking to their dolls or their playmates with the precise words, tone of voice, and facial expressions you have used yourself.

If you swear or become insulting when you are angry, then your children will do the same—not only at home but with other chil-dren. If you teach your children to use profanity they may not be welcome at your neighbor's home. In fact, other parents may not allow their children to play with yours. To me this seems particularly unfair, since your children will really have no ability to evaluate the effect of their profanity on other people, and therefore will be unable to change it.

If you would like your children to acquire habits of neatness, then you must make a genuine effort to be neat yourself. If you're the type of father who leaves the newspapers, dishes, cups, and clothing in a trail behind you, then don't bother insisting on your children tidying up after themselves. They will respond to your words as if they were noise. When they reach thirteen or fourteen years of age and are capable of verbally describing your hypocrisy, they'll be quick to point it out. Meanwhile, they won't have learned any habits of neatness through all your years of criticism and orders. If you really and truly want your children to develop habits of neatness and order, then you must clean up your own act first.

The powerful effect of modeling on children's behavior is most impressively and sadly seen in the case of abused children. Even though people who were abused remember with horror being beaten by their parents, when they themselves become parents they are likely to abuse their own children. They have learned through modeling that the way to deal with frustrating situations is to beat the child. Because their only models for childrearing were their own parents, other ways of handling the situation simply do not occur to the abusive parents.

A considerable body of research on modeling indicates that parents who use physical punishment as a means of control have children who are themselves more aggressive than children of parents who use other means of control. If you spank your child when you are frustrated or angry, then you provide your child with a model of how to behave in frustrating or annoying situations. Therefore, you should seriously consider means of control other than physical punishment, such as the time out procedure explained in the next chapter. Of course, we are all human and we all make mistakes, but if you make a genuine effort to model behaviors which you hope to see in your child, and not to model behaviors which you don't want your child to acquire, then you will certainly be a more effective parent.

Modeling and TV Violence

A number of studies on the effects of viewing televised violence have shown that seeing violence *does* cause increased aggressive behavior in some children. When childrens' level of aggressiveness is already high, then viewing television violence tends to increase their aggression even further. Boys seem to be affected more than girls. Most of these studies were done with nursery school or older children, and we do not know the factors that contributed to their existing levels of aggressive behavior. However, it is clear that at least some children are affected by viewing aggressive scenes on television. In play situations following this viewing they strike more frequently at their peers and get into more aggressive encounters of all kinds.

Furthermore, studies have found that cartoon representations of aggression have at least as powerful an influence on child behavior as realistic displays of aggression by an adult or child actor. This means that if your child views cartoon characters repeatedly hitting, slapping, and smashing one another, your child's level of aggression is likely to increase. Particularly if your child seems to learn aggressive behaviors easily, you need to be extra careful about what your child sees on television.

Modeling in Sex-Role Socialization

You want your children to be as free of rigid ideas of masculinity or femininity as possible and to be able to develop all parts of their personality. You hope that your daughters will be athletic, assertive, competent, achievement-motivated, logical, and decisive. You want your sons to be nurturant, sensitive, and loving in their relationships.

How can you encourage this and still be certain that they have a good feeling about their own sex? How do you teach boys to be boys and girls to be girls?

You as a parent will serve as a model of masculinity or femininity. Your boy will imitate his father, and your girl will imitate her mother. You sometimes see the effects of this very strikingly when you meet the parents of your friends. When you meet someone's father or mother and you see the son or daughter in their facial expressions, posture, and the way they laugh, you are seeing the results of modeling.

To promote the feeling of similarity to you as the same-sexed parent, you should spend time with your child in activities which your child enjoys. These may not be the activities you hoped your child would enjoy. Sensitively responding to the interests and desires, likes and dislikes of your child will prevent you from making mistakes in modeling sex roles.

If you are the mother of an active, robust girl, it's better to run and climb trees with her than to try to make her enjoy wearing frilly clothes and baking cookies. Your active and energetic daughter is more likely to identify with being female and enjoy being female if your shared activities are ones she enjoys. Similarly, boys who are mild-mannered and quiet in temperament may prefer indoor play to outdoor play, may prefer baking cookies inside to riding tricycles or playing ball in the yard. If you as a father insist on rough-and-tumble play or more traditionally masculine activities with your mild-mannered son, this may be disruptive for his sex-role identification. If your son prefers being in the kitchen to playing ball, you and he can make pancakes together on Sunday morning. What is important is that your son enjoy activities with his father and that you provide a model of masculinity to which he is attracted. The particular activity you do together is not important, and need not be traditionally "masculine."

If you are a single mother of a boy or father of a girl, promote a relationship between your child and a same-sexed relative or friend who can be a model for your child. Big Brothers and Sisters organizations have been formed in recognition of the importance of same-sex modeling.

Sex-role socialization is somewhat more difficult for boys in our culture because it is usually the mother who takes time off from her work or career to stay home with young children. Boys spend very little time with their fathers, and there are few other models of masculinity, since most babysitters and teachers are women. Furthermore, the female role is likely to be seen as very attractive both to little boys and to little girls, particularly between the ages of eighteen months to two and a half years when gender identity is being established.

Many boys are attracted to the "frills" of women, but it is best to tell a little boy that nail polish is for girls and that boys just don't wear nail polish. The same is true for lipstick, other cosmetics, and dresses. To permit your son to use these cosmetics may encourage him to feel like a girl or prefer and model after the female sex and interfere with his sex role development.

Although you want to teach your little boy that girls are people, too, and that they can be good company, I think that it is a mistake to have him play primarily with little girls. When boys at the critical age of eighteen months to three years play frequently with little girls who have all of the cosmetics and frills which our society has designated for use by girls, some boys become particularly attracted to this sex role. This can create problems for their sex-role identification.

It is important that boys spend time with other little boys and that they enjoy the play. Fireman suits, policeman suits, and cowboy outfits all help promote an attraction to the male role. While many parents worry about toy guns, swords, and bows and arrows potentially promoting violent behavior, these are the "frills" of the boy's outfit. Many peaceful, nonviolent men ran around for years wearing a double-holster gun belt and a cowboy hat. As my son, Ian, said at age two and a half when he begged for a gun, "It's only a toy Mom. It won't hurt anybody."

It is helpful to read stories which have an attractive main character who is the same sex as your child. Traditional fairy tales such as Cinderella or Snow White do not provide much of a role model either for boys or for girls.

Once your boy's sex-role identity and sex-role preference are clearly established, playing with girls more often is no problem, although usually by this time he'll prefer to play with other boys.

You may have questions about the consequences of giving traditionally boys' toys to girls and vice versa. Can there by any harmful effects if boys play with dolls and dishes and girls play with trains and trucks? The answer to this question is that it depends. When a child is noticeably attracted to cross-sex activities or more interested in main characters of the opposite sex in stories, this can indicate that the child is not identifying well with his or her own sex and may signal a problem. Until you see signs that your child is clearly identifying with his or her own sex, you may want to discourage cross-sex activity or playing with opposite sex friends frequently.

Do not worry about the over-simplified, rigid, and cartoon-like image your child has of masculinity and femininity in the early years. You child will gradually distill an image of masculinity or femininity from a wide variety of sources: from you and other significant people, from television heroes or heroines, magazine pictures, billboards, and so on. As children mature, their ideas become increasingly complex. A two-and-a-half-year-old girl to whom wearing a dress signifies femaleness may become a feminist crusader. A three-year-old boy who insists that dolls are for girls may become a house-husband. Your child's ultimate freedom from sex-role stereotypes is a matter of a life of opportunities to develop all parts of his or her personality. The models you provide of competence and nurturance are far more important in the long run than which toys your child plays with.

Playgroups and Other Children as Models for Behavior

You are probably already aware of how much children imitate each other. However, it is not only the behavior of other children your child observes, but also the *consequences* to the behavior that your child observes, that determines whether or not your child will imitate that behavior.

A considerable body of data on "observational learning" indicates that the consequences to the model determine whether or not the observing child will imitate the behavior. If the aggressive behavior of a child model gets the model a toy or any other reward reinforcing to the child observer, the observer is likely to imitate the behavior. If the behavior of the child model is followed by some consequence viewed by the observer as negative, the observing child is not likely to imitate the behavior.

If you have a playgroup on a regular basis and the parents can agree on appropriate consequences to certain common transgressions, then you can use these findings to an advantage. For example, when a child pushes another child, parents can agree to say, "No, you cannot push children. You might hurt them. You have to sit outside the playroom in time out for awhile." When the onlooking children observe the consequences to the aggressive behavior, they will be unlikely to try it themselves.

Similarly, if parents will agree to loudly praise prosocial behaviors such as sharing, taking turns, and cooperating, the observing children will be more likely to imitate these behaviors. All the parents should be alert for desirable behavior and call attention to it so that nearby children notice the praise. For example, you say quite loudly, "Ruth is sharing her toys with Sam. Thank you, Ruth, that's good sharing."

The important element here is that parents *consistently* respond to the agreed-upon misbehaviors with the agreed-upon consequence. A push must be a push whether or not the pushed child falls or cries. The same consequence must always follow the grabbing of a toy, whether or not the child grabbed from protests.

The usual situation is that different parents do *not* respond similarly or consistently. In these circumstances your child may persist in undesirable behaviors that you yourself consistently punish. If your child gets pushed or sees another child being pushed and the pusher gets away with it, your child will be likely to imitate that pushing behavior.

Choosing Your Child's Friends

Because it is so clear that children do imitate the behavior of their peers, you will want to be certain that your child has models for desirable behavior. You won't be able to choose your child's friends for very long, but in the early years I believe it is wise to do so.

The self-control of a two, three, or four year old is not very strong. If your child is often in the company of a peer who has not learned to obey instructions, then that child's behavior can weaken your child's self-control. For example, I was once in line to get into a restaurant with my son and his friend, both three and a half. The boys were near the door and I told them, "Don't go out that door. There are cars outside." Ian's friend looked at me and walked out the door as if I had said nothing. Ordinarily, Ian would not have gone out that door after my instructions. But, seeing his friend leave, he looked at me, looked at his friend, and followed him. This meant that I had to leave the line, lose my place, and follow the children. When this happens you must provide some consequences, such as time out or going home. Otherwise you will teach him that he can imitate his friends' bad behavior with no consequences.

Similarly your son can be encouraged in the positive behaviors he has already learned by being with children who behave well. If he is with friends who play cooperatively and share, these behaviors will continually be modeled and rewarded. You would be wise to surround your child with peers and playmates who have already developed some of the positive behaviors you would like to see strengthened in your own child.

Of course, you will not find any more perfect children than you will find perfect adults, so you have to weigh the advantages and disadvantages of each situation. It is not necessary that you find a perfectly behaved companion for your child. Just find one whose parents have similar expectations for their child's behavior and who provide effective consequences.

Peers as Models for Fearless Behavior

A peer who is fearless can be a very powerful influence on your child's feelings about many situations. If you structure the situation well, you can have a peer model help your child learn to swim, to feel comfortable around animals, or to approach any other feared situation such as amusement park rides.

The best child model is one who is the şame age and a friend of your child. It is also best if that model is doing something that is just slightly ahead of what your child is able to do. You want to have the courageous child model behaviors in small steps, prompt your child to imitate the model, and then reinforce your child. For example, if you are trying to encourage your daughter to put her face in the water, it's a good idea to have her observe a peer who has just learned to put his in, blow bubbles, and come up smiling. Don't show her a boy who is diving off the side of the pool and swimming the length of it. She will see that child model as quite different from herself and be less likely to be affected by his behavior.

To promote fearless behavior when your daughter is anxious, you must be very patient and let her stay some distance away from the fear stimulus. Let her observe her fearless friend from dry land. Let her watch this friend smiling and enjoying himself in the water. In her own good time, let your daughter approach the pool and try some of those behaviors. You can prompt her when you see she's just about ready to do it herself, but do not push her. If she is truly afraid and you push her, you will strengthen the fear.

If you are at a pony ride and your son is afraid to get on the pony, let him watch his friend get on the pony. Simply observe.

As he sees his friend smiling and having a good time, he may begin to express some interest in the pony. Sit him on the back of the pony with his friend, and if he continues to seem comfortable, move him to his own pony to sit for a time. If he objects, feels tense, or acts frightened, then back up again and allow him to watch his friend. If you can repeat the situation, he will gradually become more confident and likely to want to ride the pony himself.

Modeling Is Superior to Instruction

Rather than simply telling, actually *show* your child what to do. For example, assume your daughter is passive and does not protect herself when someone pushes her or takes a toy away from her. If you simply say to her, "Tell Johnny not to push you. Tell him not to do that," the appropriate words and inflections may not occur to your child. For this reason she may not be able to do as you have instructed her. You will be more effective if you model the assertive statement for her, saying, "Tell Johnny, 'Don't push me Johnny.'" Then prompt her to imitate you. This way you help her to learn specific words she can use, and you show her the effective tone of voice, facial expression, and posture that should accompany a self-protective, assertive statement.

Rather than instructing your son: "Tell Johnny that's your truck," model a statement for him. Say to him, "Tell Johnny, 'No! Don't take that, it's mine.'" Rather than saying, "Go ask Johnny if you can have the truck," model a statement such as, "Ask Johnny, 'May I have that truck when you're done?'" Whenever possible try to give your child the precise words that he can use rather than instructions. The use of modeling is far superior to instruction in teaching both the verbal and nonverbal aspects of a complicated behavior.

Modeling Talking As an Alternative to Whining

If your daughter whines when she could just as easily talk, it may be that she has not yet learned to verbalize the uncomfortable sensations she feels when she is thirsty, hungry, or tired. To help her learn to express her needs in words rather than whining, you may have to model the words for her and prompt her to use them at those difficult times. It is best to explain the new rules to her ahead of time: "I want you to talk to me, not whine. I won't pay any attention to whining. I will only hear talking." Then model the appropriate behavior. When your child stands before the sink and whines that she wants a drink of water, say, "Stop! I want you to say 'water.' Don't whine. Say 'water.'" When she says the word in a more peaceful tone of voice, immediately give her some water and say, "That's nice. You asked me nicely for water like a big girl." Lavishly praise her for inhibiting the whine and expressing herself in words.

Role Playing

Sometimes children need some real practice in learning to become appropriately assertive. Even adults often have this problem, that's why they enter assertiveness training groups! You can help your child to become effectively assertive by practicing at home the words your child could use in a difficult situation.

One parent described a problem her child was having at preschool with another three year old who loved wrestling. Her David would be playing quietly by himself. The other little guy, Tyson, would come up behind him and grab him around the neck and tackle him in a playful manner. David did not like this wrestling at all but would say nothing and suffer the attack quietly. He began to hate going to nursery school because of this feeling of helplessness when Tyson was around.

I suggested to his parents that they pretend to be at nursery school and ask David to pretend he were Tyson and attack his father. When David attacked his father as Tyson had attacked him, his father would model a self-protective statement: "I don't like that Tyson! Stop it, stop it right now!" After David attacked his father and Dad had modeled these self-protective statements several times, they would trade places. David would be himself, his father would pretend to be Tyson, and David would practice stopping the attack with these statements, saying to his father, "Stop that, Tyson, I don't like it. You stop it right now!" After practicing the words, strong tone of voice, and appropriate facial expressions at home, David was able to use the same words and tone at nursery school and put an end to Tyson's unwelcome attacks. Only one weekend of practice made a significant difference in David's feelings about going to school. Because he had a behavior he could use, he no longer felt helpless when Tyson was around.

Role playing and rehearsing assertive words or behaviors can help your child cope with teachers as well. If your daughter is one who sits and waits for the teacher to notice that she needs some help with her boots or her work, then she may need some help in learning how to ask the teacher for assistance. The two of you can pretend you are at school. First let your daughter be the teacher and you be your daughter. You say to her, "Let's pretend you're the teacher, and I am you and we are at school. I can't put on my boots by myself, I just can't do it. I'm going to say, 'Mrs. Ward, will you help me put on my boots? I just can't do it!' What would Mrs. Ward say? Now you are Mrs. Ward. What do you say?" Prompt her to say, "Keep trying, you can do it." Then you respond, "No, I can't. I tried and tried and I can't do it. I need help, I just need help." Then trade places and ask your child to be herself, and you be the teacher. Give her the objection, "You can do it. Just keep trying," and see if she can respond assertively. If she cannot, then trade places again so she can hear you model the assertive response again: "No, I can't! I just can't do it. I tried and I just can't." Keep trading places until she can ask for help.

Being able to ask a teacher for help in academic work can sometimes be the difference between a child who is happy and doing well at school and one who is lost. This is so important that you may want to practice with your child even if your child never complains, just so you know that your child can ask for help when necessary. As we all know, "the squeaky wheel gets the grease."

Another time when role playing can be effective is teaching a child how to respond positively to a new sibling. With dolls and doll-play you can rehearse the way to behave with a new baby. You can model gentle touches, a quiet, playful voice, and a way to hold the baby. This way when your newborn comes home for the first time, your older child will already know some ways to behave and you can begin to reward them immediately. Knowing how to treat a newborn baby is not something most two, three, or four year olds will know unless you deliberately teach them, and modeling can make it much easier for them to learn.

Conclusion

It is worthwhile to spend the time and the effort to model for your child behaviors that will be naturally reinforced by other people. If you model such things as the way to initiate play, the way to ask a friend for a toy, and the way to ask for help, then these behaviors will be rewarded not only by other children but also by their parents. If you model and reward polite behaviors such as saying "please" and "thank you," people will respond more positively to your child. When you teach your child behaviors that will be maintained by the natural reinforcers of friendship and the warm responses of other people, you teach social skills which will be lasting. They will continue to evoke positive reactions long after your training.

12

Decreasing Undesirable Behavior

Extinction

Sometimes before you realize the pattern, you will have rewarded whining. Other times you may be forced by circumstances to reward behavior you would not normally tolerate. For example, when your baby son is ill you may not want to let him cry at bedtime, so you let him stay up and hold him until he falls asleep in your arms. You might do the same when you are in somebody else's home or when someone else is ill in your own house. Once the circumstances are changed and you are home again or the illness has passed, your son will let you know that he preferred the other circumstances, and you might have some bedtime tantrums. This kind of behavior calls for the extinction procedure. Extinction simply means that you ignore a behavior until it goes away.

The Williams Study

A very famous study by Williams used the extinction procedure to eliminate bedtime tantrums in a two-year-old boy who had been ill for most of his first eighteen months. When the boy was ill, he understandably got a lot of attention. He learned to control his parents' behavior by crying. When he had recovered his health, he continued to demand the special attention and care he had received while he was sick. His parents began to feel that he enjoyed controlling them at bedtime and that he was fighting sleep.

The pattern that had developed was as follows: Either the parents or the aunt had to sit with the boy at bedtime while he fell asleep. Usually he took between an hour and a half to two hours to fall asleep and during this time he required that his parents or the aunt pay full attention to him. If the parent or the aunt should be so inattentive as to try to read, the boy would scream. Occasionally, the parents or the aunt would become tired or bored with watching the child fall asleep and would slip out of the bedroom before he was sound asleep. How foolish of them. The boy would then have a tantrum, and they would have to begin the whole bedtime ritual all over again.

In desperation, the parents went to see Dr. Williams about the boy's bedtime tantrums. Dr. Williams recommended an extinction procedure. The parents were advised to take the little boy to bed, lovingly tuck him in, and then to leave the bedroom and close the door. They were told to leave the child alone to fall asleep by himself. The parents were told that the boy could be expected to cry, but eventually he would stop crying. Over a number of days the length of time he cried and the intensity of his crying would diminish.

The results of this treatment were as follows:

On the first day he screamed for 45 minutes and finally fell asleep.
On the second day he didn't scream at all.
On the third day he screamed for ten minutes.
On the fourth day he screamed for seven minutes.
On the fifth day he screamed for three minutes.
On the sixth day he screamed for two minutes.
On the seventh day he *didn't cry at all.*

He didn't cry on the eighth, ninth, or tenth day. By the tenth time he was put to bed, he smiled pleasantly and the parents said that he made happy sounds as he was falling asleep.

So far this seems pretty easy, but something quite predictable happened the next week. About a week later, when the boy was put to bed, he once again cried. In the research this reoccurrence of a behavior is called *spontaneous recovery.* Although we have given this research finding a special name we don't really know the reason for it. We only know that it is a very reliable and predictable event. About a week after a response has been extinguished, the response will recur even though it has not again been rewarded. Usually this behavior lasts only for one or two trials and then once again disappears, provided that it is not rewarded again.

Unfortunately for this child, the aunt was not aware of this phenomenon, and, when the boy cried that time a week later, she went back to his room and sat with him until he fell asleep. This one reward for his tantrum behavior resulted in having to do the *entire procedure* over again. The next time the boy was put to sleep, he cried for fifty minutes before going to sleep, the second time for eleven minutes, the third time for seven minutes, the fourth time for twenty minutes, the fifth time for ten minutes, and the sixth time for three minutes. The seventh, eighth, and ninth times he didn't cry at all and by the ninth time, he was happily going off to sleep.

Extinction and Continuous Reinforcement

One consistent research finding is that when a response has been rewarded on a continuous basis and then the reward is withdrawn, the response will extinguish very quickly. Knowing this, you can make some intelligent decisions about what kind of bedtime rituals you want to begin and how you want to end them. You can rock your baby girl to sleep, sing her to sleep, or perform any other ritual, as long as you do it on a regular basis. When you decide that rocking her to sleep is beginning to take a little too long, and you want to discontinue the procedure, be certain that you are ready to endure the extinction procedure. Get your baby ready for bed, sing to her or rock her for as long as you feel you would like to, then put her in bed awake, regardless of her protests. To stiffen your resolve, it may help to sit and read the Williams case while she screams it out.

Extinction and Intermittent Rewards

Behaviors rewarded intermittently are difficult to extinguish, as this case will illustrate: One family came to my office complaining that their fourteen-month-old girl, Kim, was keeping them awake nearly the entire night and then sleeping half the day. The couple was desperate, their marriage was on the verge of splitting up, and they both looked extremely tired. They described a classic example of rewarding bedtime tantrum behavior by a variable interval schedule.

For the first six months bedtime was no problem. The mother would either walk or rock Kim to sleep, which usually took no longer than five minutes. When she was six months old, however, she began to take longer and longer to fall asleep—anywhere from twenty minutes to an hour. When the mother would try to put Kim down before she was sound asleep, she would awaken as she was being put in her crib. When Kim screamed and grabbed onto her mother's arms, her mother would pick her up and begin rocking her again. It would take another twenty minutes to an hour and a half for her to fall asleep again. As Kim grew older, she took longer and longer to fall asleep and became more and more likely to wake up when she was put into her crib.

One night when she was about eight months old, her mother decided to let her cry it out, after having walked her for two and a half hours. Kim cried for about half an hour. Then her father couldn't stand it any longer, and he picked her up. Both parents were concerned because lights were going on in the neighbors' homes, and the screaming was keeping people awake.

After several more nights of walking Kim for nearly three hours each night, the parents decided again to let her cry it out. This time she screamed for an hour and a half before her mother began to worry about what the neighbors thought and picked her up.

After that, the parents were even more variable in the way they handled the situation. They would let her cry for minutes or hours depending upon the advice they had received from friends that day and their own frustration tolerance that night. By the time I saw the couple, Kim was fourteen months old and was keeping everyone awake until around 4:00 a.m., when she finally fell asleep in her parents' arms, on the sofa, or on the living-room rug. The parents would then pick her up and put her in bed. Unfortunately, her father had to go to work with very little sleep and daytime deliveries, and phone calls kept her mother awake. Kim slept peacefully until around 1:00 p.m.

Because Kim had been rewarded for crying longer and louder through the months, the extinction of her tantrum behavior was very arduous. The parents had to be prepared to let Kim cry for the entire night and not to return to her under any circumstances. On the first extinction trial, Kim cried for approximately four and a half hours. We had kept her awake for most of the day before this first extinction trial, and she was extremely tired. The second night she cried for three hours and woke up during the night three more times, each time crying for another half hour. On the third night she cried for close to two hours. The fourth night she cried for an hour and a half. By the sixth night she went to bed quite peacefully. The taming of a tyrant is so much more difficult than preventing your child from becoming one!

Accidentally Using a Fixed-Interval Intermittent Schedule

When my daughter Sherri was an infant, I was aware of research on the effects of continuous reinforcement and therefore rocked her to sleep every night until she was about six months of age. As often happens, when she reached six months she began to take longer and longer to fall asleep — sometimes as long as twenty-five minutes — and began to wake up as I put her in bed. I decided that I would rock her or walk her no longer than fifteen minutes, and she would simply have to go to sleep on her own after that. Knowing that she would protest, I was prepared to let her cry it out. Because I had rocked her on a continuous reinforcement schedule the extinction went very rapidly. Sherri cried only about ten minutes on the first night, less than five minutes on the second night, only two or three minutes on the third night, and not at all after that. I was confident and happy about the procedure.

Within a week a new problem arose. After she had been quietly in bed for fifteen or twenty minutes Sherri began to cry. Thinking that there must be some problem with a diaper pin, or that perhaps she was ill, I returned to her room to check on her. I found everything normal and again rocked her and put her down to sleep. She stayed quiet for another fifteen minutes or so and then began to cry again. Again, thinking there must be some new problem, I went to her room.

Sherri had learned that if she waited fifteen minutes before crying, then her crying would be rewarded. It took me some time to recognize the pattern of behavior that had developed. But once I was certain that her crying was not in response to any pain or discomfort, I was able to extinguish that crying as well. I simply did not respond to those cries at fifteen-minute intervals, and, after only two nights, she no longer cried when she was placed in her bed.

The Child Who Knows Extinction

Although the first extinction of tantrum behavior is usually very long and upsetting, there are many rewards for you if you can endure the crying and resist the urge to reward the behavior. Once you have gone through the extinction procedure a few times your child will recognize it and won't cry as long.

An example of a parallel situation that you can probably appreciate involves using a pay phone. If you put one or two coins into the telephone and you don't hear the rewarding dial tone, you won't be likely to put any more money in that telephone. You know from experience that if you don't get a dial tone immediately, you probably won't get it at all. Children who are experienced with the extinction procedure know that if crying and tantrums do not get rewarded immediately, they probably won't get rewarded at all. Therefore, tantrums or crying are very short-lived.

Young children also learn to tell the difference between people who will reward their crying or tantrum behavior and people who won't. Very quickly they learn that a person who doesn't respond immediately to their whining or crying won't respond at all. Therefore they don't whine and cry at the babysitter's house or for the unresponsive parent. However, they may whine and cry frequently for you if they have learned that you will reward it.

Prepare Yourself for Extinction

When you no longer reward a behavior you have been rewarding, it will *increase* before it starts to decrease. Things will actually seem to be worse before they get better. For example, if your girl has learned to whine at you to get your attention when you are talking on the telephone, the first time you do not respond to her whining you should expect her to whine longer and louder. She probably feels that since low-volume whining isn't working, she may need to whine a little louder or a little longer to get your attention.

If you continue to ignore her whining and don't respond to it, eventually it will taper off. If you make a mistake and assume that the extinction procedure is not working and respond to more intense whining, you will actually reward the more intense behavior.

Another frequent result of extinction in the earliest phases is that when you no longer reward a behavior your child may become aggressive. If you have been rewarding whining and you stop rewarding it, your daughter may whine louder and then begin to cry and scream and stamp and bang things to get your attention. Her aggression is similar to your banging or kicking the vending machine that takes your money and won't give you a Coke. If you make a mistake and give in and reward her behavior you will not only teach her to be very persistent in her whining, but you also will reward the aggressive behavior. Be prepared for the outburst, wait it out, and don't give in.

Also be prepared for the response to spontaneously recur a week or so after the extinction of the behavior seems complete. If you are careful not to reward the spontaneous recurrance, it will soon drop out.

Determining the Rewards for a Behavior. If you assume that your attention has been rewarding a certain behavior, but when you stop paying attention to it the behavior does not decrease, there are a number of possibilities. It could be that *your* attention is not what has been rewarding that behavior for your child. Check to see what other possible consequences could be rewarding that behavior. Check to see that no one else in your family or household is rewarding the behavior.

When you are thinking about using an extinction procedure be certain that you are in control of the reward for that behavior. For example, ignoring your child's eating candy would probably not decrease that behavior since the reward for eating candy is the taste, not your attention. Other methods such as distraction or modeling are needed here.

Extinction Combined with Positive Reinforcement

Extinction is far more effective when you combine it with positive reinforcement of an alternative behavior. If your three-year-old boy has been whining and crying and causing trouble to get your attention while you nurse a new baby, promote another desirable behavior that you can reward during that time. Take the time to set your toddler up in some positive play activity that you can be fairly certain will hold his interest for some time. For example, give him a half a cup of flour, some water, some sugar, and some containers to mix them in. Then praise him for being such a good boy while you are busy. In the beginning it would even be worth getting up and going over to your toddler to give him an appreciative hug while you tell him how pleased you are. If he stops his play and begins to whine and pull at you, ignore the behavior. When he goes back to work with his flour and sugar, you can again become attentive, rewarding his positive play behavior by giving him a food reward or a trinket. In the beginning it is worth allowing your child to make some messes to be certain that he has something that he especially likes doing. After some time he may be able to entertain himself with some of his toys while you are busy, especially if you are careful to continue praising his positive play occasionally.

When To Use Extinction

You want to use extinction when you can let a behavior continue to occur without any undesirable consequences. For example, certain attention-getting behaviors are annoying but relatively harmless. Sometimes young children will "show-off" in front of guests or visitors. They make unusual noises, yell more loudly than usual, throw clothes over a railing, or become a little wild in their activity. As long as none of these behaviors are dangerous to them or anyone else it is probably best to ignore them, and quickly pay attention to the children when they do something normal or appropriate.

If your child picks up profanity, rather than responding to it in any way, it would be best to ignore it completely. Then be certain he doesn't hear it anymore. Sometimes it is helpful if you model another expression that your child thinks is funny to use when he drops or spills something. For example, you might say, "Bats" when you drop something. When your child drops something encourage saying, "Oh, Bats!"

Sometimes children will *demand* a glass of milk or *demand* breakfast, saying, "Give me some milk!" Sometimes a mother will respond in an angry voice, "Don't you talk to me like that! You had better ask more nicely," all the time she is pouring the milk. This rewards the demanding behavior because the child gets the milk, along with a lot of attention. It's better to explain to your daughter, "I cannot get you anything when you order me to do it. If you say, 'Get me some milk!' or 'I'm hungry, get me my breakfast,' then I *cannot* get it for you. I have to wait for you to ask me nicely. I must hear something nice like 'Mommy, would you please get me some milk' or 'Can I have some breakfast please?' before I can get you anything." Then later when she demands something to eat you can prompt her by saying, "I can't get anything for you when you ask me that way." Remind her of the new requirements the first few times. After that simply ignore the impolite demands and they will diminish.

You can expect your child to repeat an unwanted behavior several times without being rewarded before there is any apparent decrease in the frequency of that behavior. However, the extinction process does work, and eventually the behaviors that no longer get rewarded will decrease. Your child will not persist in useless behavior.

Time-Out

Time-out means time out from positive reinforcement and is something that was used by lifeguards at pools before psychologists learned about it. When children repeatedly roughhouse in an unsafe way in the water, or run to the diving board rather than walking, the lifeguard blows the whistle and requires the offending child to sit on the side of the pool for five minutes. This procedure is quite effective in changing children's behavior.

Psychologists have defined time-out as "a temporary loss of all positive reinforcers." This means that you take your child away from toys, friends, and ongoing activity and place your child in a boring setting for a specified length of time. Psychologists like to distinguish time-out conceptually from punishment because you do nothing *aversive* to your child, nor is a specific positive reinforcer removed. The *child* is physically removed from the opportunity for any rewarding experiences. The time-out procedure is a very effective alternative to punishment that you can start to use at age two.

The rules of time-out are simple:

1. Find a Boring Place

Immediately after your child commits an unwanted behavior, put your child in a boring place. At first you'll probably have to hold your two year old down in a chair, an empty playpen, or a crib. The important thing is that the setting should be boring: no toys, no friends, no interesting things to see or do.

At two and a half or three years old, your child can stay in a closed room alone. The bathroom is a good choice. It's a boring room to most children and there are bathrooms almost everywhere you go, making time-out a portable procedure.

Don't worry that your child may come to hate the bathroom. This does not occur, because nothing painful or harmful happens to your child there. In actual practice I have never heard of a case where a child had a negative reaction to the bathroom as a result of it being used for time-out.

Time-out doesn't absolutely require a separate room. When your son does something intolerable at the beach, simply take him aside, away from toys and friends, and make him sit still. If possible, face him away from the ongoing activity or anything interesting to watch.

2. Explain the Ground Rules

Say, "I can't let you do that. You have to stay here in time-out for two [or three, four, five] minutes. You have to be quiet to come out. I can't let you out if you're screaming. Screaming will *not* get you out."

3. Set the Time Limit

The number of minutes in time-out should equal the age of your child: two minutes for a two year old, two and a half minutes for a two and a half year old, three minutes for a three year old, and so on up to five minutes for a five year old. Research shows that five minutes is the longest time you ever have to use. For children five or older it seems that five minutes is as good as twenty.

Hold your two year old for the whole two minutes, counting out loud the first few times all the way to 120. After the first three or four time-outs you can count silently, but let your child see your lips move. After several more experiences of time-out you can count to yourself. For older children you can time them by setting a kitchen timer.

During the time-out you may have to remind a younger child: "Why did Mommy take you away from the playgroup? Because you pushed." Don't stand outside the room and talk to an older child, since your attention will take away from the boredom and possibly reward screaming.

4. No Release without Silence

When time is up, wait for silence before letting your child out. This is very important, because you don't want your screaming daughter to think that her screaming got her out.

Wait for four or five seconds of relative calm from two-year-old children, gradually increasing it to ten seconds by the time they are three years old.

When you first start using time-out you may have to remind your two year old after 120 seconds: "Remember, you have to be quiet before I can let you out." For older children, don't say a thing, just wait for silence. Reminding your child can actually reinforce the screaming.

5. Repeat Time-Out As Needed

If your child resumes the unwanted behavior after being let out, say, "Oh, you're not really ready to come out. You have to go back into time-out." Repeat the entire time-out procedure again. Especially persistent children can cycle through four or five time-outs in a row before getting the point. However trying this might sound, the twenty minutes it takes is preferable to a whole day or night of outright warfare.

Examples

Time-Out to Eliminate
Screaming and Tantrums

Around the age of two and a half, many children will begin to scream, whine, and try to use their voices to control their parents. When they want something that has been denied, they scream and whine even though the parents may never have rewarded tantrums. The child has noticed that this screaming is upsetting to the parent, and screaming represents a power struggle. It is as if your son has decided that if you will not give him what he wants, then he will punish you by screaming. His crying and screaming behavior may be clearly theatrical, but it can continue for long periods of time. Because he is sensitive to your moods and expressions, he realizes that he is getting the desired effect.

The use of time-out can be very effective in eliminating manipulative screaming. You say to your son as he begins to scream, "Do not scream at me, I don't want to hear that." If he continues to scream, say, "If you want to scream then you'll have to do it in time-out because I don't want to hear it." Take him by the hand and place him firmly in time-out. The procedure is then the customary one in which the timer is set for two and a half minutes for the two and a half year old. As usual he must stay in time-out until there is a period of silence. It is a mistake to stand by the door and remind him that he must be quiet to come out. Your attention will reward his screaming. Tell him only on his way in, "You have to be quiet in order to come out of time-out." If he continues to scream and cry past two and a half minutes, then he continues to stay in time-out. Only when he is quiet for at least a few seconds should you let him out.

Sometimes your son will be quiet, you will open the door, and he will begin screaming again. When this happens, you must immediately put him back into the time-out room saying, "Oh, I see you're not through screaming yet," and quickly close the door. You may have to repeat this procedure three, four, or even five times for some children who are *very* persistent. When your son tries to control your behavior through whining, screaming, or crying at you at any time of day or night, tell him immediately, "You cannot do that to me, I won't have it," and then immediately place him in time-out.

Time-Out for the Night Crawler

For a child less than two and a half years of age, I would not recommend time out for night waking. However, if your two and a half year old daughter develops or continues a habit of waking in the night, there is no reason that you have to acquire her habits! First, ask her nicely to let you sleep and to stay in her room quietly. If she insists on waking you at 3:00 A.M., crying and whining and badgering you until you get up every night, you may want to consider using time-out.

Tell her, "You cannot keep me awake like this, I want to sleep. If you continue to bother me, I'm going to put you in time-out." The next time she whines at you, put her in time-out. You must be prepared to repeat the time-out procedure again and again as necessary. Sometimes as soon as you open the door and let her out, she will whine and cry again. When this happens you must place her back into time-out. If you do not immediately put her back into time-out when she whines and cries then she has won! You will have taught her that if she can get through that brief period of solitary confinement, she can continue to whine and cry at you and keep you awake. Being firm and consistent and placing her in time-out two or three times may add up to ten minutes of unpleasantness. However, if you don't put her back in time-out after that first time, she may keep you awake for hours. Unfortunately, at 3:00 A.M. many parents find themselves losing tempers, screaming, and coming close to physical violence. I believe that repeating the time-out, as hard as it is, will be a better alternative for you and your child.

Time-Out to Encourage the Use of Medication

Sometimes your son will refuse to take important medication. It may be that he does not even dislike the taste but is using this particular arena to act out the power struggle, because he sees how important this is to you. At two and a half my son was quite capable of swallowing his vitamins in tablets, but he would refuse to swallow important medication pills. This is a situation in which you can use time-out very effectively. You may shudder at the thought of placing your feverish, sick little boy into time-out, but if he must take his medication to recover, then you must find a way for him to take it. The alternative to time-out is having at least two people hold him down, squeezing his mouth, and forcing the medication down his throat. This is stressful for both you and your child. If the medication must be taken for ten days, three times a day, then this terribly upsetting procedure will have to be repeated thirty times!

The use of time-out to encourage your son to take his medication should go as follows: You would say to him, "Benjamin, you have to take your pill. You know how to swallow it and you must swallow it. Either you swallow the pill or you go into time-out. Which one will it be? Will you swallow your pill?" If he sits there with clenched teeth and refuses to take the pill, then say, "Okay then, you'll have to go into time-out." Place him into time-out, with fever and all. After the usual two and a half minutes, open the door and ask him, "Are you ready to take your pill yet?" If he says no, then immediately say, "Okay, then you'll have to go back into time-out" and close the door again. Each time you open the door, ask the same question, "Are you ready to take your pill yet?" Sometimes children in the middle of time-out will yell, "I'm ready to take my pill." This is one time you can let him out earlier.

Time-Out at the Doctor's Office

Sometimes children who have been quite calm and relaxed at the doctor's office will begin to protest at being examined when they are in their terrible twos. When this is a power struggle or simple resistance because they "don't like" the examination, rather than the result of fear or anxiety, you may want to use time-out. Your daughter may kick and scream and fight during the examination to such an extent that the doctor cannot get a good heart reading or other accurate measure. The examination can take three times as long because she is kicking and screaming. It is a very simple matter to say to her "You have to let the doctor examine you, and if you scream you'll just have to go into time-out." When she begins to kick and scream while the doctor tries to examine her, place her in time-out in the bathroom in the doctor's office. Let her out after two and a half minutes followed by a period of calm. If she begins to scream and cry again, you place her in time-out again.

You will have to ask for the cooperation of your doctor on the first visit. Tell her or him what you are doing and ask if you can come for a visit at a time when the office is not so busy. You may have to repeat time-out three or four times and continue to remind your daughter that the doctor has to examine her before you leave the office. Tell her that as soon as the examination is over you can leave, and she can have lunch or some favorite treat. Help her think of something on the other side of the examination rather than focusing on the doctor's exam.

Although the time-out procedure is very arduous and upsetting, especially when you have a sick child, you would be wise to carry it out the two, three, or four times necessary to get cooperation. Once your daughter is familiar with your commitment to her cooperation, then on later visits to the doctor she will cooperate when you tell her, "Either you let the doctor examine you, or I'll have to put you in time-out. Which would you rather do?" Once she believes that you mean and do what you say, she will be much more likely to cooperate. You may only have to go through the procedure on one visit to the doctor's office.

Time-Out As the Alternative to Behaving Appropriately

After some experience with time-out you can give your son the choice of appropriate behavior or time-out when he balks at a nice request. For example, you might say, "Would you rather pick up these toys or go in time-out?" If you *consistently* place him in time-out when you say you will, your words will come to exercise a great deal of control over his behavior, and he will probably choose to pick up his toys. When you give him the choice of behaving appropriately or time-out, he will believe you and either stop his inappropriate behavior or do what is desired of him. When you say, "If you push again, you will go in time-out" he will know you are serious and he may control his behavior.

You can expect that occasionally he will refuse to cooperate just to test your continuing requirements for appropriate behavior, but the occasional time-out will keep your words in control of his behavior.

Punishment

Sometimes your child will do things that are not only annoying or inappropriate, but which are also aggressive or destructive. When this happens you will not be able to ignore the behavior and let it extinguish. For example, biting playmates may be very rewarding for your son — either in the form of the toy he wanted or in stopping an aggressive attack by another child. If you wait for biting behavior to extinguish, his playmate's parents may extinguish him before you extinguish the behavior! Since extinction doesn't work with biting or other aggressive acts, you may have to use a punishment procedure.

The punishment procedure involves doing something extremely aversive or unpleasant to your child immediately after your child commits some undesirable behavior. Punishment is one of the less effective means of controlling your child's behavior for two reasons. First, physical punishments like spanking have emotional side effects. Most parents feel sad, depressed, or guilty after having spanked their child. Children are usually angry and resentful of the parent. These emotional reactions tend to linger long after the particular incident has passed.

The other problem is that punishment teaches children what *not* to do but doesn't teach them what they *should* do. For example, assume that your boy picks the cat up by the tail and you follow this behavior with a spank. After you spank him several times he may not pull the cat's tail when you are there to see him. But when you leave the room, or when he and the cat are outside in the yard, he will be likely to pull the cat's tail again. The reason for this is that the cat is a highly attractive item, and your boy doesn't know the appropriate way to play with it.

By following these principles, you can use punishment sparingly, appropriately, and effectively while avoiding most of the harmful side effects.

1. Try Everything Else First

Apply what you've learned about increasing desirable behavior with rewards and modeling desirable behavior. Consider using the time-out procedure. Think of punishment as the last resort after you've tried everything else.

2. Choose an Effective Punisher

There are actually two forms of punishment. One form of punishment is to take away from your child something that you know is rewarding or positively reinforcing. For example, if your daughter thoroughly enjoys playing with sticks, frequently looks for them, and would sleep with them if you let her, then you can assume that sticks are a reward for her. If she hits her friend with a stick, and you immediately take the stick away, then removing the stick would be a punishment.

The second form of the punishment procedure is the one that most of us recognize as punishment. This involves doing something aversive or highly unpleasant to your child immediately after your child commits some unwanted behavior. For example, if your son bites his friend and you immediately give him a hard slap on the leg, you will have punished the biting behavior, provided that slap is truly a punisher for the child. One mother I talked with very effectively poured a cup of iced cold water which she kept in the refrigerator right down the back of her three-year-old son each time he tormented the baby. This proved to be an exceptionally effective punisher for him and much less stressful for the mother than spanking. You do not want to do anything that will be harmful to your child. Just something unpleasant. For example, you wouldn't want to throw water in your son's face because you might teach him to be very upset by having water in his face, which may interfere with learning to swim later on.

You know something is an effective punisher only if it actually decreases the behavior that it follows. For some children a loud noise screamed into the ear or a spank even through a thick diaper, will be enough to suppress the unwanted behaviors. For others it will not. You need to look at your own child's behavior to decide whether or not what you are doing is effective.

You must be prepared to repeat a punishment many times before you will see a decrease in undesirable behavior. Therefore, decide in advance precisely what you will do each time a behavior occurs. It must be something that you can do relatively calmly and consistently.

3. The Punisher Must Be Intense

To be effective, a punisher must be intense. Often parents will begin with a low-level reaction to a child's behavior and gradually become more intense. For example, when a jealous older brother is harassing his little brother, you might sternly say, "Don't bother your brother." When he continues to shake something in the baby's face, you say in a more angry tone of voice, "I asked you not to do that!" When he persists in bothering his brother, you may finally give him a mild slap. If he continues to bother the baby more, he will get a good, hard slap.

The problem with the above approach is that the good hard slap will not be nearly as effective administered this way as it would have been had you given him one good hard slap the very first time he bothered his brother. Research has demonstrated repeatedly that if you gradually increase the intensity of a punisher it is not nearly as effective as administering the punisher in its full intensity the first time.

4. Punish the Behavior at the Beginning

Another finding is that punishment is far more effective if you administer it at the beginning of the unwanted behavior. If you allow the behavior to continue for some time your punishment will be much less effective. Punish the unwanted behavior the *instant* you see it beginning.

5. Punish the Behavior Immediately

For the punishment procedure to be effective you must administer the punisher immediately after your child commits the unwanted behavior. Especially with young children, withdrawing a privilege later on in the day will have no effect on an undesirable behavior that happened earlier. For example, tell your daughter that her friend must go home immediately after her grabby, unsharing behavior, and then actually ask her friend and parent to leave (it is helpful if you discuss this with the parent ahead of time so you don't hurt anyone's feelings). If you tell her that her friend cannot come to play tomorrow because she hasn't been sharing today, you will make her angry or upset but you will do nothing to change her grabbing, unsharing behavior in the future.

6. Never Sweeten a Punisher

Another very important precaution is to make sure that you never pair up positive reinforcement with punishment. It is especially undesirable to first punish your son and then to sit him down on your lap and lovingly explain to him why you had to do it. This sequence of behavior teaches him that he has to endure some discomfort in order to get your intense, undivided attention. This practice is probably the reason why some children seem as if they are "begging to be punished." For them, being punished has come to signify that they will get lots more attention.

You certainly will want to give your son explanations about your behavioral requirements and what it is you expect of him, but do so at some other time, not immediately following the punishment. Also, try to maintain a calm and controlled attitude as you punish a behavior—your angry and frustrated expressions of exasperation can sometimes be very interesting and therefore rewarding to your child.

7. Punish Every Instance of the Behavior

Once you decide that a particular behavior is entirely unacceptable and that you must resort to punishment, then from that point forward you should punish *every instance* of the behavior. The research on punishment clearly indicates that occasional punishment is not nearly as effective as punishment that follows every instance of the unwanted behavior (Kircher, Pear, and Martin). This means that when you decide that you will punish biting, you must stay right with your son with your punisher ready when he is interacting with his peers, so that you don't miss any occasions. If he bites two or three times and gets away with it, then your punishment will not be nearly as effective.

8. Model Alternative Behavior

Because of all of the potentially harmful effects of the punishment procedure, you want to be certain that you maximize its effectiveness when you use it. One way to increase the effectiveness of punishment is to help your child to develop an alternative behavior through the use of positive reinforcement. In the example of a girl pulling the cat's tail, you would deliberately model and then reward an alternative way of interacting with the cat, since these behaviors may not occur to your daughter. Show her some appropriate play behaviors, such as throwing paper balls to the cat, petting it softly, or dangling a string for it. Simply rewarding these desirable behaviors may eliminate the need for punishment altogether. If rewarding these appropriate behaviors is not enough, you can then punish inappropriate behavior of pulling the cat's tail, knowing that your child has some alternative behaviors to fall back on.

Sometimes you only need to redirect a behavior and not eliminate it altogether. For example, assume your son is inclined to hit other children with the sticks he loves to carry. The next time he has a stick you can help him to redirect the behavior by prompting him, "Hit the ground with the stick." When he does so, you can positively reinforce him by saying, "That's right, that is very good. You hit the ground." Encourage him to bang the fence and to hit stones with the stick and positively reinforce those behaviors: "That's good. It's good to hit the stones with the stick." Each time he hits his friend with the stick, however, you should immediately take the stick away and not give it back to him on that particular day, explaining to him, "We don't hit our friends with the stick. If you hit people, I have to take the stick away."

Punishment alone is particularly ineffective in the case of aggressive behavior of young children. If you analyze the purpose of the aggressive behavior you often find that your child has not yet learned some important necessary alternative behaviors. Your little boy may not have learned how to ask for what he wants, defend his rights with words, or get the attention of a friend.

When the purpose of aggression is to obtain a toy from a friend, in addition to preventing the aggressive behavior you should also teach the desirable behavior. Say to the child, "No, don't grab that toy from Evan. Ask Evan, 'May I see your truck for a minute? I'll give it right back.'" (See also the chapter on Modeling.)

Sometimes your daughter may hit or bite to prevent some other child from taking a toy away from her. To successfully eliminate this aggressive behavior, you must teach and positively reinforce some other appropriate self-protective and assertive behavior at the same time. Teach her to say, "No, this is my toy. Don't take it!" If she can't say something, teach her to hold the toy behind her back. Praise her when she successfully hangs onto her toy without biting or hitting.

At times your son may push or try to take a toy from a child who seems uninterested in him in order to get his attention. In this case, he needs help in thinking of ways to effectively get the attention of that playmate. Tell him, "Let's see if Mike wants to play cars with you. Ask him, 'Mike, do you want this car?'" If you are careful to teach alternative, desirable behaviors, you will be more successful in eliminating aggressive behaviors.

9. Restructure the Situation

Are there certain settings or times in which your child consistently misbehaves? Is your daughter particularly tired, hungry, jealous, or in need of attention at certain times? When you discover a pattern, try to restructure the situation to eliminate the feelings that promote her unacceptable behavior.

For example, I arranged a preschool in my home for my son, Ian, while I was teaching. When I came home from teaching, all the other parents returned to pick up their children. Many parents, teachers, and children wanted to speak to me. My son also wanted my attention since he had been away from me for six hours and other mothers were attending to their children. On the first few days after school, as I discussed with the teachers the events of the day or parents asked me questions about the program, Ian began to behave in some very undesirable ways. He became hyperactive and aggressive with the other children, slamming doors and throwing things.

It would have been simply inadequate to punish this wild behavior in this particular situation day after day. When I analyzed the situation, I decided that Ian was probably feeling quite neglected and was expressing through his bad behavior a very appropriate need for my attention after having been separated from me for six hours.

The solution to such a problem is to first try to change the situation which promotes the aggressive behavior. For me this meant arranging to speak to the teachers by telephone later on in the day and minimizing the conversations with parents when I first arrived at home. Changing these conditions was enough to eliminate the unacceptable behaviors. When I got home Ian eagerly showed me the work he had done at school that day.

Negative Reinforcement

Many people misunderstand the term negative reinforcement and use it when they mean to use the word punishment. As psychologists use the term negative reinforcement it refers to a procedure which actually increases behavior.

You may have accidentally employed this procedure yourself. Assume that your daughter is writing on the wall with her crayon, and, as you approach her to take her crayons away (a would-be punishment procedure), she says, "I'm sorry, I won't write on the wall. I'll write on the paper." As a result, you don't take her crayons away, and she then returns to coloring on the paper. What you should expect in the future from this sequence of events is that 1. There will be no decrease in her tendency to write on the wall, but 2. There will be an increase in her tendency to say, "I'm sorry" when she expects to be punished. Because you provided no aversive consequence to writing on the wall and since she did not lose her crayons, she will be just as likely to do it again as if you had permitted her to do so. Because she was able to avoid losing her crayons by saying, "I'm sorry, I won't do it again," she will be likely to say, "I'm sorry" in other similar circumstances because it averts punishment.

Sometimes you might accidentally use the negative reinforcement procedure because a particular event such as taking a bath, washing hair, or having a diaper changed becomes aversive to your child for a period of time. Your son may kick, scream, and thrash around trying to avoid having to get a diaper changed, or having his hair washed or combed, or having to take a bath. If his kicking and screaming is effective in avoiding having to get into the bathtub, or if it avoids having the diaper changed, then he will be much more likely to kick and scream in the future. You will have negatively reinforced his kicking and screaming by ceasing to do whatever it is he didn't want done. He will have learned that kicking and screaming can stop you, that he can avoid or escape whatever he finds unpleasant by increasing his kicking and screaming.

Over the years, I have seen many children who had a high rate of saying, "I'm sorry" along with a high rate of hitting other children, grabbing toys, screaming, and other highly unacceptable behaviors. Usually the sequence of events that taught the child to say, "I'm sorry" was this:

1. The child misbehaved.
2. The parent approached the child with a threatening facial expression and posture, looking as if he or she were ready to deliver some serious consequence.
3. The child would avoid any consequences by saying, "I'm sorry."

Sometimes parents even encourage a boy to say, "I'm sorry" by grabbing him by the arm, squeezing it tightly, dragging him over to his playmate, and saying through clenched teeth, "Tell him you are sorry." The child will be able to escape the arm squeeze and avoid any further physical punishment by saying, "I'm sorry." The effect on the child's behavior is that he continues to hit other children, to grab their toys, and to behave in an unsocialized fashion, but to follow each transgression by saying, "I'm sorry" whenever there is an adult present.

My feeling about "I'm sorry" is that these words should be ones that have some real significance and meaning to your child. If your son accidentally hurts someone and you can tell by his facial expression or his posture that he is truly sorry, you can help him learn to apologize by asking him, "Do you want to tell Casey that you are sorry that you hurt him? You can tell Casey that you are sorry if you want to." Then you can tell him yourself, "Joe is sorry, Casey. He didn't mean to hurt you." This way your son will learn to say these words when he is remorseful and not to mouth them to avoid punishment for his behavior. When you force a child to say, "I'm sorry" you may just as well force him to say, "Goobliegook" because the words have no meaning to him whatsoever. He will only be saying those words to escape your wrath.

In a home visit to one of my clients I observed this sequence when two sisters were playing and the older one hit the younger. As their mother approached them the older girl began to pat her crying sister softly. The mother responded to the nice touches and said, "That's right, play nicely with your sister." The older child, through many repetitions of this sequence, had learned to pat her sister nicely in order to avoid the punishment. But she continued to hit her and grab her toys and otherwise terrorize her much of the day. She had learned to immediately follow each hit or other behavior which made her sister cry with some gentle stroking to avoid the negative consequences.

In order to change the frequency of an undesirable behavior you have to ignore your child's saying, "I'm sorry" or the gentle stroking and provide some aversive consequences to the behavior. Remove a seized toy, put your child in time-out, or provide whatever other consequence you have decided upon. Remember that when you have decided that you must provide some punishing consequences for unacceptable behavior, it is important that you don't allow your child to escape or avoid the consequences. Once your child has committed the crime, saying "I'm sorry," begging, pleading, crying, or promising to reform *should not move you.* You will know that what you want is fewer unacceptable behaviors, not more begging, pleading, or promising.

Spoiling

In raising young children the *timing* of parent attention is a critical factor. Always consider the question, "If I do this now, what behavior will I reinforce?" To avoid the pitfall of unwittingly using an intermittent schedule of reinforcement, be certain always to evaluate your daughter's behavior before you attend to her or reward her.

If you have the time and inclination to rock your son to sleep or to play with him, then there is no problem with doing so, so long as you are not rewarding tantrums or badgering behavior. It is foolish to refuse to rock a child for fear of conditioning a habit, because habits maintained on continuous reinforcement are easy to extinguish. If you have a great deal of time to play with your children, then enjoy it and ignore warnings from relatives that you may be spoiling them and teaching them to demand too much attention. As long as you respond with either a prompt yes or a definite no and teach your child to discriminate and accept the occasions when the answer is no, then your child will not be "spoiled."

A child will exhibit behavior people refer to as "spoiled" when you reinforce tantrum behavior rather than civilized requests. When you find yourself being controlled by tantrums and obeying a child's requests for fear of the reaction if you say no, the child is "spoiled."

I believe that the term "spoiled child" should be reserved for children in whom tantrum behavior gets positively reinforced and not used to describe children to whom a parent pays a great deal of attention.

So long as you do what you want to do and you are not controlled by tantrums, you may indulge your child as you wish. We are all individuals and have different needs and tolerance levels for our children's behavior. There is no single correct formula regarding which behaviors should be reinforced, but many people seem to feel that they have the formula and will not hesitate to advise you.

You will be the one to decide the behaviors which you find the most important to establish or eliminate. You will never be able to please everyone, and your child will never be perfect. Also in some situations you will be weighing the relative importance of your control of your child's behavior versus your child's creativity. The most important factor in using behavior modification successfully is to *think things through* and make decisions about behavior in advance so that you will not be influenced by well-meaning friends and family or your own fluctuating moods.

13

Choosing Behavioral Goals for Older Children

What Kind of Behavior Do You Want to Require?

One way of deciding this most important question is to consider the kinds of behaviors that work well for children in school. After extensive interviews with twenty teachers, whose students ranged from four-year-old preschoolers to third and fourth graders, I distilled a number of behaviors that teachers agreed upon as important to a child's adjustment in school. Most teachers agreed that

1. Children need to be able to share school equipment. This means that they cannot act as if something that is school equipment belongs to them.
2. They must treat school materials with respect. This includes not only desks and school supplies, but books and materials that other children have brought in to share with the classroom.
3. They need to be able to speak for themselves, to ask questions when they don't understand something, and to ask for more information when things are unclear.
4. The child needs to be able to be quiet when either another child or the teacher is speaking.
5. Children especially need the ability to *listen attentively* while either the teacher or a classmate is speaking.
6. They need to be able to *concentrate* on the task at hand, and
7. They need to be able to pay attention and to follow directions.

Teachers described the emotional characteristics of children who thrive in a classroom situation and a number of clear characteristics emerged. Children who thrive in the classroom have these abilities:

1. They are able to consider other children's feelings, and they are empathic and compassionate in their dealings with children. Teachers described them as kind, considerate, helpful, warm, and friendly.
2. They are also described as *assertive,* able to verbalize their feelings, whether they are happy, sad, or angry. It is not that these children do not cry or have their bad moments, but they are able to verbalize or articulate their feelings without being abusive to other people.
3. Children who do exceptionally well in the classroom have an ability to bring people together and *negotiate.* They do not need all the praise. If someone else has organized a game, and some participants are not happy about it, the successful child is one who is able to suggest some modification of the game so that everyone is happy and able to participate. This ability, to work for group harmony rather than to obtain praise and admiration, is a prominent feature of successful children.

Then teachers were asked to describe behaviors that characterized children who are obviously *unsuccessful* or *maladapted* in the classroom. The most frequently cited behaviors were 1) Children not sharing equipment and acting as if equipment belonged to them. 2) Stealing school equipment or other children's belongings 3) Angry, physically abusive and verbally abusive behavior to other children and 4) Being unable to sit in one place for a required amount of time, and 5) Being unable to finish a task.

By studying the behaviors that teachers agree are characteristic of a well-adjusted student and of a student who has problems in the classroom, you can establish some goals for your child's behavior in that setting. From birth until two and a half, you and you alone have to live with the behavior of your child, and therefore you can decide, on the basis of your own preferences and personality, what behaviors you will or will not allow. But, because you must send your child out into the world, you will want to teach him the behaviors that will be required in the environment to which you will send him. After he reaches two and a half, regardless of your individual values or your own tolerance for certain kinds of behaviors,

I think it is wise to look at your goals for your child's behavior in terms of the settings where you will send him. Your goal will be to promote the behaviors that will help him get along as well as possible with his teachers and his peers.

Socialization for Older Children

The ability to get along well with peers is characteristic of children who do well in school. As parents, you want your children to be well-liked, to have friends at school and in the neighborhood. By four years of age some children seem to be very well liked and some children are significantly less well received by their peers.

There is data that tells what makes some children more popular than others. A number of studies have found that there are specific things that well-liked children do. You can help your child to learn to do them. Well-liked children know how to act friendly to a new child in school or on the playground. They are likely to ask the new child questions, to give him information, and to invite him to visit. They suggest games and play that their peers like and join. They are likely to give praise to their friends when they do something well: "That's a nice picture" or "I like that building" or "That's a good tower." They play constructively and cooperatively. They are able to work as a team; they would, for example, suggest working together to dig tunnels rather than protect their own space. They seem to understand the rules of their agemates, and know how to *take turns* and *compromise*. They are usually described as generally positive in their peer interactions and as knowing how to have fun and come up with good ideas for playing.

One behavior that is strikingly absent is aggressive behavior. Well-liked children are rarely aggressive. Popular children seem to agree more with other children when playing than do unpopular ones. When they do disagree, well-liked children seem to be able to offer some constructive alternatives along with their disagreement.

Popular children have strategies for entering into a group of ongoing play. First, they stand on the sidelines and figure out what the flow of the activity is. Then they make some statement that shows that they approve and want to particiate in the kind of exchanges and play that are going on. The well-liked child is often helpful! "Here's a bucket that you could use." He is also very likely to initiate interactions by asking "Can I play with you?" or "Will you play with me?"

Children who are rejected by their peers are likely to be socially inept. Researchers have described unpopular children as "lacking knowledge of peer norms or values." (Ladd and Oden). Often they act inappropriately, doing things such as standing on the table in the lunchroom, or they are distractable, hyperactive, or aggressive. They have trouble handling conflicts or disagreement and are much more likely to hit or push a child who takes their ball than to solve the problem verbally. They will disrupt other children's play with their unsuccessful attempts to enter into it, such as toppling the children's blocks in order to get attention. When they do sit down to play with someone they often will play uncooperatively — insist on building tunnels by themselves and complain if someone tries to work in their spot. They may not stick to their task but may wander off to do something unrelated. They may talk a lot, but it isn't communicative. Sometimes they ask questions and then give their own answers rather than waiting for an interaction; "Do you like handball, I don't like it. I'd rather play back stop." Unpopular children express disagreement by giving commands without giving any alternative — "No, don't put it there" — and by crying or whining. Unpopular children are often described as *bossy* in disagreements.

Very often an unpopular child will try to initiate a relationship by just hovering silently around a group of playing children or by making aggressive or inappropriate responses. In this way he is off to a bad start before he even begins. When trying to enter into an ongoing game or group at play, and unpopular child is likely to 1) Disagree with what's going on: "That's not how you play that" and 2) Make statements about himself and his opinions that don't relate to what's going on: "My dad's going to buy me a new fishing rod." These strategies are not successful, and the child is rejected or ignored.

The problem with rejected children is that they have a very high chance of staying rejected for a great number of years. This isn't because the children in the groups remain the same, but because even in new groups of different children the rejected child tends to remain at the bottom of the social scale. Those who are not liked in one group tend to not be liked in another group.

Rejected children are likely to be rejected all through childhood, and their interactions with children tend to stay negative. One important reason to do someting to alter the behavior of the rejected child is that rejected children seem to have a lot more behavior problems than their agemates. Boys in particular are likely to become increasingly aggressive over time, and this adds to the likelihood of their being rejected even more frequently, creating a cycle of aggression and rejection.

Not only does the unpopular child have problems in childhood, but research has found that children who are unpopular with their peers are more likely to have a number of problems later in life. These problems are serious ones: dropping out of school, delinquency, being discharged from the military for bad conduct, and mental health problems. The children who are at risk are the *rejected children* rather than the ignored ones. Children who interact very little with their peers are not necessarily at greater risk of problems than the more sociable child. But there *is* a relationship between the children who are rejected by other children and later problems. This means that simply getting your child to interact with other children is not going to solve the problem of the disliked child. It isn't because he doesn't have enough interactions that he has problems, it's what he does when he plays with children that is the problem.

There is some encouraging research, however, that indicates that even children who have already developed a lot of negative social behaviors and are reliably rejected by their peers can be successfully coached to learn behaviors that increase their likability. They can learn *to play more cooperatively* and *to pay attention, to share, to communicate, to give support and encouragement to their peers,* and, as a result, to increase their social status among their friends. Most of the research was conducted with children in the third and fourth grade who are eight or nine years old or older. If children already nine and ten years old can learn to be more skillful socially, parents can certainly teach their younger children some of the same skills.

First you many want to observe your child with her friends a number of times. Try to go to her school and sit on the sidelines while she plays at lunch recess. Take the following checklist along and evaluate her skills. Do the same in the neighborhood and at home when she invites friends to play. Then you can work with her and coach her in her social skills.

Desirable Behaviors

____	1.	Asks questions
____	2.	Gives information
____	3.	Invites child to visit
____	4.	Makes good suggestions for play
____	5.	Gives praise to friends
____	6.	Expresses appreciation
____	7.	Plays cooperatively
____	8.	Shares
____	9.	Takes turns
____	10.	Compromises
____	11.	Is *agreeable* to friends' ideas, rather than argumentative or bossy.
____	12.	Offers alternative ideas when disagreeing
____	13.	Successfully enters ongoing play
____	14.	Can initiate play
____	15.	Communicates well—waits for and responds to friends' comments

Undesirable Behaviors

____	1.	Behavior that is inapproprate to the occasion.
____	2.	Easily distractable
____	3.	Hyperactive—runs from one thing to another
____	4.	Aggressive—hits or pushes
____	5.	Disruptive
____	6.	Plays uncooperatively—whines or complains if someone tries to participate
____	7.	Talks without communicating or interacting
____	8.	Disagrees negatively—without alternatives, bossy
____	9.	Inappropriate ways to initiate or enter group of play

You can help your child learn to ask questions by making suggestions to her: "John's ball looks new, why don't you ask him when he got it and who got it for him." Encourage her to give information: "It would be nice if you would tell Barbara about the games you play at recess and where you play them." Help her pay attention to the interests and likes and dislikes of her peers. Ask "What games do the kids seem to like at school?" "Who else plays backstop?" "Who likes to play handball?" "Maybe you could ask Kelly to play a game of handball today if you want to play with her."

You will want to work on your child's communication skills between the ages three to six. It is not enough for him to be able to use words and sentences, he needs to be able to communicate clearly. Help him learn to use full descriptions: "Hand me that big brown rock with the orange flecks in it." To teach such clarity in communication is a fairly simple process: ask him to give clear descriptions that tell you exactly what he wants to do: "You want some baking soda? Tell me how you would like to play with it and exactly what you will do." Play "describing games" in which you both think up as many adjectives as you can to dscribe toys, furniture, rocks, and so forth.

Also teach him to *exchange information* by asking questions of other children. "Ask Tony where he got that nice transformer." With continued coaching your child will become a skilled question-asker, which is a very important social skill that he will use through adulthood. "Where do you live? What school do you go to? What grade are you in? Do you like your teacher? Can you ride a bike?" Help him learn to ask these kinds of questions and then wait for and respond to the answer.

Another skill that helps children to make friends is *establishing a common ground*. Children need to be able to find something that they can do together. The technique is a sort of mutual interview to find some shared interests. Barbara might say, "Do you like water guns? I have two of them." "Do you like to ride bicycles?" "I like to play kickball on the garage, do you?"

Another process by which children make friends is disclosure of feelings. When a child expresses her own feelings and vulnerabilities, the friend is likely to do the same, which allows a feeling of shared experience to develop. Some opinions that children might share with each other are such things as, "I hate school, do you?" As they get to know one another they can reveal more: "I'm afraid of the dark so I sleep with a light on." "I'm afraid of the ocean. I'm afraid I'll get knocked over by the waves."

Another important skill is that of reciprocating in conversation. Help your child learn to add to or comment on what his friend says to encourage his friend to continue to speak. Reciprocity develops when he first shows interest in what his friend has to say and then adds to the conversation. This is distinctly different from the age of parallel play in which children simply speak egocentrically. In a reciprocal conversation, Zachary might say, "Did you see Casey's sister's hair?" and your child would answer "Yes, I think she's a punk rocker." If your child answers with an unrelated comment,

"My dad's going to buy me a new computer," he needs coaching. In positive reciprocity there is an interaction; your child adds to the comment that was made and keeps the conversation going.

You will also want to teach your child *conflict resolution:* the ability to negotiate and compromise so that the play can go on and feuds can end. When you have one bicycle and one scooter and two children who both want the scooter, your child may suggest "All right, I'll ride the bicycle to the store, and you can ride the scooter. Then we'll trade, and I'll ride it back."

In the previously mentioned studies, unpopular children who were coached by an adult in these behaviors improved their ratings in the classroom. A year later, in different classrooms, their status was even higher than it was immediately after coaching. Only six sessions over the course of a month made lasting changes in these children's behaviors. This is most encouraging. As a parent you can have far greater influence on your children if you carefully consider what it is they need to learn and instruct them on the kinds of behaviors that will make them more likable to their peers.

Behavioral Goals and Temperament

With regard to the issue of temperament, you certainly have to realize that temperament contributes to child behavior. But you also must recognize that temperament is not the *only* determinant of your child's behavior. Environmental factors such as the way you respond to your child, your requirements for her behavior, and the behaviors that you allow will shape the way her temperament gets displayed as she gets older. Your role as a parent of a difficult child is particularly important because statistically the difficult child is more likely than other children to develop later behavior disorders. But your child's inborn temperamental differences will be constantly interacting with the environment. Her temperament will be expressed in a certain style of behavior but the pattern of behavior she develops will be influenced by the environmental circumstances and the consequences which follow her behaviors. This means that you can have a well-adjusted child despite her being a difficult baby. However, all parents, particularly those with difficult babies, must be *aware* of *their goals* for their child's behavior, and assess their progress and evaluate their goals every few months. With continued attention you can teach your children those behaviors that will help them to adapt to the situations they will enter when they venture out into the world.

I like to think about temperament in children as similar to different breeds in dogs. The chihuahua and the German shepherd are both dogs, but the nature of the breeds is clearly different from the beginning. You wouldn't expect a German shepherd to stay indoors all day because you recognize that a big dog needs lots of room to run and exercise. You wouldn't expect him to sit in a small car for an entire day while you run your errands; this would be too confining for him. Neither would we expect a chihuahua to guard our home for us. Yet both of these animals can be trained to be obedient, they both can be trained to sit, lie down, stay, and to heel. There are certain requirements you must make of all dogs if you want them to be acceptable around people. Both breeds can be trained not to jump up on visitors or furniture and to accept some strangers in the house. Some breeds need more lessons or training to learn these behaviors, but all can learn them.

Children, too, respond differently to the same patterns or same types of parenting because of inborn temperamental characteristics. You must consider the characteristics of your child that make him unique. However, for his own growth, you must still insist upon and require certain important behaviors. You will want to be certain of progress toward increasing maturity, particularly with behaviors that are going to be required and expected of your child in school and in social situations.

The Easy Child Becoming A Person

It is true that most easy children do not develop behavior problems. Of course, a series of tragedies, abuse, or neglect, as well as routine inconsistency or inappropriate demands can result in behavior problems even with a very adaptable child. However even with loving parents, problems can result from differences in behaviors allowed or required by parents and those allowed or required in other settings such as school and in relationships with peers. When there is a conflict between your values regarding behavior and the behavioral expectations of the child's friends and teachers, your child will suffer.

One child I treated was obviously of an easy temperament, but he had trouble adusting to school from kindergarten until third grade and had difficulty relating to his peers. His parents brought him to therapy because he was expressing an increasing anxiety about going to school and was becoming school-phobic. The problem took a while to sort out, but by observing his behavior at school and at home, it became apparent that Joseph had unrealistic expectations regarding the amount of time and attention people should pay to him when he spoke. Because Joseph was an extremely bright child, he had a lot of complicated, involved, and usually very intelligent thoughts about things. At school he expected and persisted in trying to get the teacher to listen to long and involved answers whenever she asked a question. The teacher expressed her feeling that Joseph was like a self-centered adult who only wanted to hear himself talk. In his conversations with other children, his descriptions of things he had done or would like to do were always far longer than they had patience for. As a result, Joseph was ignored by his classmates, and his teacher avoided calling on him in class.

Home observations gave some clues as to the origin of his problem. Joseph's parents were very loving and *very* involved. They were very impressed with Joseph's verbal abilities. As a result, whenever Joseph spoke at home, they stopped their conversation immediately and both parents' eyes would focus on Joseph. Joseph was allowed to talk and explain and go on with his description of things for however long he desired. In fact, Joseph monopolized 90 percent of the family's conversation time at dinner, and whenever Joseph was in a room with either or both of his parents, he did about 90 percent of the talking. In a home observation, I noticed that Joseph would not even continue his speech unless he had his mother's undivided attention. He would say, "Mommy, mommy, mommy" until she stopped doing whatever she was doing and *looked* at him; then he would continue with his conversation. Joseph repeated this kind of behavior with the children on the playground. To initiate play or speak to them, Joseph would pull on their sleeves or call their names until they looked at him. He would say, "Paul, Paul, Paul, Paul" until Paul looked at him. Then he would begin to talk. If Paul looked away, he would again start saying, "Paul, Paul, Paul." Eventually Paul would tire of this requirement for eye contact and run off, leaving Joseph very unsatisfied. Joseph's well-meaning, very loving parents had taught Joseph some very unrealistic expectations regarding the amount of attention he would get when he spoke. They were both interested in their son but sacrificed their own need for adult conversation and for attention from one another to focus on Joseph. In so doing, they taught Joseph some behaviors that did not work at all in the school environment or with his friends in the neighborhood.

Being an easy child—adaptable, good-natured, loving, and friendly—doesn't mean that the child will *automatically* learn to take turns in talking. *Sharing,* one of the requirements that most teachers cited as important for children in a classroom, includes being able to share talking time as well. One of the important skills for a child, regardless of temperament, is that the child be able to listen to other children and *interact,* with a give and take in verbal exchanges. This means that your rights as parents are important not only for you but for your child. If you have only one child, it is particularly important that you as parents consider your own needs as well as the needs of your child. In our child-centered culture, it is a common mistake for parents to be overly indulgent and put their children's needs above their own. Oftentimes this is *not* in your child's best interest. You should remember that it will be easier for her to share and be compassionate with you than with friends later, so training in these abilities is best begun at home.

Andy was another child whose parents taught him behaviors which were not adaptive to the classroom. Andy's parents were concerned with their children's individuality and with the school system teaching children to be "sheep." They encouraged creativity, and Andy was quite creative in his art-work—constructions with scraps— and had novel ideas about science and experiments. At home, his parents allowed defiant and disobedient behavior and described Andy as being independent and an individual. Andy was rarely *required* to comply with his parents' requests for order or for following rules. When Andy went to school, he was unwilling to take instructions from his teacher, he was unwilling to follow the regulations on the playground, and he disregarded the rules in learning situations in school. He wasn't able to finish his work when he didn't *feel* like doing it. If Andy had not been required to attend a public school, if his parents had planned to instruct him at home, their training would not have been a problem. Unfortunately, Andy attended public school, the usual six hours a day. Andy's "uniqueness," creativity, and disregard for the rules of the teachers and the school system resulted in his being sent to the office as punishment, his being kept after school to finish his work, frequent parent-teacher conferences, and repeated negative interactions with his teachers.

When Andy was brought in for therapy, both he and his parents were objecting to the requirements of the school system. They objected to the requirement of certain paperwork, which they viewed as a waste of time, and the requirement that children progress through a sequence of readers when Andy's reading was at a higher level. The point here is not whether the parents were right or wrong. They might have been perfectly right about the inadequacies of the current public school system; schools often do not appreciate creativity or uniqueness. The issue here was that Andy was becoming more and more hostile and aggressive, feeling very alienated and dissatisfied for six hours a day, five days a week. He was unable to get along with his friends on the playground and was in an endless power struggle with his teacher. Andy suffered because at the age of seven, he was unable to make a discriminaton between independent thinking and disobedience to necessary rules. While Andy's parents wanted to teach independence and creativity, they taught him a contempt for authority and inability to follow rules. As a result, his academic progress was delayed; his spelling, reading, and math were all well below his capabilities. His feelings of self-esteem suffered as a result of the frequent negative interactions with his teacher.

Andy's parents would have done better to teach him some ways of being creative while *also* being able to follow the rules and go along with the group when necessary. Even a temperamentally easy child will suffer from a disparity in values or behaviors taught to him at home and those required at school. You will want to think about where you will send your child, what he or she will have to live with, and be certain not to teach your child to behave in ways that are distinctly different from those that are going to be required at school or in relationships with his peers.

The Slow To Warm Up Child Becoming a Person

The child who characteristically reacts to new situations with initial withdrawal and then slow adaptaton needs help in learning to cope with new settings and people. As opposed to the difficult child, the slow to warm up child will usually show a *quiet* withdrawal from a new situation and then gradual adaptation to it. Although her first negative reactions will be on the quiet side, this youngster needs to have repeated exposures to new situations and be allowed to adapt slowly and in her own way. Take her to many new situations where she has the opportunity to make her gradual warm-up, and she will begin to recognize her own pattern. She will learn that she eventually does warm up, relax, and enjoy new places.

When she is four years old, you can explain to her in a gentle way that though she tends to feel uncomfortable in new situations at first, gradually she gets used to it.

You might stay with her at parties when you can and allow her to hang around with the mothers for most of the time until she learns how to handle birthday parties. She would probably have to be at camp for a week before she would be able to enjoy it, so it wouldn't be worth it for you to send her for one week only. Keep her in some organized activity during the summer instead of letting her have a whole summer away from organized activity, children, and teachers, so that she remembers how to get along in that kind of situation. Be patient and allow her to adapt in her own time and without a lot of pressure. You may want to try team sports to allow her to learn to get along in groups. For example, there are soccer leagues for children as young as five. Also t-ball and basketball leagues begin at age six in many cities.

You must remember not to be discouraged by her initial withdrawal from new situations. Your slow to warm up child is not going to be happy about soccer practice, t-ball, or any other practice on the first day. It will be almost certain that she will not want to be in the group or continue the sport after the first practice. If you require that she try it six times before she decides whether or not she wants to continue, she may be thoroughly enjoying herself by the sixth time. If she wants to give it up after having tried it six times, she probably just doesn't like it.

If your youngster has a pattern of initial withdrawl and gradual adaptation, you will want to help her expanding her horizons as much as possible. Without the benefit of repeated opportunities to adapt to new situations, you child may be very tense at the beginning of each new school year, avoid most social situations, and become socially isolated. So continually take her to new places; try ballet, rope skipping, or art classes. The more she adjusts and meets new people, the less glaring this behavioral style will appear. Help your child move along in the direction of increasing maturity and better social development. Rather than avoiding situations your child finds difficult, develop a plan to help her progress in those areas.

The Difficult Child Becoming a Person

If your child has a difficult temperament you will want to give a considerable amount of thought to your goals for her behavior and the direction you want to take. The problem is to strike a balance between recognizing the individual behavioral style and responses of your temperamentally difficult child and yet requiring that she continually make progress in developing the behaviors that will be required of her. You need to make some demands for change and growth so that your child will become competent in handling life problems. In order to grow and develop she will need to experience some stress. *It is not possible for your difficult child to grow and mature without experiencing some upsetting demands.*

Problems can result from either being too rigid and demanding or too indulgent with a difficult child. I have focused on the importance of being flexible, patient, and understanding with a difficult infant from birth to two and a half or three. Because a young baby really is not reasonable and cannot change his moods or schedules, it makes sense to be somewhat indulgent in the early years. It is easier for everyone if you simply recognize the nature of your baby and adapt to his needs for consistency in scheduling naps and meals and avoiding unnecessary car trips. However, after your child reaches the age of three, you really need to start making demands for mature behavior; your child needs to begin developing the socialized behaviors that will enable him to get along in school and in social situations.

The trouble is that as you make demands for increasingly mature behavior, your difficult baby will *respond intensely and negatively to the stress.* His reaction will be punishing to you. If you ask him to do something he doesn't want to do, he will make you pay for it by whining, crying, withdrawing his love, or tantrum behavior. It is far more difficult to require the mature behaviors and far easier to give in to his tantrum or refusal. It is easier for you to allow him to remain at the level he is on than to ask him to go forward. Unfortunately, you do him no favors when you give in to his terrorist behaviors. This is why it is so important to *think through the goals* for your child and to keep him moving in a direction of increasing maturity. You have to be brave and strong and prepared for the intense negative reaction when you insist on progress.

Sharing and Cooperative Play

What kind of behaviors might you want to require of your child? For your two and a half year old, you will probably want to think about requiring *sharing and cooperative behaviors*. Although you may have been teaching sharing behaviors by rewarding them, there will be times when your difficult baby refuses to share. Because she responds so intensely when someone touches her new bicycle or new records, it would be much easier to give into her and put away the new toys when someone comes to visit. While it might be all right to put away one special new toy she has not yet played with, this can easily evolve into a pattern in which your difficult baby will want you to put away any toy another child begins to enjoy. This tactic can develop until any time a visiting child wants to play with a toy, the difficult owner will say, "Mommy, put this away." If you continue to put away toys because your daughter doesn't want to share them, the child will never develop the ability to share. It is easy to come up with rationalizations or excuses for giving in to a difficult baby. One mother said, "I want him to *want* to share and if I force him he may not *want* to." This is an excuse, a way of avoiding his tantrums, and, it is not good for him. Remember that children who are the most successful with their peers in school are ones who can share both equipment and their own things with other children.

Successful children also are able to cooperate and work together. The difficult baby will probably have trouble cooperating. He may want to play *alone* with his blocks in his own way. Because the normal developmental step would be for children around age four to begin cooperative play, it is important that you teach your child to be able to cooperate. If he has a friend to play at his house, *require* him to play cooperatively. When he is building a tower or block construction and cries that he doesn't want his friend to add a block, this is an antisocial and undesirable response. Sit down with both children and instruct them in cooperation and taking turns. Your child may cry and protest and refuse to play with the blocks. *Let him cry and protest while you continue to play with the other child in a cooperative way.* When his tantrum doesn't work and he begins to cooperate, reward the behavior. It is tempting to look at his desire to play alone as independence, or reframe the behavior and think about it as a need to be creative. It is better for your child if you face the real problem. He needs to learn to give in to the desires of his friend regarding where the construction should go or how it should look. He needs to learn to consider the feelings and wants of that visiting child and modify his own wants accordingly. Certainly you're not asking that your child make *only* cooperative structures and that he *never* be allowed to be creative and individual. But if he is playing with a friend, his refusal to play cooperatively is not likely to be a result of an intense need for creativity and individuality; it's more likely to be a result of his not wanting to consider anybody's desires but his own. It's easier for us as parents to attribute more sophisticated or socially desirable motives for our chldren's behavior than to recognize the selfishness and immaturity of the behavior. But, to promote your child's growth and development and increase his ability to get along with peers, it is very important that you teach him to play cooperatively.

Teaching Cooperation to the Difficult Child

You can sit down with your child and teach him how to cooperate. First prompt cooperation: "Okay, Jason, you wanted a block here. Now where do you want yours to go, Danny?" "Okay, now Danny had a turn. Now Jason, where would you like the next one to go?" and "That's good, you're taking turns and you're cooperating." Use the word *cooperating*. "Yes, you are cooperating, you are working together. Together you are making something, that's cooperating."

As your child makes progress you might consider using some primary reinforcer, a couple of raisins or some crackers and cheese or chips. Tell him, "I'm so happy you're cooperating! Let's have a little party while we're working on this together. It's fun to do things together; we're cooperating." Then use the word *cooperating* in another activity. Take them to the beach or the sandbox to make sand castles and encourage them to cooperate. If your child objects and doesn't want a stone or shell in a certain place, you must teach him to regard his friend's feelings. "That's Danny's turn, he wants to put the shell there. He likes it there, and we're doing this together. Danny's feelings count because we are cooperating." If he cries and hollers and has a fit and tries to remove it, then you simply push him aside, saying, "No, Danny wants to have it there, and it must stay there." You cannot give in to Jason's wishes to remove the shell or stone just because he cries and whines and acts unpleasant. If you do teach him to disregard his friend's feelings and that only *his* feelings and wants count, he will not be a good friend to anyone when he gets to school.

Remember that your difficult child *can* eventually adapt to and conform to consistent rules just as an easier child can. Her first reaction may be negative and intense, but she eventually will adapt to a rule if you are consistent. You will realize the truth of this if you think about the fact that you *never* allow your daughter to put things in light sockets, play with the stove, or lean out a high window. She may have protested when you refused to allow her to put things in the light socket, but you were firm and clearly meant business. Therefore, she learned that she must *never* do that thing and now abides by the rules. If you have the same degree of firmness and consistency with your rules for mature behavior, you will find that your difficult child will adapt, will abide by the rules, and will develop increasingly mature behavior.

Your rules must be simply and clearly conceptualized and stated: "When you have a friend here to play, you must share your toys, you must share." It is not a question of whether she feels like sharing today or if she's in a good mood and wants to share. The rule must be "If you have a friend to play, you must share your toys or your friend will go home." If this is the rule, your child will know it. If you will not allow her to grab toys away from another child no matter how many tantrums she throws, then she will learn that she cannot grab things away from her friends. If you sometimes give in to her tantrums, because you make excuses for her behavior, she will *not* learn the rule. If you allow her to be possessive of a toy you think she likes especially well or you allow her to be possessive of her toys because she seems tired and under the weather today, then you reward her uncooperative behavior and make it far more difficult for her to learn the mature behaviors. Would you, because she is tired, allow her to put a metal wire into the light socket? Just as you would not allow this kind of behavior with matters of safety, you must not allow this kind of behavior in matters of learning mature behavior either. *The rules must be consistent.*

If you insist on sharing and cooperation, she will adapt to the rule. The arguments about who gets first choice of cookie, which chair at the table, the prettiest glass or cup will end. She will have a social skill that will help her whenever she has someone to her home and will teach her to think about what her friend would like and to offer that. She will have learned to think about what someone else wants rather than what she alone wants.

Teaching Consideration to the Difficult Child

When your child is five years old (or even younger), you can begin to help your child develop concern for the feelings of his friends. When he is having a friend for lunch or dinner, talk to him about what his friend likes to eat. "Let's call him and find out what he likes for lunch. You talk to your friend about what he would like to have. You can give him some choices." His guest should determine the lunch menu or the movie they watch.

Depending on your child's progress between six and seven, you may want to introduce the rule "Guests first." When you are serving your child and his friend cookies or pieces of fruit, his friend should select the ones he wants *first*. Of course, your difficult one may complain that his guest got the bigger one and throw a tantrum. You must insist firmly, "Guests choose first which ones they want, and that is the rule." When it comes time to take turns doing something with a toy, going down a slide or riding a bicycle, the simple rule should be "Guests go first." Then you will have no more discussion about who will go first. Your difficult child will *always* want to be first unless you teach him this rule. If you try to do things fairly by flipping a coin, he will be happy if it comes up his turn, but will be very unhappy if it comes up the other child's turn. It is easier and more helpful to him to ask him to follow the simple "Guests first" rule. You can explain that this is the way grown-ups do things. Tell him that when you have guests for dinner, you offer them the best seats so they have the nicest view from the window. Teach him that having friends over means that you treat them nicely and try to make sure they have a good time. Tell him that the way he can do that as a little person is to let guests go first.

In the beginning of this training, your difficult child may have a tantrum. She may cry and say that you are thinking more about someone else's feelings than hers. You may have feelings of guilt; you may begin to think that perhaps you *are* being unkind and unfair to your own child. But you must think in terms of your goals for your child's behavior. You are thoughtful of your child. You conduct a great deal of your life according to her wants and needs. You treat her very nicely. She must learn to treat other people nicely as well, and she won't learn this unless you require her to do so.

Some parents think that if they treat their own children with respect and consideration, modeling alone will teach their children to do the same with others. *This is simply not true.* Your child needs to be encouraged and, at times, required to attend to the needs and feelings of others for her empathy to develop. Otherwise you will teach her that everyone needs to think about *her* needs only. If you don't act as if her friends' needs are important, she will not notice her friends' needs.

Your difficult child's intensely negative reactions make it difficult for her to learn to be empathic. And so you really need to concentrate on her development of this capacity if you consider it important. An easy child, who does not feel so intensely about anything, finds it far easier to consider the wants and needs of someone else. You must help your difficult child develop the habit of thinking about the needs and feelings of other people and the ability to suppress her own feelings. Everyone needs to know how to control him- or herself; everyone needs to learn to restrain our negative feelings at times in order to get along with people. The emotional intensity that a difficult child experiences makes living and learning such lessons a difficult process. But don't let your empathy for your child cloud your vision of what is best for her. The easiest thing to do with a difficult child is to indulge her, spoil her, and put off requiring mature behavior. You truly show your love for your child when you help her develop a potential for getting along well with people. You know that in the long run she will be happier because of it. If you avoid the issues when she is little, you will face more difficult ones later.

Withdrawal As Weapon

Sometimes a difficult child learns to express her intense negative reactions by withdrawal rather than tantrums. This happens when tantrums are not rewarded but withdrawal behavior gets lots of pleading or attention. One family came in for therapy after the child's behavior ruined a beautiful seventh birthday party. For her seventh birthday, Maria invited five little girlfriends to a pool party. Maria's mother decorated the house with crepe paper and balloons, organized several games, made a homemade checkerboard cake, and she and Maria made ice cream. On the day of the party, Maria was having a wonderful time until she won a game of pin-the-tail-on-the-donkey. Her mother pointed out that she had a table full of presents and that the game prizes were for the guests. Maria wanted one of the prizes, and her reaction to her mother's argument was intense and negative. She announced, "Well, then I don't want to be at the party." She went to her room and refused to come out.

Her friends missed her and took turns trying to talk her into coming out. Her mother begged and pleaded with Maria to return to the party, but she refused. Maria had a seven-year history of manipulative control and punishing her family by withdrawing when they did not do exactly what she wanted. By age seven her reactions were so intense and negative that she could not control them, even when her behavior clearly ruined her own birthday party.

Another mother of a difficult child was giving her five year old rides across the pool on her back. After a while, she told Laurel not to hold onto her any longer because the pool was too shallow and she wanted to swim lengths. Laurel leaped onto her shoulders anyway, and her mother scraped her foot on the bottom of the pool. She screamed at Laurel, partly as a result of the pain. Laurel got out of the pool, went to her room, and closed the door. Laurel's mother expected her back after a brief trip to the bathroom and was planning to play with her some more. She went to Laurel's room and begged her to come back, but Laurel refused. She hadn't liked the tone of voice her mother had used, and she was punishing her mother by withdrawing herself. Whenever her mother tried to discipline Laurel or used a tone of voice that Laurel didn't like, Laurel would simply withdraw herself. Her mother's sweet supplications and pleas for interaction rewarded this behavior. When Laurel was rewarded for her intense negative reaction, she was prevented from learning anything about other people's feelings. As Laurel's mother became aware of the pattern, she realized the degree to which she had been controlled by Laurel's withdrawal and began to simply ignore Laurel when she withdrew, letting her stay in her room and miss the swim time. When the withdrawal didn't work, Laurel stopped withdrawing. Laurel had the opportunity to learn more about other people's feelings and reasons for raising their voice at certain times. Naturally, changing long-practiced patterns of behavior is difficult; preventing such patterns is best.

On her eighth birthday, Dana's family took Dana and three friends to Sea World. Dana became upset with her mother and refused to enter the park, saying that she didn't want to go. Dana was willing to miss Sea World, to make her mother and father and other girls very upset, and to have all of them miss Sea World because of her intense anger. Dana's mother and father pleaded with her for an hour in the parking lot while all of the girls waited. Finally, Dana agreed to accompany them after being bribed by her mother to enter the park. She was promised to have some friends spend the night the following weekend if she would enter Sea World. Is there a better solution? Absolutely yes! If her parents were thinking about Dana's behavior *in the long run* rather than at that very moment, they would have allowed Dana to experience the consequences of her behavior. Her mother and father should have agreed that if Dana didn't want to go into the park, she didn't have to. Then either the mother or the father should have taken Dana home with a baby sitter and returned to the park with the other three girls. If giving in to such intense anger had resulted in a loss of enough positive reinforcement, Dana would have become less likely to do it again.

Events such as took place on these two birthday parties are the kinds of things to expect if you beg and plead with children in response to temper tantrums. If you reward their fits over little things or respond to their intense anger and withdrawal, you will find yourself in increasingly strenuous and stressful situations. As they get older, the consequences of their negative reactions become even more far-reaching, and you and other people suffer enormously as well. It is very important, therefore, that you don't reward this kind of intense negative reaction. It is far easier not to reward this kind of behavior in a young child than it is to change a seven or eight year old when the consequences are far more wide-reaching.

If, when you insist that your three year old play cooperatively with his friends, he says, "Well then I'm not playing," then let him go. You play with his friends and let your little one play alone. If he intensifies his negative reactions and screams and cries, then consider time out or sending his friends home.

Be careful that you don't fall into the trap of not asking for mature behavior from your difficult one in an attempt to avoid stressful situations. Some parents become very clever at anticipating all the objections of their difficult one and have learned never to say no if they can possibly avoid it. For example, they would expect him to want the prize at the birthday party and have extras. Unfortunately if your goal is to avoid saying no to spare your child frustration, he will never learn to behave maturely. His friends will not have the same goal for him, and he will not be able to get along with his peers. Parenting a difficult child is difficult, but you must have the courage to face his negative reactions. Conviction in a well thought-out plan of behavior will help you to keep your child moving in the direction of increasingly mature behavior.

Intense Negative Reactions

Your difficult child typically has intense negative reactions when frustrated. Therefore, you must expect cries, screams, and tantrums any time he is frustrated. It is, therefore, especially important that you be firm and consistent and that you insist upon compliance with your requests. Once you hand him the key and teach him that he can control the family with his tantrums, you will make this behavioral tendency into an established personality trait. If you don't allow this intense negative reaction to control your behavior, but instead you make realistic demands of your child and insist that he yield to them, he will be less likely to show behavioral problems as he develops.

Because a difficult baby will have such strong negative reactions when he is frustrated or not given what he wants, you will be tempted to reward the tantrum in order to stop it. You need to be very careful not to reward tantrums. If you aren't, you might be terrorized by your little one as Melissa's parents were. At the age of two Melissa was already terrorizing her family. She would refuse to wear clothes, and succeeded in not wearing them by screaming violently and flailing her arms about when her parents tried to dress her. She began to protest being dressed at about a year old, and her parents soon became intimidated by her intense reactions. Because they stopped attempting to dress her when she protested, Melissa learned to protest more and more violently whenever her parents tried to do something displeasing her. Melissa wore clothes very infrequently and the entire family suffered from keeping the house uncomfortably warm all the time. They were housebound because Melissa would neither put her clothes on nor keep them on at birthday parties, stores, or parks. When Melissa wanted candy, she screamed, cried, stood up on boxes and chairs to get what she wanted, and persisted until she got it. Her parents were intimidated by the intensity of her reactions, and, in order to reduce the tension in the family, they would ultimately give in to her terrorist tactics. Eventually Melissa controlled the entire household. Her parents placed very few limits on her and made very few demands for mature behavior in order to avoid her intense negative reactions.

A home observation revealed that Melissa's behavior was a result of shaping. At times her parents would decide that it was necessary that Melissa wear some clothing. They would attempt to dress her forcibly until Melissa intensified her tantrum behavior, when they would decide that it really wasn't worth it and put the thermostat up a little higher. In so doing, they taught her that to be successful in getting her way she needed to become more and more vigorous in her protests. This became a predictable pattern of behavior. Another time Melissa wanted M & Ms while her mother was trying to fix dinner. Melissa got a stool and began to climb up on the counter, screaming and crying. Her mother took the stool and then the chair away. Melissa continued to get more unstable items to pile up to reach the M & Ms. Eventually her mother became so stressed and irritated by Melissa's crying and persistence that she got the bowl of M & Ms down and gave Melissa two, saying, "just two and no more." Of course after Melissa finished those two M & Ms, she was back again screaming and crying and trying to get up to the cupboard where the M & Ms were kept. Eventually, her mother gave her the bowl of M & Ms and that was her dinner. Her terrorist tactics paid off in a big way that time. The bottom line is that you must not reward negative reactions or they will get more frequent and more intense! For the difficult child whose reactions are often intense and negative this is most important. When those intense negative reactions don't work, your child will learn to comply.

To be certain that you teach your child compliance rather than tantrums, you want to be sure that you only make requests of him that *you intend to enforce*. If you ask him to pick up his toys, then consider it as important as asking him to take a metal wire out of a light socket and insist that he do it. There is a contest of will here that you want to win in the early years with a child of this difficult temperament. If you settle the issue when your child is between the ages of two and four, then you'll have a fairly easy time during the school years. If, instead, you teach him that he can avoid complying with your wishes if he screams loud enough, you may have problems controlling him for the rest of his life.

Withdrawal from New Situations

Your difficult child will have a tendency to withdraw from new stimuli or new situations and to adapt slowly. You can teach him to cope with his anxiety in new situations instead of avoiding them. Prepare for a new event with rehearsals and as much support from friends as you can arrange. When he begins nursery school, plan an extended time to walk around the grounds with him, observing the children at play and the various activities. Let him meet the teacher and see how she or he treats the children. Give a neighborhood child a ride to school for a week or two so that he knows someone going in.

Expect that your child will have a difficult time adjusting to the new school but insist that he must attend school in spite of tantrums. Be certain that his negative reaction does not allow him to escape the situation, or he will never learn to adjust. If you expose him to new situations and new social groups on a regular basis, doing whatever you can to ease him into the situation, then you can help him to develop certain behaviors and *self-talk* that he will be able to use in any new situation.

If your child starts nursery school at age four, then the following summer you may want to enroll her in a summer camp program just so she stays in practice with new situations and people. Again, as with a slow to warm up child, you want to prepare her and make the new situations as familiar as possible. Try to arrange for a same-age friend to attend the summer camp program as well. Take the children there together, and introduce them to the camp setting, the activities and program. If you can, stay with them for the first time or two so your child can relax and notice the fun that other children have. Then leave her at camp even though it means more tears and more anxiety for several days. You may be tempted to keep her at home since she doesn't have to go to camp and she's so stressed. Remember, she will benefit from the opportunity to adjust to a new situation in the summertime. That way when school begins in September and she is faced with a new classroom, new teacher, and perhaps even new school, the intensity of her reaction will probably not be as great.

Even if she had gone to camp, at the beginning of each school year she will show some tension and fear, and it will take her some time to adjust. But now that she has recently experienced her own gradual adjustment to the camp situation you can remind her, "Remember how scared you were at the beginning of camp and how you cried and then how you met new friends and liked it? You made friends with Ruthie, and you met Clay, and remember how much you got to like your camp teacher. Lots of times we are scared of something new and we learn later that there really isn't anything to be afraid of. There are new people to meet and fun things to do and after a while you will feel good just like you did at camp." Begin from the time your child is four years old to help her understand her own reactions so she can learn to cope with them.

It's not uncommon for children of a difficult temperament to show such an intense negative reaction to school that they become physically ill on school mornings. One kindergarten girl I treated was sick every Monday morning. Her single mother was particularly loving and nurturing and spent most of every weekend with her daughter, shopping and having lunch, going to the parks or to the zoo. Nearly every Monday morning, Sharon would develop a stomachache and throw up on the way to school. Fortunately for Sharon, her mother had to work, so she couldn't turn around and take Sharon home. She took Sharon to school and called later to see how Sharon felt as the day progressed. Of course once she got to school, Sharon was fine. The upset stomach and vomiting on Monday mornings were clearly anxiety-related. But interestingly, Sharon was wonderfully well-adjusted at school. When I observed, she seemed quite happy most of the time. The other children particularly liked her. In fact at times there were children pulling on Sharon's clothing trying to have her stay longer when her mother arrived. It is easy to imagine that if Sharon's mother were to return home with Sharon when she threw up on a Monday morning, Sharon could develop a pattern of being sick at the thought of going to school on any day. Many children do exactly that.

If you know that your little one has trouble with new situations, then you want to make sure that you *give him the opportunity to continue to experience new situations on a regular basis.* Don't let him stay away from new situations because of intense negative reactions. Your goal should be to give him assistance and guided practice in dealing with new situations rather than letting him avoid them.

The Persistent Child

Persistence is an inborn temperamental trait independent of the easy, difficult, or slow to warm up classification scheme. A persistent child is one who gets very involved in an activity and doesn't like to give it up once he is involved. When the child is doing something that you want him to do, you enjoy this personality trait. If he is trying to put on his clothes and get dressed, he will struggle with his shirt until he finally figures it out. If he is trying to do a puzzle, he will stay with it and work at it until he finally gets it together. If he's trying to learn to ride a bicycle, he will try and try, in spite of skinned knees and elbows, until he finally gets it. But when the persistent child refuses to stop drawing his pictures to get ready for bed or does not want to stop shooting baskets to go home, you might call it being uncooperative or disobedient.

If your child is persistent, he needs to have some warning before you ask him to stop what he is doing. If he's in the middle of doing a puzzle or drawing, try to give him as much time as possible to finish up. Show him the clock, what time it is, and the time at which he must finish. He'll be much less able to get up the moment you suggest it than a child who is not so persistent.

It is very important that your child learn to discriminate those situations where *persistence is not appropriate.* If you have a persistent child, you will not want to say no until you have really thought it through. If you say no too quickly and then change your mind after your child begs you, then your persistent child will learn to beg until you are ready to lose your mind. You can teach a persistent child to be an absolute pest who never gives up and badgers you until you're ready for physical violence if you reward his begging at all. Teach him instead that when you say no, you mean no and that there is nothing he can say to change your mind. Make it easy for him to know when persistence is a desirable thing and when it is not appreciated. Don't give him inconsistent messages about whether persistence will work. His persistence will work for him when he is trying to learn to ride a bicycle and when he is trying to do a puzzle, but make it clear that his persistence will not work to control you.

The persistent children who are brought for therapy are those whose parents have taught them to become more and more and more persistent by systematically shaping that behavior. One mother told her son that he couldn't spend the night at his friend's house. He begged and pleaded, and she continued to say no, that it was impossible, that he had been sick and needed to stay home. He then whined and complained some more. After crying, whining, and complaining for fifteen minutes he threw all the clothes off his bed and lay there sobbing. Then he begged one more time, and this time she said, "Ok, if it means that much to you, go ahead." We can be sure that there will be future occasions when he will badger, cry, scream, and carry on to do something that his mother absolutely cannot allow him to do. Perhaps it will be something truly dangerous and undesirable. Only this time *he* won't know the difference, and he will continue to badger her until she ends up spanking him, punishing him, or at least screaming at him. It would have been better for him not to be allowed to spend the night after she had said no than to teach him that this kind of persistence would be rewarded.

Be careful to teach your child to discriminate the times at which this trait is not acceptable. Begging and pleading after no has been the answer is something you won't want to reward. Instead, teach him to accept no for an answer. His teachers will appreciate it at school, his friends' parents will appreciate it when they try to limit his behavior at their homes, and you will have done him a big favor.

14

Behavior Modification Techniques for Older Children

Behavior Modification with Children Four through Seven

Remember when you were so pleased when your child began to talk and to walk and all the attention you gave her for these wonderful new behaviors? Remember when you were teaching her to use the potty and pick up her toys? You were very encouraging, and your encouragement seemed to inspire her to continue to try to please you. Unfortunately, many parents forget to continue to be encouraging and attentive to their children's positive behaviors and simply take them for granted. When this happens they may find that some very important behaviors are not happening. Frequent complaints from parents include the child's unwillingness to help with household chores, unwillingness to do schoolwork, or failure to be cooperative about dressing or eating breakfast in order to be ready for school on time. If you have such complaints, you probably have forgotten to be positive and reward your child for her cooperative or helpful behavior and instead have fallen into the trap of noticing her more often when she dawdles, does not pick up after herself, fails to do her chores, or is not ready on time.

One of the things you know is that attention is a powerful positive reinforcer for most children. It almost doesn't matter what you say, as long as you are focusing your voice and your attention on her, she'll do more of whatever it was that got you to focus on her that way. So, if she dawdles and you attend to her by criticizing or yelling, you still attend to her.

The best parents with the best intentions will make mistakes and wish to change some of their children's behaviors when they get to be four, five, and six or older. Without even noticing what you were doing, you may have reinforced or rewarded certain habits of defiance or verbal argumentativeness, or you may have failed to reward children for participating in the family work.

You can use the principles of behavior modification to treat troublesome behaviors before they become a serious problem as well as use these principles to teach some desired behaviors that are missing. Most undesirable behaviors, such as tantrums, physical aggression, crying, and whining, can be changed by changing the pattern of reinforcement. Desirable behaviors such as cooperative helpfulness and positive sibling interactions can be established by using positive reinforcement. The procedures referred to in the discussions of *prevention* of problem behaviors are easily used to *change* patterns of reinforcement when you realize you are not getting what you want.

Changing Children's Behavior

Table Manners: An Example

Sometimes a whole new set of behaviors can emerge just by using your son or daughter's sense of being an actress or actor. For example, if your son has been eating with terrible manners—fingers in the food and food on the face and table—you might ask your five or six year old to see if he can eat like royalty, like Prince Edward or one of the members of the royal family. Your child will, of course, have heard fairy tales and seen pictures of princes and know about kings and queens. You may want to set your table elegantly for his meals during your training time and simply remind him each time, "Let's see if we can eat like royalty, holding our forks just so, taking very small bites, cleaning our faces after every second or third bite." As your son hams it up for you, continue to notice this royal behavior, "Oh, I see you're dabbing your lips like a prince and oh, what small bites. I noticed you cut that big piece into little bites so you could have a princely bite. Yes, that is very elegant, the way you rest your knife on your plate and change hands before your put your fork to your mouth." Continuing this game over a period of time and frequently commenting about your child's royal eating habits can be a cue for his behavior even when he is not with you. When he has been invited to have dinner at a friend's home, you might remind him to use his royal manners and he will then be more likely to be able to remember all those things that he's been practicing at home. A number of behaviors will occur to him when he thinks about having "royal" manners. After continued praise, he will remember to take small bites, wipe his mouth frequently after bites, be certain to place his knife against his plate while he puts a bite in his mouth, and keep his food on his plate.

You might try to use this approach with a variety of behaviors first to see if the spirit of acting and fun can encourage your child to develop some of the behaviors you would like. Of course, if these don't seem to be enough to interest him, then you would want to try something more structured, such as charts and systems of stars and points.

Using Charts, Checks, and Stars for Children Four Years and Older

Your child of four years and older is able to think about the future. He is now able to look forward to the evening, a trip tomorrow, or the weekend. Now you can use a promise of rewards later to help him do what he must do now. Checks or stars help him make the connection between his behaviors now and the rewards later. In an obvious place, such as the refrigerator door, you can post a chart where certain activities or desirable behaviors are listed. Each time your son does one of those desirable things, he himself can make a check or put a star on the chart. You will probably have to read the chart for him and show him where to put the star or check. A sample chart which could be used for a four year old is given below.

Ian's Chart

Good Manners	M	T	W	TH	F	SAT	SUN
Breakfast uses fork or spoon							
takes small bites							
keeps food on plate no food on floor no food on shirt no food on place mat							
holds glass with two hands							
wipes face and hands with napkin							
Dinner uses fork or spoon							
takes small bites							
keeps food on plate no food on floor shirt, or place mat							
holds glass with two hands							
wipes face and hands with napkin							

Ian can get seven stars per meal or fourteen each day. When he gets six, he can trade them in for something special.

For a six year old, you can list each desirable behavior and the points that she can earn for each behavior. An example of a point system for a six-year-old girl is given below.

Shawn's Program

	M	T	W	TH	F	SAT	SUN
feed and water the cats (2)	2						
feed and water the dog (2)	2						
play ball with dog (4)	4						
take out trash (2)	2						
Total	12						

If Shawn gets ten points, she can watch one hour of TV that night or have one hour of games with Mom or Dad, have an hour craft-type activity or baking in the kitchen, or go out for an ice cream cone. If she gets fifty points from Monday to Friday, she can have a friend spend the night on the weekend.

State Behavior Positively

There are a number of principles that were discussed earlier that you want to think about when making a chart to help your child be good. First of all, you want to try to state the behaviors positively rather than negatively. For example, assume that each time you refuse to do something your daughter wants you to do, or each time you say no to her, she has a tantrum. The behavior that you are looking for is *taking no for an answer with a good attitude*. On your chart and in your discussions, you should say that you will notice when she does accept no for an answer without a tantrum. You decide on a number of stars or total number of points for this acquiescence, which your child will be able to trade for certain privileges. Below is a sample worksheet to help your state behaviors positively.

Sample Worksheet for Restating Behaviors in Positive Terms

Problem Behavior	Desired Behavior
1. My child is disobedient translates to:	does what is asked
2. My child is undisciplined translates to:	comes when called
3. My child is disruptive in school translates to:	pays attention when teacher gives instructions
4. My child is restless translates to:	concentrates on one activity until it's finished
5. My child bothers and annoys other children translates to:	keeps hands on his own desk doing his own work
6. My child can't sit still translates to:	is busy with quiet activity on plane or bus etc.
7. My child is irritable translates to:	responds with a smile when someone bumps him unless it's clearly an aggressive act
8. My child is easily aroused to intense anger translates to:	has patience when things don't work right—tries again and again to negotiate turn taking or trades
9. My child fights with other children translates to:	uses words to resolve problems
10. My child has temper tantrums translates to:	accepts "no" for an answer with good attitude
11. My child shows off to get attention translates to:	has skill of social conversation to get attention from visitors
12. My child talks back translates to:	accepts verbal reprimand agreeing with the behavior required—says "O.K.," "I understand."
13. My child has a short attention span translates to:	stays with a game or activity for increasingly longer period of time
14. My child cries over minor difficulties translates to:	uses words and discussion to express disagreement, wants or needs

15. My child lacks self-confidence translates to:

can ask to join a group of children playing

16. My child is distractable translates to:

concentrates on *finishing* a designated part of a job or homework, then play as a reward

17. My child is hyperactive translates to:

can sit quietly in school and run and be active outside

Select the Reinforcers

Ask yourself, "What does my son like to drink or eat? What kinds of things does my son like to do at home? Does he like craft activities, art activities, baking or cooking, or building things in the garage? What does he like to do in the yard? Does he enjoy playing ball or some other sports activity, planting a garden, or barbecuing? What activities does he like to do in the neighborhood, such as going for a walk or a bicycle ride, going to a neighboring park or to a video-game room?" Consider such things as watching television, listening to records or tapes, sitting and talking, or playing cards or games. Favorite activities that are farther away, such as going to the beach or a water-slide park, a movie or sporting event, could be done once a week.

If a number of activities would be rewarding, you want to offer your little ones activities that include an interaction with you. This means that if your child would enjoy playing a board game with you, this is better than using TV time as a reward.

If things have become too tense between you and your child, and interaction doesn't sound like fun to one or both of you right now, then start with TV or things you can give to your child. Later on when you are feeling better about each other, you can change to activities you'll both enjoy. You might consider toys and games, books and art supplies to trade for a number of stars or points. They need not be expensive to be reinforcing to your child. Consider nail polish, perfumes, special little hairpieces or ribbons or barrettes, belts, special kinds of shoelaces, little belt clips, balloons, jacks and jump ropes. Novelty items such as goofy glasses, silly putty, special pencils with your child's name printed on them, school supplies like special erasers or pencil boxes, paper clips, glue and tape.

One important thing to remember is that what your son or daughter does tells you whether or not you've got a good reinforcer. If your child's behavior doesn't change, the chances are that you don't have an effective reinforcer. Not using an effective reinforcer is one of the greatest important setbacks to most attempts at changing children's behavior. You can never assume that an item or an activity is a reinforcer without some demonstration that it does in fact change the child's behavior. Remember, any activity or event is a reinforcer only if it increases the behavior that it follows.

Example: Eliminating Tantrums

1. Describe the Behavior You Want. Assume your child has a tantrum every time you deny him something he wants. First, explain the new program to him: "Travis, we decided to help you learn how to take no for an answer. It is very important that you learn to act like a big boy when someone tells you no. You can't always do what you want or always have what you want."

2. Show him the chart and explain how he can get stars. "So, I have a special chart here that I have made for you. You will get stars when you take no for an answer like a big boy. When you say 'Mommy I want a cookie,' and I say 'No, Travis, it's too close to dinner time. You can't have a cookie now,' I will look at you to see how you take the no for an answer. If you go away and play with a toy like a big boy, we will put a star on this chart right here. If you walk away and read a book, we will put a star right here. If you accept a carrot instead and say 'OK, Mom' like a big boy, then we will put a star on your chart."

3. Tell him or decide together what the stars will trade for. "When you have five stars I will play a game of checkers or Candyland with you. If you have two stars, you can watch a half hour of cartoons. If you have four stars, we can go for a bicycle ride to get an ice cream. Every time you take no for an answer like a big boy, you will get a star. At the end of every day, you can trade in your stars. At the end of a week, if your stars add up to fourteen, you get a special treat. We can go to the zoo on Saturday morning and you can bring a friend, or we can go swimming in a pool, or something else you pick. I will give you a list of things that you can pick from to do on Saturday morning whenever you have fourteen stars."

For a young child, it is good to use pictures along with the words on the chart to help him remember the rewards. For example, cut out a picture of a checker game and Candyland game from a toy catalog, a picture of Donald Duck or other Disney character for cartoons, and a bicycle for the bicycle ride.

Travis Takes No for an Answer

Mon	Tues	Wed	Thurs	Fri	Sat	Sun

2 stars = a half hour of cartoons
4 stars = bicycle ride to get an ice cream
5 stars = a game of checkers or Candyland

Example: Refusal to Comply with Requests

By the time they are six, seven, or eight, many children are quite capable of getting themselves dressed, brushing their teeth, getting ready for school, bed, or their bath. They may not do so simply because their cooperative behaviors get them very little attention whereas their moping and dawdling get them lots. When you find yourself nagging and badgering your child—"Come on now, get ready for bed. It's time to get ready for bed. I want you to go upstairs now and get ready for bed"—until you are forced to yell and scream, you probably need a program to *reward compliance with your requests*. With a child of five or six or more, you can make a chart.

1. *Describe the behavior you want.* First explain to your seven year old what the program is. For example, say, "Lily, I would like to help you learn how to be more cooperative so that I don't have to be yelling at you and nagging you anymore. I have bought you a watch, and this is how to set the timer so you will know how many minutes have passed."

2. *Show her the chart and explain how she can get points.* "What I'm going to do is put a chart here on the refrigerator and give you points for cooperating when I ask you to do something. You get points for when you do what I ask you to do *right away.* If I say to you, 'Lily, would you please get your clothes on for school,' and in *ten minutes* I look at you and you are all dressed—socks on, shoes on, shorts and shirt on—then you will get three points. When I say that your breakfast is ready, and you come to the breakfast table to sit down and eat *within three minutes,* you will get another point. If you are all through eating your breakfast *within fifteen minutes,* then you'll get another point. I will say to you, 'Lily, I would like you to brush your teeth and comb your hair now, because we have to leave in five minutes.' If you are ready to go *in five minutes,* then you will get another two points."

3. *Tell her or decide together what the points will trade for.* "At the end of that day, you can trade your points for a game of Monopoly with Mom and Dad or an hour of television, a bicycle ride to get an ice cream or something else we agree on." You and Lily together can decide on the activities or things for which she wants to trade her points and the number of points she needs for each.

4. *Break down the behaviors.* It is too much to expect a six- or seven-year-old child to be conscious of time and to get dressed and organized for school without reminders. You really must have small tasks and specific time limits for each task for her until she gets to be around ten or eleven. It is unreasonable to say to a seven year old, "I want you to get up, get dressed, have breakfast, and be ready to leave for school by 8:20." Most children, particularly boys, are far too distractable to concentrate on the clock. They need to be reminded: "It's time to get on your clothes," "Now it's time to eat breakfast," "Now it's time to brush your teeth and get your lunch and papers together." If your child cooperates with these reminders the first time, life can be much smoother in the morning.

Lily Gets Ready for School

	M	T	W	TH	F
Dressed for school in ten minutes, socks, shoes, shorts, shirt	3				
Comes to breakfast when called within three minutes	1				
Eats breakfast within fifteen minutes	1				
Brushes teeth and combs hair within five minutes	2				
Total	7				

7 points = Monopoly game, or
1 hour of T.V., or
bicycle ride for ice cream.

Example: Teaching Responsibility for Homework

Today, there is a lot of emphasis on giving children homework, and teaching good study habits is a real concern for a lot of parents. If you child is not doing his homework, you want to break down doing homework into a lot of smaller behaviors. The first important behavior is that your child brings his homework home. Therefore on your chart, you should include *brings home homework assignment*.

It's a good idea to give your little one a special little notebook wherein he writes down his homework assignment. That way, you know what it is, and your child remembers what it is. If he brings home the notebook with the assignment written down and the required books and papers to do the assignment, he gets two points (one for writing the assignment and one for the books!). When he sits down at his desk or table, opens the book to the right page, and has his pencil and paper ready to do the homework, he gets one point. Because getting started is such an important step, starting the assignment gets two points. Actually completing the assignment will give him five points. Asking for help so that he understands his homework will be rewarded with your attention and help. Remember that he gets the points for bringing the book home even if he never does the homework and that you give the points when he sits and opens the book even if he never completes the homework.

These points cannot be taken away. Your noticing the wanted behaviors and his putting the points on the chart will help both you
and your child to concentrate on the desired behaviors. Once he
starts his assignment, you should acknowledge his behavior right
away, "I see you've decided to get right into that assignment and
get it done. You've already gotten one-third of it finished!" Again,
you and your child will decide together on the things or activities
the points will earn. See if your company, sitting down at the same
table to do bills or read, while he does homework will reward his
concentration.

Homework

	Points	M	T	W	TH	F
Brings home homework assignment	1					
Brings home needed books and papers	1					
Sits down at desk with book, paper, and pencil	1					
Starts assignment	2					
Finishes assignment	5					
Total Points	10					

Example: Problems at School

Sometimes your child will be having some problems at school.
How can you help him behave more appropriately? First, you must
have a conference with his teacher to find out just what he is doing
or is not doing that is causing trouble. Your child may be speaking
out loud, talking out of turn, disturbing other children, making animal noises in the classroom, but, whatever the trouble, you will
want to state your goals in a positive way. He will be rewarded for
being quiet, raising his hand to speak and *concentrating on his schoolwork.* You and the teacher may agree to break the day into one half-
hour segments. Your child will be supplied with a chart of these
blocks of time. When a half hour passes without the undesired behavior, your child must ask the teacher to put her initials next to
the problem-free block. Each initial can earn a star or a point which
can be traded for special privileges as in the previous examples.

8:30–9:00	9:00–9:30	9:30–10:00	recess
10:30–11:00	11:00–11:30	11:30–12:00	lunch
1:00–1:30	1:30–2:00	2:00–2:30	

Most teachers will be happy to cooperate with a program such as this, since it takes only a second of their time to initial a square and they appreciate the results.

Some social problems at school can be treated similarly. In one family, I treated a six-year-old girl who was very domineering, controlling, and a leader in her class. When she decided to have a club, all the girls wanted to be included. Denise told the girls what to draw and what color it should be. If one of them failed to follow her rules, that girl was not allowed in the club. This tyrannical behavior was not good for Denise or for the other children. One child, Sharon, cried several times a day because of Denise's behavior. After a conference with the principal in which Denise's power over Sharon was described as a serious problem, her mother agreed to use a report chart for her daughter at school. Denise took a little card to school very day in her lunch box. Because she changed teachers every hour (an unusual setting for first graders), she brought this card to the teacher at the end of every class. The teacher would sign his or her name to the statement, "I did not make Sharon cry in class today," if, in fact, Denise did not cause Sharon to cry. If all five teachers signed, Denise was given special privileges. If she did not have all five statements signed, then she was not allowed to watch television, was not allowed to have a friend over, and was not taken anywhere special for ice cream or any other treats. That Sharon was a child who cried for little or no reason (probably having had it reinforced by her parents) was actually quite helpful to Denise in getting her tyrannical behavior under control.

Sharon's Chart

	Mrs. Roberts	Mrs. Weiss	Mr. Lambert	Mr. Hughes	Mrs. Angioni
Monday					
Tuesday					
Wednesday					
Thursday					
Friday					

Please sign this card if I did not make Sharon cry in class today.

To review the most important steps in setting up a point system:

1. Try to state the behavior in positive terms.
2. Break the behaviors down into small behaviors over small periods of time.
3. List the behaviors on a rough copy chart.
4. Decide on number of points for each desired behavior alone or with your child.
5. Decide on privileges and the number of points for each alone or with your child.
6. Make the final chart listing all desired behaviors, stars or points for each behavior, and the reinforcers and their costs in stars or points.

Young children should not be given global requests to "get ready for bed" or "get ready for school." Explain the program very carefully to your child, show him exactly what will happen if he does what you've asked him to do, and make sure he knows the privileges he will earn from the points or stars. *Make sure he knows he won't be allowed to have those privileges unless he earns the points.*

Will He Always Want a Reward?

Many parents worry that using a chart system teaches a child always to want payment for what he does and takes away from the child's sense of participating in family life. While it is true that your son will initially be doing his part with the idea of getting something tangible in return, you can safely expect that eventually he will find pleasure in doing things simply to be helpful as your response becomes more and more positive. Over and over again in clinical practice, I find that children who have been working on point systems for some period of time will eventually cross certain activities off the chart and simply say, "You don't have to pay me for this one. I'll just do it anyway. I like walking the dog."

One mother asked her seven-year-old daughter to help keep a crawling baby within a unfenced grassy area so that the parents could talk and offered to pay her for her help in babysitting. The girl said, "You don't have to pay me. I'll do it because I want to." Her mother expressed her appreciation: "That's so nice of you, Kimberly. I really appreciate that. That gives me time to talk to my friends." The mother of the infant was especially pleased, saying: "Such a giving and generous child. You must be proud of her being so willing to help. That's a rare thing these days."

Occasionally, a child whose parents use a reward system ends up wanting always to be paid with consumable reinforcers or some tangible item for whatever he does. My experience has been that this happens when parents forget to express their appreciation along with the tangible reward. If you remember to express encouragement and enthusiasm for your son's cooperation as you give the tangible reward, eventually the appreciation and attention he gets for cooperative behavior is likely to become more important to him than the tangible rewards he earns. At that point, the tangible rewards become insignificant and are usually discarded.

15

Teaching, Preventing and Eliminating Fears

As you may have noticed, newborn babies are quite fearless. The only things that really frighten them are the sensation of falling and sudden loud noises. In the beginning, no babies are afraid of the dark, large dogs, spiders, or planes flying overhead. Yet all of us have known of children who by three years of age are afraid of at least one of these things. Most childrearing books suggest that it is quite normal for children to develop many fears between the ages of one and three and to grow out of some fears and develop new ones through preadolescence.

How is it that such fearless babies acquire so many fears by the time they are three years of age? Is it necessary that they acquire so many fears? The methods of behavior modification used in the treatment of phobias by clinical psychologists offer some answers to these questions. Although it may be "normal" for children to develop fears, you can easily apply the methods of clinical psychology to prevent them from developing fears or help them overcome mild fears they may have already developed.

The Case of Albert and the Rat

A very famous study conducted in 1920 by two psychologists named Watson and Rayner describes the way some fears may be acquired. In this study the authors took a nine-month-old boy named Albert and tested his reaction to a white laboratory rat. As you would expect, Albert was not afraid of the rat. In fact, he seemed to enjoy the creature. They also tested his reaction to a variety of other furry items such as cotton wool, a rabbit, a dog, and a monkey. Albert was not afraid of any of these.

Next, the authors tested Albert's reaction to the sudden loud noise of a steel bar being struck behind his head. He was frightened. They then paired the rat with the loud noise in this way: they would present the rat to Albert and then immediately, within a half second, they would make a sudden loud noise behind his head with the steel bar. Albert started and began to cry. The rat was taken away and Albert was comforted and consoled. Once Albert was calm again, they sat him back down on the table, presented the rat to him, and immediately struck that steel bar behind his head. Once again, Albert started and cried.

The authors repeated this procedure seven times. By the eighth time, as soon as Albert saw the rat he began to cry and tried to crawl away — so fast that the authors had trouble catching him before he crawled off the table. Albert had learned to fear the rat after *only seven pairings* of the rat and the sudden loud noise.

Five days later, Albert was shown the rat again and he was just as frightened. Another really interesting finding was that now Albert was afraid of *all* of those furry objects that had never been paired with the sudden loud noise. His fear had generalized to the rabbit, dog, a fur coat, cotton wool, and a white beard. Poor Albert, he left the hospital before his fears could be treated, and no one knows what happened to him.

Teaching Fears

You might wonder why we are talking about teaching fears, since no parents in their right minds want to teach their child to be fearful. However, if you think a little further, you'll realize that you *do* wish to teach your children to be afraid of events or situations that could be life-threatening. For example, you want your children to stay away from the street, light sockets, hot stoves, and other similarly dangerous situations.

The case of Albert shows that to teach a child to fear an originally neutral situation, you should pair it with something frightening. When your one-year-old boy begins to head for the street, you should let out your "emergency shriek." If you are close enough when he starts to step into the street, you can scream a sudden, loud NO directly into his ear. By repeatedly pairing the street with a sudden, loud noise, the street becomes frightening and your child will avoid it. The same method would work for the light socket or for the hot stove.

Some parents may reason that the conditioning or learning is automatic. The first time your daughter touches a hot stove and gets burned, she learns to fear the stove. But because you cannot control the degree of the burn your daughter will receive during such a learning experience, it is probably wiser and safer to teach her to fear the stove with your voice or a spank rather than waiting for her to be taught by the heat of the stove.

Teaching caution with dogs requires more careful and different training, because you don't want to teach a fear of *all* dogs. To develop caution instead of fear, teach your son to ask the owner, "Does your dog bite?" rather than telling him, "Don't touch the dog, it might bite." If you use an emergency tone of voice as your child approaches a dog, you may create a fear of not only that particular dog, but of all dogs, which can later develop into a serious problem.

To be able to use your voice to teach fear of dangerous situations you must not overuse your emergency shriek or frequently scream NO. If you do so, your baby will adapt to it and will not be afraid of that voice any longer. You want to save it for those situations where you really do have an emergency or an important lesson to teach. As always, babies show individual differences that are important to consider. Right from birth, some babies startle very easily, and others are much more difficult to frighten. If your baby startles easily, a loud noise or an emergency shriek will probably be quite enough to teach your baby to be afraid of the street, light sockets, and other dangerous things. If you happen to have one of those babies who is less easily frightened, then you may need to resort to a good hard slap in these situations. Slap once, hard, on the skin and not through a thick diaper, the instant your child steps into the street or reaches for the stove.

Another reason to look very carefully at the case of little Albert is that it can teach you what *not* to do. On many occasions I have seen parents who desperately wanted their children to enjoy something like a swimming pool, the ocean, or horses when the children were obviously afraid. One time at the beach, a mother was determined her boy would enjoy the ocean. She had bought him a very nice rubber raft and was very eager for him to ride on this raft. The child was not at all excited about getting on this raft. In fact he was terrified of the ocean. The mother, trying to help her child overcome his fear, slapped him on the rear end, forcibly put him on the raft, and screamed at him to stop his crying — all in the hopes that he would enjoy the ocean.

Of course, you are thinking to yourself that you would never be so foolish. What she was doing was teaching her child to be more frightened of the ocean than he was already by pairing up the ocean with all of her own unpleasantness. Perhaps you would not make this mistake, but you might make others. You might find yourself in situations where you feel your child is unnecessarily frightened: crying on the first day of nursery school, being reluctant to walk into a birthday party, or refusing to go on a ride at an amusement park. Even *you* may lose patience and become inclined to yell at your child or even force your child to participate. As we learned from Albert, this can only make your child more emotionally upset and will do nothing to teach your child to be more relaxed in the situation.

Eliminating Fears

The Case of Peter and the Rabbit

What can be done about a fear once it has been developed? Is there any hope for Albert and children like him or must they remain fearful of furry objects for the rest of their lives? In another famous study, Jones demonstrated that you can teach a child other emotions to replace the fear.

In this study the psychologist tried to eliminate a fear of rabbits in a little boy named Peter. She thought that if she could create in Peter some very positive emotions, such as the good feelings he might have while eating ice cream, and very gradually introduce the rabbit, beginning far off in the distance, then some of the positive feelings that he had for the ice cream might become associated with the rabbit. Peter was seated at a table with his bowl of ice cream, and the rabbit was shown to him from the doorway, far enough away so that Peter continued to feel comfortable. Gradually, over an extended period of time, the rabbit was brought nearer and nearer to Peter as he ate. Finally, Peter was eating his ice cream while petting the rabbit.

How long does a process like this take? Treatment could take an hour, days, weeks, or even months. The intensity of the fear, the intensity of the positive emotion, and other temperamental and individual differences are important factors. With a very mild fear and a strong positive emotional response, you might be able to countercondition a fear in an hour. When a child's fear is intense the counterconditioning can take a period of weeks or even months.

Can you use anything but ice cream to countercondition a fear? There are many things that will create positive emotions in your child, and you will be the best one to know those things that make your child happy, relaxed, or content. Good feelings might come from your son eating something he enjoys, laughing at the silly faces you make, playing with a favorite toy, or hearing a happy song. Warm, safe, and secure feelings will come from being close to you or in your arms. Other things that make some babies feel relaxed or comfortable are sucking on a pacifier or drinking a bottle. You don't need something unusual or out of the ordinary but only something effective in producing a positive emotional state. You will know if what you have chosen is effective by your baby's reactions.

Preventing Common Fears

Fear of Water in the Face

If you are like most parents you will be eager for your baby to learn to swim. Unfortunately many babies are really quite terrified of getting water in their faces by the time they are brought to a swimming class.

For most children, the most important and difficult part of learning to swim is being able to tolerate water in the face. Many parents inadvertently teach their child to fear water in the face because of the great efforts they make to keep the baby's face dry while bathing or washing hair. My mother-in-law showed me a way to wrap a washcloth around my fingers to prevent water from splashing in my baby's face.

In order to teach your baby girl to be able to accept and even to enjoy water in her face, do exactly the opposite. Begin pouring water over her face from the first time you bathe her. Remembering the case of Peter and the rabbit, be sure that you have only positive feelings going on in your baby. To do this, you want to make sure that your room is comfortably warm, that your baby is not tired or hungry and has no other unpleasant feelings. Then gradually pour water over her face while she is feeling calm and relaxed and comfortable. Take her in your arms into a comfortably warm tub and gradually, over a period of months, pour more and more water over more and more of her face. Start with her cheek, then wet her forehead, and then pour water over her eyes, being very careful not to have her breathe in or swallow any. Later, when she is more aware, you can take her into a well-heated pool or spa with the whirlpools turned off. Then, hold her and play with her and bounce her up and down in the water.

When you are convinced by a smiling and happy face that she is having a wonderful time and that she loves the water, you can think about submerging her face. Only after many times of obvious delight with the water should you submerge her. Give your baby some signal that you will always use before you put her face in, so she learns to hold her breath on that signal. For example, say "one, two, three" and then blow in her face and dunk her under for just a brief second. When you lift her up, smile at her and continue to bounce her and play with her. Only put her under one to three times during your first session, depending on her reaction. Even if your baby gets happy immediately, there is no reason to continue to submerge her. She has a long life to learn to swim.

It is best to take your baby in the water at least twice a week, if possible, and to submerge her at least once each time as she is beginning to accept having water in her face. She may cry the first time you put her under, particularly if she chokes on the water or gets a big drink. After the third or fourth time, if you are very careful to make sure that she is relaxed, comfortable, and having a wonderful time playing with you in the water between dunks, she will probably accept going under without being upset.

It is important that you pay attention to your *own* baby's reactions as you teach her. This is especially true if you see other babies who are more relaxed in the water than yours. There are some babies who come up grinning after their first dunk and never become frightened or upset. Good for them. If your daughter is one who seems a little upset by getting water in her face that first time, then you must make certain that you get her comfortable and go very slowly. What you want to do is teach her to enjoy the water — not to keep up with her friend.

An important point here is that you can teach your baby to be *afraid* of the water just by going too fast. If you leave out the fun and laughter and playtime and only dunk her, you might teach her to be afraid of the water. Remember, you are trying to pair up strong positive feelings with the water to keep fear from developing. You want to teach her that the water is fun and means happy times.

There are many methods of teaching a child to swim, and all of them are effective with some children. You as the parent, however, will be the best person to teach your daughter to accept water in her face. The stronger your baby's initial fear reactions, the better it is that *you* be her teacher in the early phase. You may not have the skills to teach her to swim, but you certainly have the skills to be able to teach her to accept and tolerate water in her face.

To keep your daughter dunking her face in the water regularly, buy water toys that sink rather than toys that float. If her toys are at the bottom of a tub, spa, or pool, she may be willing to put her chin, mouth, part of her nose, and finally her whole face under water to reach them.

Fear of the Dark

Many adults are uncomfortable in a completely dark room and therefore assume that an infant will be afraid as well. This is absolutely not so. Newborns are fearless of the dark. They have just come from a very dark place where they were very happy for nine months! Therefore, it is a mistake to keep a night-light in your boy's room when he goes to sleep. By doing so you will only teach him your own fears. It is best to simply put him into bed, turn off the lights, and have him accustomed from the beginning to sleeping in a completely dark room.

Even if you never put on a night-light and always try to keep your son comfortable about being in the dark, he may start to show some anxiety about the dark as he gets close to two and a half years of age. One mother told me that she noticed her daughter had developed some fear of the dark only after realizing that for some time her child had been getting up to turn the light on after she had been tucked in bed. If you should notice such behavior or if your son expresses some concern about being in the dark, there are some things that you can do to keep him comfortable about being alone in a dark room.

Sometimes the problem is related to being *alone* in the dark and your boy may be very comfortable if you are in there with him. If your child feels comfortable and relaxed lying beside you in the dark, then you can use your ability to create feelings of warmth and security to interfere with his fear of the dark. Lie down with him at bedtime and tell him homespun, pleasant stories in a completely darkened room. Stay until he falls asleep. After some time (days or weeks), you tell your baby that you have to get up for just a second to check something that you forgot and you will be right back. You leave for a few seconds and then hurry right back and lie down next to him. Wait a while, then give him some other reason for leaving and tell him you will be right back to check and see that he is okay. You then go out for another thirty seconds and duck right back in and say, "I'm here to check, I just came in to see if everything is okay. I have to do something [wash my face, put in a load of wash, feed the dog] but I'll be right back. Don't call me because I'm going to come right back. You don't have to call me." Then, you leave the room for a minute or so and then pop back in again: "Oh, I just came back to check to see if you were okay. I have to go put on my robe and slippers. I'll be back again." Very gradually increase the number of seconds between your return visits to the room until you are staying away longer and longer periods of time.

Increase your time away randomly so one time you might come back after ten seconds and the next time you come back after a minute and then the next time perhaps thirty seconds and the next time after a minute and a half, so that your child is not timing the instant of your return.

You want your son to be able to relax and give in to his sleepy feelings rather than to be tense, anxious, and worried. When he feels safe and secure with the thought that at any time you will be coming in to check, then he will relax and fall asleep. In the beginning, you may actually wake him up when you tell him, "I just came in to check on you." That's fine. That further reinforces his notion that you are nearby and that you will be in to check.

This procedure should be continued for days or weeks or even months depending on the intensity of your child's fear. If your baby expresses some distress about the length of time that you have been gone, this means that you have gone too fast and that you should decrease the number of seconds that you are gone from your baby's room. This may mean that you drop back to staying out of the room for only five seconds. Increase the length of your stay away only as much as you can while still keeping your baby completely calm, secure, and comfortable in the dark room.

Continue this procedure of checking on your baby until he finally falls asleep. If you continue on a nightly basis, after a while, the frequency with which you check will decrease, and the length of time between visits will increase as your baby learns to feel calm, relaxed, and comfortable in the dark. Finally you will not have to make any checking visits at all.

Separation Fear at Bedtime

If your daughter protests her bedtime when she is obviously tired, or if she continues to call you in a dozen times after being tucked in, she may have some anxiety about being separated from you. The same procedure as outlined above works very nicely here. That is, take the child to bed and tell her stories so that bedtime becomes associated with a sweet time spent with Mommy or Daddy. Tell her stories about your own childhood, some of the naughty things you did as a child, or anything she seems to enjoy. Then leave for increasing lengths of time as she feels comfortable and secure. Tell her, "Don't call me. I'll come in and check on you if you *don't* call me. If you call me, I won't come, but if you're quiet and lie there like a big girl then I'll come in and check on you in just a few minutes." Then again, depending upon how long she will stay quiet, you will adjust your length of time between visits. Perhaps you'll stay away for a minute or two minutes or perhaps five minutes, depending on your child.

It is true that this checking procedure is very time-consuming and disruptive and keeps you hanging there in the hall outside your baby's room for long periods of time in the beginning. However, in the long run it is very well worth your effort and trouble. Ultimately your baby will learn to stay in bed without calling you, to relax, and to go to sleep, and you will have years of pleasant bedtimes to reward you for your early effort.

Fear of the Shower

There are certain advantages to being able to bathe a child in the shower. You may visit places where there is no bathtub and there are times when a shower is just more convenient. Take the baby into the shower with you and turn it on very lightly to reduce the noise. If you begin this in early infancy, your baby will not develop a fear of the shower.

If your son already shows some fear of the shower, you may begin by taking him in the *bathtub* with you with the shower dripping only slightly. Continue to take him in the bathtub with you daily. As you play with him in the water and he experiences feelings of relaxation and security that come from being with you, very gradually increase the spray in the shower. Be certain to never increase the spray of the shower to a degree that creates anxiety in your baby. Gradually, the spray of the shower will become associated with the positive emotions of relaxation, security, and fun and will not frighten him.

Fear of Loud Noises

Although it is certainly not a good idea to constantly expose a child to loud noises, whenever there is an opportunity it is wise to take your son gradually closer and closer to some construction machinery or some other loud machinery while you are holding him in your arms so that he becomes able to tolerate the loud noises without feeling frightened or anxious.

Fear of Separation

Before your baby girl becomes specifically attached to you, leaving her with a second person is easy. She doesn't seem to notice whether she is with Daddy or Grandma or a babysitter. Once she has become specifically attached to you (usually to the mother at age six months), she will find your leaving her upsetting.

There are a number of factors which influence the degree of upset your baby will feel when you leave. Some difficult babies develop specific attachment as early as four and a half months of age and will cry and refuse to eat with anyone else. Many easy babies seem to trust most people from the beginning. Another factor is the amount of time you have available for playful interaction. The more time you have to play with your daughter, the more attached she will be to you and the more distressed she will be when you leave her. A related factor is the amount of time a second attachment figure has for play. If both parents have a great deal of time at home, then your baby may develop multiple attachments. If she is left with a second attachment figure when her favorite person leaves, she will not be so upset.

If your daughter is one who seems to be very upset by your leaving, then you can ease her anxiety and stress by using the same counterconditioning methods as were used with Peter and the rabbit. The way in which you will handle these separations will, of course, depend upon whether you need to leave the baby to go to work or to get some personal time alone and on the temperament and the reaction of your baby to your leaving.

When a mother must leave for work, somehow she manages to do so even if the baby screams, and babies usually do become adjusted to the second caregiver. On the other hand, you might be able to make the separation a little easier for both of you if you use some of the methods described here. This section is important both for the working mother and the mother who is at home and finds herself unable to walk out the door and leave her baby screaming.

As with Peter and the rabbit, the approach in dealing with separation and anxiety is to make the experience of separation as positive for your baby as you possibly can. This means that you will want to focus more on helping your baby girl feel positive emotions when she is with her babysitter than on trying to decrease her attachment to you. You want your baby to learn three things: 1. That she can cope with the fear she feels when you leave, 2. That she can have a reasonably happy time while you're gone, and 3. that you will return.

To help her learn these things, you will want to focus on the second point. Teach her that the person you leave her with will not only take care of her but will also have some enjoyable, interesting, and delightful experiences for her. Leave her regularly and frequently with the second person and make certain that this person has a plan of entertainment for your baby every time. Particularly in the beginning, the second caregiver must give your baby some very exciting and interesting experiences to create the positive emotions that counterbalance the fear or sadness she feels when you leave.

Make the Process Gradual. There are three factors in this situation that you want to change gradually. One factor is the familiarity of the caregiver to your child. In the beginning you want to leave your baby with the most familiar person. Gradually you will leave your child with less and less familiar people until finally you may be able to call a babysitting service and have your child accept a friendly stranger for the evening. For example, you might graduate from leaving your son first with Daddy, then with Grandma, then with the mother of a friend he sees regularly, and so on.

If you are a single parent or if you are alone with your son most of the time, you should help him become attached to the mother of one of his agemates. If you get together with his friend and mother several times a week, take exciting excursions together, and help with the needs of one another's children, you can promote a feeling of affection between your friend and your child. If this attachment develops, then the fear or anxiety your baby will feel when you leave him with his friend's mother will probably be minimal.

The second factor which you will want to deal with in a gradual manner is the place or the circumstances in which your boy and his caregiver will be while you are gone. You will graduate from the most exciting and positive circumstances you can dream up to the least excitng. Exciting an eight-month-old is fairly easy. Taking him out for a stroller ride while he eats his teething cookie and you throw bird seed to the pigeons is usually quite exciting. To help him get through the first separation experience, the caregiver should keep up the excitement for the entire time you are gone. Have the caregiver take your baby to the store to buy an ice cream cone or a piece of fruit to eat on the way home. Have them bring along some bread to feed the birds or some peanuts for the squirrels in the park to keep him interested while he is away. Be certain that the caregiver brings along your baby's pacifier, comforting blanket, or favorite toy.

If you carefully plan for something very exciting and enjoyable to happen while you leave your son with the second caregiver, then he will gradually feel less distressed and frightened when you leave. He will learn to trust and enjoy other people as well as believe that you will always come back. As your baby becomes attached to the second caregiver he will feel more relaxed and comfortable, and the caregiver will not need to do so many things to excite and interest him. He will no longer be fearful or anxiety-stricken when you are gone, although he may still cry and be unhappy as you are leaving.

The third factor to be changed gradually is the length of time for which you leave your baby. If you have the luxury of being able to leave your son for short periods in the beginning and gradually increase your time away, the anxiety he feels may be minimized. You may have your caregiver take him for a stroller ride and come back and find you at home only twenty minutes later. Gradually you will leave your baby for longer and longer periods of time. The important point here is that you should *not* have the caregiver bring the baby back to you screaming and upset. Be certain that he doesn't see you again until he has calmed down and begun to become interested in something that the caregiver has to offer. What you want to do is to reinforce the idea that he can have a good time with someone else. If he is miserable until the moment he sees you again, you will have reinforced his fear of your leaving.

Your child's reactions to being separated change with age. By the time they are four years old, most children are very minimally affected by your leaving. Part of the changes have to do with the baby's increasing cognitive abilities. The child who cannot think about the future has a much more difficult time with separation than one who can anticipate your coming back. The ability to think about the future usually develops by about age two and a half. Also, by the time your daughter is three and a half and getting closer to four she is becoming far more independent and has an interest in learning from and relating to other people.

Each time you have to change caregivers and leave your baby with someone new, you need to drop back a few steps and increase the positive activities for the baby while you are gone. As that caregiver becomes a trusted person for your baby, then the fun and excitement that has to be provided will be less.

When You Cannot Be Gradual. Although you may want very much to be gradual in leaving your baby, you may not be able to be as gradual as you would like. If you must work, then do your best to take your baby to the daycare center several times with you before you return to work. Get your babysitter to come to your home several times while you are still there. Do your best to arrange exciting experiences for your baby while you are gone.

If you can't make the separation experience gradual, it is not necessarily bad. There are reasons to allow your baby to experience some anxiety and stress. Because I am a psychologist and was in graduate school at the time I had my first child, I was very aware of all of these counterconditioning methods, and I was very compulsive in applying these methods in every circumstance, at times at great personal expense. I made certain always to follow a very gradual program and minimize the anxiety and tension for Sherri. I went to great lengths to have her caregiver take her to exciting places. When she was two and a half years old and entered nursery school for the first time, I spent two hours in the beginning and gradually less and less time at the nursery school with her before I would leave, until I finally could leave her at the door without her crying. Because she was a difficult baby I felt her stress was great when I left, and I worked hard to minimize it. I was equally careful in every situation in which I could minimize her anxiety.

You may be thinking that this was wonderful and desirable, as I did. However, the first time she and I went to Mexico together, I realized differently. Sherri was eight years old. Because I had been so consistently gradual and tried so carefully to minimize the amount of anxiety she would feel in every situation, she had not learned to cope with anxiety.

She was in foreign country for the first time, she couldn't speak much of the language, and I could not make anything gradual. When I left her with a Mexican family while I taught classes, she had what could only be described as a full-blown anxiety attack. It was obvious to me that she had learned no coping skills to deal with the anxiety and felt to the depth of her soul that this would be the end of her.

Most babies and children have a chance to learn when they feel stressed or anxious that this anxiety does not kill them and that the stress and anxiety does ultimately end. They learn ways of dealing with that stress, such as forcing themselves to become interested in something else, reminding themselves of other times they have coped, and trusting that the tension will leave. My daughter had not had an opportunity to learn these things.

I tell you this story because none of us should feel that we must be superhuman and eliminate *all* stress for our children. If you do your best, within reason, to minimize your baby's fear and anxiety but cannot eliminate all stress in all situations, your baby will learn some coping skills. Whenever you can be gradual and minimize the stress your baby feels, you probably should do so. If being gradual involves too much personal sacrifice or if you simply cannot be quite so gradual, your baby will learn some important things about coping with stress and anxiety. You should not be worried about being unable to keep your baby stress-free in all situations.

Eliminating Mild Fears

If your child is even mildly afraid of some situation, event, or object, you must plan a careful treatment. Although the method is similar to preventing fears, the treatment of an already established fear must be more thoughfully planned and more cautiously approached. I will describe the treatment of a specific fear of water to illustrate the treatment approach.

Fear of Water

Assume your daughter is afraid of water, and particularly terrified of the bathtub. In this case, you want to have the water gradually approach the child (as did the rabbit with Peter) while she feels calm and relaxed. You can do this by presenting the water in gradually increasing amounts as part of a daily playtime.

As always, many positive emotions could potentially replace the fear. In this case you could use the feelings of security she feels being with you and the positive feelings she gets by playing with interesting toys. The plan of treatment will be for your child to experience water in gradually increasing quantities while she continues to feel relaxed, secure, and joyful, so that finally sitting in a tub of water will be relaxing and fun for her. The procedure may take a day or two or a month or two, depending on her reactions. Try to relax, have fun with your baby, and forget about the final goal. Eventually you will get there.

Begin with a very small quantity of water, perhaps a teacupful. As you play with your daughter let her pour salt and pepper into the water and stir it around with a spoon, pretending to make soup. Next introduce some larger ingredients to add to the soup such as pieces of vegetables or toys, and suggest that a larger bowl of water would be better. With a large spoon gradually begin to pour water over her arms and hands in a playful manner, always monitoring her reactions so that she never becomes upset. If you make a mistake, move too fast, and your child becomes anxious, drop back a step until she is happy again. Then proceed slowly.

The next step would be to introduce some boats or dolls which will not fit into the bowl. Now, of course, she'll need a three-foot plastic tub of water to float her boats and bathe her dolls. As long as your little girl continues to express joy and pleasure with the increasing quantities of water, continue to try to dribble water over her arms and legs very gradually while she is playing. Encourage her to reach in to get a boat and perhaps wet an arm or her knees.

Finally you will fill the bathtub to float the toys and dolls, so they will have more room. First you and your daughter sit sideways on the edge of the bathtub. Later you put your feet in the tub and finally both of you will get completely into the tub to play.

Each time you bring in a larger container of water you should expect your child to show a little less enthusiasm or enjoyment. Be entertaining and enthusiastic, but if she balks, never insist or force her to do more than seems pleasurable or enjoyable to her.

Once your baby is comfortable and happy playing in a bathtub, you may try to introduce her to a swimming pool with very graduated stairs. On the first stair should be no more than a few inches of water. At first, she may play on the side of the pool with the toys on the first stair. Very gradually, while she is experiencing a great deal of pleasure and relaxation, you can manipulate toys to encourage her to get onto the first step in the water.

With time, she can be gradually maneuvered into deeper water. When she is loving the water, you can begin working on some preswimming activities such as wetting her face little by little. Remember, your goal is to have your child experience the water in gradually increasing quantities while being relaxed, laughing, and having fun. Therefore, it is important never to push her so that she becomes anxious or frightened. If you carefully and cautiously follow the procedure, your child should never feel afraid of water again. The emotion of fear will be replaced by feelings of relaxation and enjoyment.

Fear of Animals

Frequently children become afraid of animals of one kind or another. The animal may make a sudden loud noise, one of the species may bite them or a friend, or simply make some sudden movement which startles them. Occasionally a single such frightening experience will be enough to create a genuine and lasting fear of the animal.

To countercondition the fear, try to keep your child from ever again being frightened by the animal. You will use all your creativity and sensitivity to your child to promote positive feelings in the presence of the animal. Bring along whatever food, toys, music, or other items you know will promote a positive emotional state. To begin with, the feared animal must be far away, and the positive emotions of comfort, relaxation, or pleasure must be intense. The more intense the fear, the further away from the animal you must start and the more gradual must be the approach. Tune into your baby's emotional responses and always stay within your baby's "comfort zone." As soon as your child shows any sign of tension, back up a few steps.

Fear of Ducks. For example, if your son is intensely afraid of ducks, you might begin by driving up to a duckpond, parking your car some distance away (in the comfort zone) and merely watching the ducks from the car. After several visits he might indicate a feeling of peace with the idea of opening the door. Do so and let him relax and enjoy that. Then, after some time has elapsed he may feel comfortable about stepping out of the car. It would help to hold him in your arms, to promote a feeling of security so that he remains relaxed. With him in your arms, gradually approach the ducks, stopping frequently so that he continues to feel relaxed and comfortable. The instant he begins to feel tense or anxious you shuld back up a little bit. When he is clearly relaxed, continue to approach more slowly.

Because most children are interested in watching animals eat and enjoy feeding them, you should bring a loaf of bread and help him to throw it to the ducks. If he becomes interested in throwing the bread and watching the ducks eat, the emotions generated by interest and enjoyment will leave no room for fear. Be certain not to try this with ducks who are aggressive in pursuing the bread or you will resensitize the fear. You should first test the behavior of the ducks on your own.

Frequently the sounds of the animal are frightening to a child. The loud quacking of ducks frightens many children. To make the sounds less frightening, as you approach have *him* quack loudly at the ducks. Ask him, "What are those ducks saying?" Then *you* quack like a duck and encourage him to quack loudly like a duck. As you and he make the loud sounds of the animal at each other it may become associated with a feeling of joy instead of fear.

The rate at which your boy's fear is replaced by other feelings such as relaxation and comfort in the presence of ducks is an *individual matter*. Some factors which influence the rate of counterconditioning are the intensity of his feelings of security and comfort with you and the intensity of his interest in other activities. Some very mild fears may be counterconditioned in a day or two. Others may take weeks of continued gradual approach.

Fear of Dogs. The procedure is similar when the sight or sound of a dog produces fear. You will want to expose your child to dogs varying in size, starting with very small dogs and gradually increasing to larger ones while the child experiences positive emotions which will leave no room for fear. You might begin by holding your child in your arms a comfortable distance from a small dog. While the child feels secure and comfortable, you can walk slowly closer to the dog. Again, it may be helpful for your child to have something to throw to the dog to eat, such as a dog biscuit.

It is best to expose your daughter to dogs who are obedience-trained. Help her tell the dog to sit. Then ask her to give the dog a biscuit for being a "good dog" when he sits. This gives her a feeling of control over the dog, which is incompatible with the feeling of fear. Once she experiences the feeling of control over the dog, then you may work on developing feelings of joy and pleasure associated with dogs. Help her throw a ball to a dog who retrieves. The dog's retrieving behavior may seem interesting or even funny to her and these feelings are incompatible with fear. The size of the dog should gradually be increased, and with each increase, the gradual approach procedure should be repeated.

If the barking of the dog scares your little girl, make a tape recording of dogs barking. Play the tape of the barking at home on a very low volume while you make certain she feels relaxed. Perhaps she can eat her favorite food or play a favorite game with you while listening. Being certain that she remains comfortable and secure, gradually increase the volume of the dog barking.

During the treatment period it is especially important that your child not be allowed to reexperience frightening events. If there are dogs in the neighborhood or in the park which have frightened your child, avoid those places until you are ready to gradually approach them in the same systematic way.

Because of the fact that there are some dogs who do bite, which may have contributed to the development of your girl's fear in the first place, teach her to stay away from strays and to ask important questions. Help her to ask the owner, "Does your dog bite?" before approaching a strange dog. Once your child learns that although some dogs *do* bite, most dogs do not, then her counterconditioning will proceed much more easily.

Once your daughter is feeling comfortable with the sight and sound of various-sized dogs, encourage her to pet dogs, beginning with the small ones and working up to larger dogs. Be certain that the dogs she will pet are not so frisky that they will knock her down. That could recondition the fear. Teach her to ask the owner, "Will you hold your dog so I can pet him?" If she is not verbal enough to accomplish this, then you should ask for her. When an owner agrees to hold the dog for her, again she gets a feeling of control over the situation. The feeling of control cannot occur at the same time as a feeling of fear.

Many people attempt to countercondition a dog phobia by buying children their own puppies. This seldom works because most puppies go through a very unpleasant stage during teething when they bite anything and everything. In addition, most puppies are too frisky and are likely to knock your little one over and may even increase your child's fear. Furthermore, even if they do get along, your child may still fear anything but the family dog.

Fear of the Wind

If your son is afraid of the wind, avoid taking him out in strong winds. Begin to countercondition his fear of wind by taking him out in very mild wind while you provide activities which make the wind fun. Activities which may create feelings of joy to compete with fear might be blowing bubbles, flying helium balloons on long strings, or flying a kite.

Fear of Sudden or Unknown Noises

One mother described a widespread fear of noises which resulted from one frightening experience. The parents took their two-year-old girl to a July fourth fireworks display. Dana was terrified of the fireworks, and the fear generalized to other noises for months later. Whenever some unknown noise occurred, even a little one such as a tapping or knocking of the car, the child was obviously distressed and anxiously said, "noise, noise." The louder or more sudden the noise was, the more terrified she became.

To treat a fear of noises, you want to gradually introduce low-volume noises along with some very positive emotions and then gradually increase the volume of the noise. For example, you can use a clear plastic popcorn popper so your baby can see the corn pop as you jump up and down holding your child saying, "pop, pop, pop" each time a kernel pops. This way she will be excited and happy when she hears the noise instead of being frightened.

Next, you can make a tape recording of the corn popping and play it back, first at a low volume, and gradually increasing the volume. To be certain she stays calm and happy with the sound you can say, "Let's listen to the corn pop and pretend we are popping." Again, you can hold her in your arms and jump with each pop or hold hands and jump together, saying, "pop, pop, pop," and laughing.

You then can introduce a new noise using all your pots and pans and a spoon. Let your baby bang and crash the pans as loudly as she wishes. Then make a recording of her pan drumming. Later, you can play the recording along with some music and dance to the noises.

Now you can play a noise game. Together you can record other noises around the house such as the washing machine, the toilet flushing, the garage door opening. You will then say, "Let's play a game and see if you can guess what is making these noises." Gradually you will increase the volume of these sounds. Continue the recording game on walks with your child to a construction site where you will record a hammer pounding a nail, someone sawing, and other construction noises. Remember always to approach gradually, attend to your child's emotional responses, and stay back far enough to keep her happy and enthusiastic about getting the recording. When you play back your recording at home or in the car make certain the guessing game is fun and that you increase the volume only gradually over many days. When she guesses the source of a sound give her some applause!

As you notice your baby becoming more and more relaxed with other sounds you are not playing on the recorder, you may want to describe the fireworks as "popcorn in the sky!" First pop some corn at home, then take your baby to a place where you can see the fireworks from far away and the noise is minimal. Play your recording of popcorn on the way to the show.

Eliminating Fears in Older Children

Helping Children Change Their Negative Thinking

Much emotional disturbance is a result of the kind of things people say to themselves. Psychologists refer to the therapeutic process of helping people to change fearful thoughts to positive coping thoughts as "cognitive restructuring." These methods are helpful in helping children cope with anxiety and fear.

The first thing to do is talk to your child about the negative things he is saying to himself that are making him anxious. Then help him formulate thoughts or sentences which make him feel more comfortable about what he has to do and reward him for saying these sentences. This helps him to learn that he can actually affect the way he feels by the kinds of things he says to himself. Ask him to say these things out loud so you will be aware of his behavior and have a chance to reward it. When he learns this lesson he will be better able to manage and reduce his own anxiety in situations when he gets older.

The methods of cognitive restructuring are easiest to understand in the context of a person's behavior, so I will describe a couple of cases in which I used these methods to help children to cope with fear.

Anxiety Reactions

A seven-year-old child had a severe anxiety reaction following the divorce of his parents. Although his mother did everything possible to increase his feelings of security, John was showing severe separation anxiety at the beginning and at the end of the school-day. His mother gave up the carpool because this was obviously too stressful and agreed to be at school five minutes before dismissal time as he begged. Even though she herself drove him to school in the morning and was always on time in the afternoon (that is, five minutes early), he was anxious and worried all the way to school and panicked each time she left him at school. He worried aloud that something would happen to her: "What if something happened to you, then who would pick me up?" "How would they know to come get me?" "What time are you going to pick me up?" He would repeat the latter question fifteen to twenty times on the way to school and many times at the door, making himself more and more anxious. He begged for her to be ten minutes early; if she agreed but only arrived eight minutes early, he would be in tears and highly anxious when she got there.

I decided to help John try to control the anxiety by teaching him to use self-talk that would take the place of his worried thoughts. I talked to him about the separation, how he was generally anxious because of it, and how we would work together to help him feel safe and secure again. I asked John if he thought his mother wouldn't come to pick him up, and he said that he knew she would. Then I asked him what he could say to himself about this to make him feel better and, with some coaching, he came up with these statements to read on the way to school in the car: "I have never been left at school. They would never just leave me at school. If my mother or father couldn't pick me up, they would make sure someone knew, and someone would take care of me. They would make sure that my teacher would take me home with her if something terrible happened. If there is some emergency and my mother will be late, she will call me. I don't have to worry about it. I don't have to worry about any of these things. My mother and father will worry about the problem. I'm just a child and I can be a child. They can worry about the problem. They will make sure I get picked up. I can trust them. They will make sure I get picked up. I DON'T HAVE TO WORRY ABOUT IT."

Then, on a three-by-five-inch card, we typed three statements:

1) I know my mother or father will pick me up by 2:55.
2) They will make sure I get picked up.
3) I don't have to worry about it.

John was to read the page of self-talk in the car on the way to school to earn one star. Then he would read the note card at the door and say good-bye for a second star, and again read the card at the end of school, especially if he became anxious.

John knew that when he got three stars in a day he could get a frozen yogurt or a smoothie or another agreed-upon treat on the way home from school.

Children can profit enormously from learning to change their self-talk as John did. Psychologists often have to teach adults to do this kind of cognitive restructuring to manage their anxiety when they have not learned to do this as a child. You can give your child valuable lessons which will help him all through life.

School Phobia: A Case Study

A seven-year-old boy named David and his mother came to see me because David was afraid to go to school. He would wake up in the morning and immediately begin whining and crying and complaining for the hour and a half before school. He cried and complained all the way to school. At school he screamed, held onto his mother's hair and clothing, and had to be physically peeled from his mother everyday for the first two months of school. Finally his mother became desperate and sought professional help.

David had had no problem attending school before this year. For the previous two years he had gone to a private school where he had friends, felt comfortable, and had a very warm and loving teacher. David was not happy about making the change to a new school and was sad to leave his friends from his old school. At the same time that he changed school, he also moved to a new neighborhood, so there were many changes in his life.

Naturally, his mother felt sorry for David having to make all of these changes at one time, and she was very sympathetic when he cried about missing his friends, being afraid of the new school, and having no new friends. Unfortunately the love and attention he got for being afraid of his new school seemed to reinforce his fear enormously until at times he made himself physically ill in the morning. Because David was so well-adjusted at his previous school and seemed to adapt easily to most situations, I thought I'd try the simplest analysis first. It seemed that David had been reinforced for his unhappiness and his worry by sympathy and attention from the time he got up in the morning until the time he got to school. Even though his mother said encouraging things, it was his crying and fear that got the attention.

When David started the new school there was plenty of reason to be afraid. There were many unknowns—new school, new teacher, new children. I reasoned that since the school situation was no longer unknown, his fear could simply be a habit rewarded. The solution seemed to be to find a way to change the pattern of reinforcement and arrange for his mother to reward positive thoughts toward school.

When children are frightened they are saying scary things to themselves—David probably was thinking "I don't have any friends," "I like my old school better," "I miss my friends," and so on. If you want to change children's fear, then it is important to help them change the things they say to themselves—this helps them cope with the fearful situation.

I asked David what he could say to himself to make him feel better about going to school. I asked him if it helped to think "I know where I'm going." He said it did and then after talking some more about the good parts of school David came up with many more things to say to himself which would get in the way of fear. I put half of these ideas on each of two three-by-five-inch cards for David to read.

Card I	**Card II**
1. I know where I'm going.	1. I'm meeting new friends.
2. My teacher is not mean.	2. I'm going to get my work completed.
3. The kids in the room like me, especially John and Geoffrey.	3. I'm going shopping for new friends.
4. My work is not hard.	

These statements were comforting to David and helped him focus on the positive aspects of school. He really did feel good when he completed his work and he really was getting a chance to meet some new people at school.

Next David and I started the "Breakfast Game," a game we made up after I learned that most of David's old friends were gone from his old school anyway. Part of David's problem was remembering all the fun he had had the past two years with his good buddies and imagining that the fun was still there. The breakfast game involved his mother talking to David as he ate his breakfast. She sat with him at the table and said, "David, picture walking on the playground at your old school, and as you walk up to Nicholas to say hello to him and to play with him, POOF—Nicholas disappears in a cloud of smoke and he is gone. Now picture yourself walking up to Ian, and as you walk toward him looking forward to playing with him, POOF—up he goes in a cloud of smoke. Now I want you to imagine in your mind that you walk up to Mitchell, looking forward to playing with him, and all of a sudden, POOF—Mitchell disappears in a cloud of smoke. Now picture running up to Paul and you're running really fast, happy to see him and POOF—Paul is gone. You look all around the playground and all of your old friends are gone, they've all disappeared, they're not there anymore at the school. Now I want you to picture going to your new school and walking up to Geoffrey. You see him there with a great big smile, and he starts walking toward you, and as you get near him, he says 'Hi David, come on, let's play.' Now I want you to picture walking into the school yard, and as you walk into the school yard, you see your new friend John. You go up to John and ask him if he would like to play, and John gives you a big smile and says 'Yes David, let's play keep away,' and you all play together and have a good time."

There were two purposes to the Breakfast Game. One was to remind David that his old friends were no longer at the school and to focus on the new friends at his new school. Secondly, playing this game was an activity which kept him busy, and got him lots of attention for practicing thoughts that buried his fear and whining, crying, and moaning about how he didn't want to go to school.

The cards with positive statements and the Breakfast Game gave David *something to do that got in the way of fear* during the hour and a half between when he woke up and when he went to school. It wouldn't have worked for David's mother to simply withdraw her sympathy. It was necessary for her to give David more attention for coping behavior than he got for fearful crying.

I developed a chart for coping behavior to be rewarded by attention and other positive reinforcers for David.

David received one star for reading card I, one star for reading card II, one star for playing the Breakfast Game at home, and one star for reading the cards and playing the Breakfast Game in the car. If he did not cry at school, he got one star, if he said good-bye like a big boy and turned around and walked up the stairs, he got another star, and if he turned around and smiled and waved good-bye as he went in he would get another star. Altogether he could earn seven stars in a day.

Together, David and I and his mother determined the activities that would be most rewarding to him and for which he could trade his stars. David could trade in six stars for one ice cream cone after school, a half-hour at a video game room, baking cookies with his mother, building a birdhouse, getting a video to watch at home from the video store, or playing a game of Monopoly. David would be able to choose from this selection of reinforcers each day that he got six stars. When David had eighteen stars (three days of six stars per day) then he was allowed to have a friend from school come to his house and to take that friend to a special fun restaurant for dinner. When he had thirty stars (six stars a day for five days) he could invite a favorite friend to go to a movie and spend the night.

The program was immediately effective, and by the third day David was getting an ice cream nearly every day. Because David got to have friends to his house for special treats when he got many stars, he began to develop closer friendships. Six months later his mother reported that things were perfect—no more fears or tears about school—and everyone was happy.

David's Chart

	Monday	Tuesday	Wednesday	Thursday	Friday
Get out of bed and read card I					
Get dressed and read card II					
Play Breakfast Game during breakfast					
Read cards and play Breakfast Game in the car					
No tears at school					
Say good-bye like big boy					
Smile and wave good-bye					

Possible total number of stars = 7

6 stars = *Choice of:*

      1 ice cream after school

      Half hour at video game room

      Baking cookies in evening with mom

      Building birdhouse

      Getting movie video for evening

      Game of Monopoly

Three days of 6 stars = 18 stars = friend Geoffrey comes to play.

Five days of 6 stars = 30 stars = David, friend, and mom go to a movie.

Conclusion

The methods of classical conditioning and counterconditioning involved in emotional learning are really quite simple, as you have just seen through the examples in this chapter.

To successfully apply these methods to your own child requires a great deal of sensitivity and creativity. You may not follow any example exactly as described with your own child. The more sensitive you are to your daughter's emotional expressions, and the more capable you are of making your son laugh or generating his interest in the environment, the more effectively you will create emotions to compete with fear.

There is no *one* right way to handle a fear, and your guide should be your own child's reactions to what you try. Children are all different, and you must attend to your own child's likes and dislikes to successfully teach positive emotional reactions. Some babies will be more cautious, timid, and fearful from the beginning. With such children you must proceed slowly, patiently, and cautiously, constantly attending to their expressions and being willing to move back a few steps as necessary. If what makes one child laugh and enjoy the water makes yours cry, don't do it! Remember, your goal is to teach your child to enjoy or at least be relaxed in the water or at school or in the dark, not to become like other children. Accept your son for who he is. Help your daughter to enjoy herself and become the most she can be. You will enjoy her and you both will be happier.

Bibliography

Ainsworth, M.D.S. "Attachment as related to mother-infant interaction." In J.S. Rosenblatt, R.A. Hinde, C. Beer, & M.C. Busnel (Eds.) *Advances in the Study of Behavior* (Vol. 9). New York: Academic Press, 1979.

Ainsworth, M.D.S. "The Development of Infant-Mother Attachment." In B.M. Caldwell & H.N. Ricciuti (Eds.) *Review of Child Development Research* (Vol. 3). Chicago: University of Chicago Press, 1974.

Ainsworth, M.D.S., Blehar, M.C., Waters, E., & Wall, S. *Patterns of Attachment: A Psychological Study of the Strange Situation*. Hillsdale, N.J.: Erlbaum, 1978.

Albert, M.L., & Obler, K.L. *The Bilingual Brain*. New York: Academic Press, 1978.

Bandura, A. *Aggression: A Social Learning Analysis*. Englewood Cliffs, N.J.: Prentice-Hall, 1973.

Bandura, A. "Social learning theory and identification processes." In D.A. Goslin (Ed.) *Handbook of Socialization Theory and Research*. Chicago: Rand McNally, 1969, 213–262.

Bandura, A., & McDonald, F. "Influence of Social Reinforcement and the Behavior of Models in Shaping Children's Moral Judgments." *Journal of Abnormal and Social Psychology*, 1963, 67, 247–281.

Bandura, A., & Walters, R.H. *Adolescent Aggression*. New York: Ronald Press, 1959.

Barstis, S., & Ford, L. "Reflection-Impulsivity, Conservation, and the Development of Ability to Control Cognitive Tempo." *Child Development*, 1977, 48, 953–959.

Bauer, D. "An Exploratory Study of Developmental Changes in Children's Fears." *Journal of Child Psychology and Psychiatry*, 1976, 17, 69–74.

Baumrind, D. "Authoritarian vs. authoritative parental control." *Adolescence*, 1968, 3, 255–272.

Baumrind, C. "Childcare Practices Anteceding Three Patterns of Preschool Behavior." *Genetic Psychology Monograph*, 1967, 75, 43–88.

Baumrind, D. "Current Patterns of Parental Authority." *Developmental Psychology Monograph*. 1971, 4(1), 1–102.

Baumrind, D. "Effects of Authoritative Parental Control on Child Behavior." *Child Development*, 1966, 37, 887–907.

Baumrind, D., & Black, A.E. "Socialization Practices Associated With Dimensions of Competence in Preschool Boys and Girls." *Child Development,* 1967, 291–327.

Becker, W.C. "Consequences of Different Kinds of Parental Discipline." In M.L. Hoffman & L.W. Hoffman (Eds.), *Review of Child Development Research,* Vol. 1. New York: Russell Sage Foundation, 1964, 169–208.

Belsky, J., & Steinberg, L. "The Effects of Day Care: A Critical Review." *Child Development,* 1978, 49, 929–949.

Benedict, H. "The Role of Repetition in Early Language Comprehension." Paper presented at the biennial meeting of the Society for Research in Child Development. Denver, 1975.

Bennett, E.L., Rosenzweig, M.R., & Diamond, M.C. "Rat Brain: Effects of Environmental Enrichment on Wet and Dry Weights." *Science,* 1969, 163, 3869 825–826.

Berenstain, S. & J. *He Bear She Bear,* New York: Beginner Books, 1974.

Bower, T.G.R. *Development In Infancy,* Second Edition. San Francisco: W.H. Freeman, 1982.

Bower, T.G.R. *A Primer of Infant Development.* San Francisco: Freeman, 1977.

Bowlby, J. *Attachment and Loss, Vol. I. Attachment.* New York: Basic Books, 1969.

Bowlby, J. *Attachment and Loss, Vol. II. Separation: Anxiety and Anger.* New York: Basic Books, 1973.

Bowlby, J. *The Making and Breaking of Affectional Bonds.* Suffolk: Richard Clay, Ltd., The Chaucer Press, 1979.

Bowlby, J. "The Nature of the Child's Tie to his Mother." *International Journal of Psycho-Analysis.* 1958, 39, 350–373.

Bowlby, J., Boston, M., & Rosenblath, D. "The Effects of Mother-Child Separation: A Followup Study." *British Journal of Medical Psychology,* 1956, 29, 211–247.

Bronfenbrenner, U. "Some Familiar Antecedents of Responsibility and Leadership in Adolescents." In L. Petrullo & B.M. Bass (Eds.), *Leadership and Interpersonal Behavior.* New York: Holt, Rinehart & Winston, 1961, 239–271.

Bronson, W.C. "Developments in Behavior With Age Mates During the Second Year of Life." In M. Lewis & L.A. Rosenblum (Eds.), *The Origins of Behavior: Friendship and Peer Relations.* New York: John Wiley & Sons, 1975.

Brown, P., & Elliot, R. "Control of Aggression in a Nursery School Class." *Journal of Experimental Child Psychology,* 1965, 2, 103–107.

Bryan, J.H., & Walbek, N.H. "Preaching and Practicing Generosity: Child's Action and Reaction." *Child Development,* 1970, 41, 329–353.

Cameron, J., Livson, V. & Bayley, N. "Infant Vocalizations and Their Relationship to Mature Intelligence." *Science,* 1967, 157, 331–333.

Chandler, M.J. "Egocentricism and Antisocial Behavior: The Assessment and Training of Social Perspective Taking Skills." *Developmental Psychology,* 1973, 9, 326–332.

Charlesworth, R., & Hartup, W.W. "Positive Reinforcement in the Nursery School Peer Group." *Child Development,* 1967, 38, 993–1002.

Chess, S., Thomas, A., & Birch, H.G. "Behavioral Problems Revisited." In S. Chess & H. Birch (Eds.), *Annual Progress in Child Psychiatry and Development.* New York: Brunner/Mazel, 1968, 335–344.

Condon, W.S., & Sander, L. "Neonate Movement is Synchronized with Adult Speech: Interactional Participation and Language Acquisition." *Science,* 1974, 183, 99–101.

Crandall, V., Dewey, R., Katkovsky, W., & Prestion, A. "Parents' Attitudes and Behaviors and Grade School Children's Academic Achievements." *Journal of Genetic Psychology,* 1964, 104, 53–66.

Dale, P.S. *Language Development: Structure and Function.* (2nd edition) New York: Holt, Rinehart & Winston, 1976.

Debus, R.L. "Effects of Brief Observation of Model Behavior on Conceptual Tempo of Impulsive Children." *Developmental Psychology,* 1970, 2, 22–32.

Doman, Glenn, *How to Multiply Your Baby's Intelligence.* Philadelphia: The Better Baby Press, 1979.

Durio, H.F. "Mental Imagery and Creativity." *Journal of Creative Behavior,* 1975, 9(4), 233–244.

Eastman, P.D. *Are You My Mother?* New York: Beginner Books, 1960.

Eimas, P.D. "Speech Perception in Early Infancy." In L.B. Cohen & P. Salapatek (Eds.) "Infant Perception: From Sensation to Cognition." *Perception of Space, Speech and Sound.* (Vol. II) New York: Academic Press, 1975.

Fantz, R.L. "Visual Preference and Experience in Early Infancy: A Look at the Hidden Side of Behavior Development." In H.E. Stevenson, E.H. Hess, & H.L. Rheingold (Eds.) *Early Behavior.* New York: Wiley, 1967, 101–224.

Farran, D.C., & Ramey, C.T. "Infant Day Care and Attachment Behaviors Toward Mothers and Teachers." *Child Development,* 1977, 48, 1112–1116.

Feshback, N. "Studies of the Development of Children's Empathy." In B. Maher (Ed.), *Progress in Experimental Research.* New York: Academic Press, 1978.

Fisher, C., Kahn, E., Edwards, A., & Davis, D.M. "A Psychological Study of Nightmares and Night Terrors." *Journal of Nervous and Mental Disease,* 1973, 157, 75–98.

Fox, N. "Attachment of Kibbutz Infants to Mothers and Metapelet." *Child Development,* 1977, 48, 1228–1239.

Gagne, E., & Middlebrook, M. "Encouraging Generosity: A Perspective from Social Learning Theory and Research." *Elementary School Journal,* 1977, 77, 281–291.

Garcia, E.E. "Bilingualism in Early Childhood." *Young Children,* 1980, 35, 5266.

Getzels, J.W. "Problem Finding and Inventiveness of Solutions." *Journal of Creative Behavior,* 1975, 9, 12–18.

Getzels, J.W., & Jackson, P.W. *Creativity and Intelligence Explorations with Gifted Students.* New York: Wiley, 1962.

Golumb, C., & Bonen, S. "Playing Games of Make-believe: Effectiveness of Symbolic Play Training With Children Who Failed to Benefit from Early Conservation Training." *Genetic Psychological Monographs,* 1981 (Aug.), Vol. 104(1), 137–154.

Golumb, C., & Cornelius, C.B. "Symbolic Play and Its Cognitive Significance." *Developmental Psychology,* 1977, 13, 3, 246–252.

Goodenough, F.L. & Tyler, L. *Developmental Psychology* (3rd ed.) New York: Appleton-Century-Crofts, 1959.

Gottman, J., Grongson, J., and Rasmussen, B. "Social interaction, social competence and friendship in children." *Child Development,* 46, 709–718, 1975.

Gottman, J.M. "How children become friends." Monographs of the Society for Research in Child Development, 48 (Serial No. 201), 1983.

Haggard, E.A. "Socialization, Personality, and Academic Achievement in Gifted Children." In B.C. Rosen, H.J. Crockett, & C.Z. Nunn (Eds.), *Achievement in American Society.* Cambridge, Mass.: Schenkman Publishing Company, 1969, 85–94.

Halliday, M.A.K. *Learning How to Mean: Explorations in the Development of Language.* London: Arnold, 1975.

Homme, L.E., Debaca, P.C., Devine, J.V., et al. "Use of the Premack Principle in Controlling the Behavior of Nursery School Children." *Journal of Experimental Analysis of Behavior.*

Horowitz, F.D. (Ed.) "Visual Attention, Auditory Stimulation and Language Discrimination in Young Infants." *Monographs of the Society for Research in Child Development,* 1974, 39, 5, 158.

Hutt, C., & Bhavnani, R. "Predictions from Play." *Nature,* 1972, 237, 171–172.

Jones, H.G. "The Behavior Treatment of Enuresis Nocturna." In H.J. Eysenck (Ed.), *Behavior Therapy and the Neuroses.* London: Pergamon, 1960, 377–403.

Jones, M.C. "The Elimination of Children's Fears." *Journal of Experimental Psychology,* 1924, 7, 383–390.

Jones, M.C. "A Laboratory Study of Fear: The Case of Peter." *Pedagogical Seminary and Journal of Genetic Psychology,* 1924, 31, 308–315.

Kagan, J., Pearson, L., & Welch, L. "Modifiability of an Impulsive Tempo." *Journal of Educational Psychology,* 1966, 57, 359–365.

Kagan, J., Kearsley, R.B., & Zelazo, P.R. "The Effects of Infant Daycare on Psychological Development." *Educational Quarterly,* 1977, 1, 109–142.

Kagan, J., Kearsley, R.B., & Zelazo, P.R. *Infancy.* Cambridge, Mass.: Harvard University Press, 1978.

Khatena, J., & Torrance, E.P. *Thinking Creatively with Sounds and Words.* Lexington, Mass.: Personal Press, 1973.

Kircher, A.S., Pear, J.J., & Martin, G.L. "Shock as Punishment in a Picture-naming Task with Retarded Children." *Journal of Applied Behavior Analysis,* 1971, 4, 227–233.

Kron, R.E., "Instrumental Conditioning of Nutritive Sucking Behavior in the Newborn." *Recent Advances in Biological Psychiatry,* 1966, 9, 295–300.

Lambert, W.E., & Tucker, G.R. *Bilingual Education of Children: The St. Lambert Experiment.* Boston: Newbury House, 1972.

Languis, M., et al. *Brain and Learning: Directions in Early Childhood.* Washington, D.C.: NAEYC, 1980.

Lenneberg, E. *Biological Foundations of Language.* New York: Wiley, 1967.

Likona, T. "What Optimizes Moral Development and Behavior? Where the Theories Converge." Paper presented at the conference of the Society for Research in Child Development, April 1975, pp. 10–13.

Maccoby, E., & Felman, S. "Mother Attachment and Stranger Reactions in the Third Year of Life." *Monographs of the Society for Research in Child Development,* 1972, 37 (146).

Messer, S. "Reflection-impulsivity: Stability and School Failure." *Journal of Educational Psychology,* 1970, 61, 487–490.

Midlarsky, E., Bryan, J.H., & Brickman, P. "Aversive Approval: Interactive Effects of Modeling and Reinforcement in Altruistic Behavior." *Child Development,* 1973, 44, 321–328.

Neimark, E.D., "Intellectual Development During Adolescence." In F. Horowitz (Ed.), *Review of Research in Child Development,* (Vol. 5). 1974.

Parke, R.D. "Some Effects of Punishment on Children's Behavior." *Young Children,* 1969, 24, 224–240.

Parmalee, A.H., Wenner, W.H., & Schulz, H.R. "Infant Sleep Patterns from Birth to 16 Weeks of Age." *Journal of Pediatrics,* 1964, 65, 576–582.

Pascual-Leone, J. *Cognitive Development and Cognitive Style.* Lexington, Mass.: Heath, 1973.

Patterson, G.R., Littman, R.A., & Bricker, W. "Assertive Behavior in Children: A Step Toward a Theory of Aggression." *Monographs of the Society for Research in Child Development,* 1967, 32, 113.

Richards, R.A. "A Comparison of Selected Guilford and Wallach-Kogan Creative Thinking Tests in Conjunction with Measure of Intelligence." *Journal of Creative Behavior,* 1976, 10(3) 151–164.

Ridberg, E., Parke, R., & Hetherington, E.M. "Modification of Impulsive and Reflective Cognitive Styles Through Observation of Film Mediated Models." *Developmental Psychology,* 1971, 5, 369–377.

Rosen, B.C., & D'Andrade, R. "The Psychological Origins of Achievement Motivation." *Sociometry,* 1959, 22, 185–218.

Rosenhan, E.L., Frederick, R., & Burrowes, A. "Preaching and Practicing: Effects of Channel Discrepancy on Norm Internalization." *Child Development,* 1968, 39, 291–302.

Rosenzweig, M.R. "Environmental Complexity, Cerebral Change and Behavior." *American Psychologist,* 1966, 21, 321–332.

Rosenzweig, M.R., & Bennet, E.L. "Effects of Differential Environments on Brain Weights and Enzyme Activities in Gerbils, Rats and Mice." *Developmental Psychobiology,* 1970, 2, 87–95.

Rutter, M., *Maternal Deprivation.* Baltimore: Penguin Books, 1972.

Siegel, A.E., & Kohn, L.G. "Permissiveness, Permission, and Aggression: The Effects of Adult Presence or Absence on Aggression in Children's Play. *Child Development,* 1959, 36, 131–141.

Singer, J.L. "Television, Imaginative Play and Cognitive Development: Some Problems and Possibilities." Paper presented at the American Psychological Association Meeting, San Francisco, August, 1977.

Slobin, D.I. & Welsh, C.H. "Elicited Imitation as a Research Tool in Developmental Psycholinguistics." In C.A. Ferguson & D.I. Slobin (Eds.), *Studies in Child Language Development,* New York: Holt, 1973, 485–497.

Thevenin, T., *The Family Bed: An Age-Old Concept in Child Rearing.* Minneapolis: Tine Thevenin, 1976.

Thomas, A., Chess, S., & Birch, H. "The Origin of Personality." *Scientific American,* 1970, 223(2), 102.

Thomas, A., Chess, S., & Birch, H. *Temperament and Behavior Disorders in Children.* New York: New York University Press, 1968.

Thomas, A., Chess, S., Birch, H., Hertzig, M., & Korn, S. *Behavioral Individuality in Early Childhood.* New York: New York University Press, 1963.

Toner, I., Parke, R.D., & Yussen, S.R. "The Effect of Observation of Model Behavior on the Establishment and Stability of Resistance to Deviation in Children." *Journal of Genetic Psychology,* 1978, 123, 283–290.

Torrance, E.P. "Creativity and Infinity." In G.A. Davis & R.F. Warren (Eds.), *Psychology of Education: New Looks.* Lexington, Mass.: D.C. Health, 1974.

Ullman, L.P. & Krasner, L. *Case Studies in Behavior Modification.* Chicago: Holt, Reinhart, & Winston, 1965.

Wallach, M.A. "Ideology, Evidence, and Creative Research." *Contemporary Psychology,* 1973, 18, 162–164.

Wallach, M.A. *The Intelligence/Creativity.* New York: General Learning Press, 1971.

Wallach, M.A. & Kogan, N. "Creativity and Intelligence in Children's Thinking." In R.K. Parker (Ed.), *Readings in Educational Psychology* 43:3, 360–370. Reprinted from Trans-Action, 1967, 4.

Wallach, M.A., & Kogan, N. *Modes of Thinking in Young Children.* New York: Holt, Rinehart & Winston, 1965.

Walters, G., & Grusec, J. *Punishment.* San Francisco: Freeman, 1977.

Watson, J.B. & Rayner, R. "Conditional Emotional Reaction." *Journal of Experimental Psychology,* 1920, 3, 1–14.

Williams, C.D. "The Elimination of Tantrum Behavior by Extinction Procedures." *Journal of Abnormal and Social Psychology,* 1959, 59, 269.

Wright, D. *The Psychology of Moral Behavior.* Baltimore: Penguin Books, 1971.

Zelniker, T., & Oppenheimer, L. "Effect of Different Training Methods on Perceptual Learning in Impulsive Children." *Child Development,* 1976, 47, 492–497.

Index

Special Offer

$2 discount when ordering New Harbinger Books or cassette tapes using the coupon on this page

You get $2 off the total price when ordering from the list of books below (with a full money back guarantee). Or send for our complete catalogue of books and tapes and get the same $2 discount on orders made from the catalogue.

The Relaxation & Stress Reduction Workbook, $12.95 paper, $29.95 cloth

Thoughts & Feelings: The Art of Cognitive Stress Intervention, $11.95 paper, $29.95 cloth

Messages: The Communication Book, $11.95 paper, $24.95 cloth

The Divorce Book, $10.95 paper, $24.95 cloth

Hypnosis for Change: A Manual of Proven Hypnotic Techniques, $10.95 paper, $24.95 cloth

The Better Way to Drink: Moderation & Control of Problem Drinking, $10.95 paper

The Deadly Diet: Recovering from Anorexia & Bulimia, $10.95 paper, $24.95 cloth

Self-Esteem, $11.95 paper, $24.95 cloth

Beyond Grief, $11.95 paper, $24.95 cloth

Chronic Pain Control Workbook, $12.95 paper, $24.95 cloth

Rekindling Desire, $10.95 paper, $24.95 cloth

Life Without Fear: Anxiety and Its Cure, $9.95 paper, $24.95 cloth

Visualization for Change, $11.95 paper, $29.95 cloth

Guideposts to Meaning, $10.95 paper, $29.95 cloth

Controlling Stagefright, $10.95 paper, $24.95 cloth

Videotape: Hypnosis for Relaxation, $24.95

Starting Out Right: Essential Parenting Skills for Your Child's First Seven Years, $12.95 paper, $24.95 cloth

Big Kids: A Parents' Guide to Weight Control for Children, $10.95 paper, $24.95 cloth

Personal Peace: Transcending Your Interpersonal Limits, $10.95 paper, $24.95 cloth

___ Please send me a free catalogue of your books and tapes. By using this coupon I will be entitled to a $2 discount on orders made from the catalogue.

___ Please send to me the following book(s). Enclosed is my check.

Price

Name_____ less $2 discount   − $2.00

Address_____ sales tax if Calif. res. _____

_____ shipping/handling   + 1.25

total   _____

Send to: New Harbinger Publications, Department B, 5674 Shattuck Ave., Oakland, CA 94609